from,

Bertrucey

Lincoln Journal Star

presents

The Best of the
Big Red
Running Backs

SPORTS PUBLISHING INC.
CHAMPAIGN, IL

Coordinating Editor: Julie Koch
Director of Production: Susan M. McKinney
Production Coordinator: Jennifer L. Polson
Book Design: Michelle R. Dressen
Dustjacket Design: Joe Buck

All photographs courtesy of Journal Star Library.

ISBN: 1-58261-001-0

Printed in the United States.

www.SportsPublishing.com

Acknowledgments

I would like to thank longtime *Lincoln Journal Star* sportswriter Ken Hambleton for being the driving force behind this book. His insight into the Husker football program helped tremendously in the compilation of *The Best of the Big Red Running Backs*. Mike Pearson of Sports Publishing Inc., *Lincoln Journal Star* publisher Bill Johnston, editor David Stoeffler and sports editor John Mabry have made it possible, and SPI's Susan McKinney and Jennifer Polson made it a reality. I couldn't have done it without the help of *Journal Star* librarians Pat Sloan, Judy Foreman and Susan Steider, and the stories and input from my co-workers: Steve Sipple, Curt McKeever, Ron Powell, Mark Derowitsch, Ryly Jane Hambleton, Jeff Korbelik, Steve Hill, Todd Henrichs and photo editor Ted Kirk.

A special thank you to former Nebraska Coach Tom Osborne and current Coach Frank Solich for their observations in this book. They both have played a major role in helping Nebraska reach the pinnacle of the college football world.

Julie Koch
Coordinating Editor

The Best of the Big Red Running Backs

Contents

Foreword

The richness in the running back tradition at the University of Nebraska dates back to the great George Sauer, Lloyd Cardwell and Sam Francis in the early 1930s.

The tradition of great backs continued with Bobby Reynolds in the early 1950s. Over the past four decades, Nebraska has continued to be the home of some of the best halfbacks, I-backs and fullbacks in college football.

Although the running backs listed in this book were chosen by the *Lincoln Journal Star* and not me, I have had the opportunity to work with many outstanding backs, including several not featured. Looking back, it is impossible for me to point out one characteristic that has allowed the best to stand out.

Great running backs have the ability to anticipate, to feel the pressure of the chaos surrounding them on the field, and to create their own path to paydirt.

They must not only take the pain that comes with the pounding of being the target of would-be tacklers, they must be willing to initiate contact and deliver hits of their own to defensive players.

Running backs must be willing to study the game, know where the holes are going to be, follow their blockers and handle their own blocking assignments when they are not carrying the ball. The ability to excel at the mental aspects of the game along with being able to meet the physical demands of college football separates these tremendous athletes from the rest of the field.

During my years at the University of Nebraska, the Husker football program has had the luxury of having a seemingly continuous stream of tremendous running backs.

The running back position at Nebraska has become coveted by the best high school backs around the nation, and yet, nearly half of all the running backs that have played for the Huskers have been from the state of Nebraska.

Whether they come from the Cornhusker State or the far corners of the country, running backs of every style have found success at Nebraska. Since 1962, Nebraska has won 13 NCAA rushing titles and five national championships.

Running backs with the slashing styles of I.M. Hipp, Jarvis Redwine and Derek Brown have fit into the Nebraska ground game, but so have backs with the power of Tony Davis, Jeff Kinney and Tom Rathman.

Roger Craig, Calvin Jones, Keith Jones and Ahman Green have carried the ball with explosive, north-south speed, while other great backs such as Ken Clark, Doug DuBose, Lawrence Phillips, Jeff Smith and Mike Rozier used their versatility in every running style imaginable to dominate their opponents.

Rozier led the nation with an amazing 2,148 yards in 1983, capturing the Heisman Trophy and helping Nebraska to a national title game. He also holds Husker career records with 4,780 yards and 49 rushing touchdowns.

As great as Rozier was as an individual player, it is important to remember that without the support of the players around him, he could never have achieved the individual honors he earned.

Like all of the Husker running backs of the Devaney-Osborne coaching era, Rozier followed some of the best offensive linemen in history. Nebraska's offensive lines have produced six Outland Trophy winners and two Lombardi Award winners.

Along with the big guys up front, most of the running backs in this book have followed great blocking fullbacks through the holes. They have also benefited from the skills of outstanding blocking tight ends and receivers who have helped to create more running room for Nebraska's backs.

Those backs have also been running the option behind such great Husker signal-callers as Turner Gill, Tommie Frazier and Scott Frost.

Along with the talented cast of Husker players on the field, Nebraska's running backs have enjoyed the stability that has come with the coaching staff on the sidelines.

From 1962 to 1997, Nebraska had only two head coaches, Bob Devaney and Tom Osborne, two of the greatest coaches in college football history. During that same 36-year span, Nebraska had only two running back coaches. Mike Corgan, who coached the Husker backs from 1962 to 1982, deserves much of the credit for getting Nebraska's rushing attack rolling with its first NCAA rushing title in 1963. He and the Huskers added three more rushing crowns and two additional titles before I took over in 1983.

Now, as I enter my first year as Nebraska's head coach and Dave Gillespie enters his first year as the running backs coach, we will work to carry on the rich tradition that Coach Devaney and Coach Osborne began.

The Husker program has been honored to have such gifted athletes fill Nebraska's backfield. At the same time, those athletes and the Husker coaching staff have been honored to play in front of the greatest fans in college football at Memorial Stadium on Saturday afternoons.

As long as we have the support of the state of Nebraska and its great fans behind us, the coaching staff plans to keep the Husker football program running so we can write a sequel to *The Best of the Big Red Running Backs*.

Frank Solich
University of Nebraska Football Coach

Introduction

One person who is not featured in this, *The Best of the Big Red Running Backs*, who deserves recognition is Mike Corgan, my running backs coach at Nebraska. "Iron Mike," as I used to call him, is the person for whom I hold the utmost respect. Mike was instrumental in the development of my mental toughness that carried me through my career at Nebraska and in the NFL.

I also believe that this book would not be published were it not for the extraordinary efforts and dedication of Tom Osborne. Coach Osborne's development of the Nebraska football program into a national powerhouse, although a crowning achievement in and of itself, should be recognized as his best. That accolade should be reserved for his commitment, caring and development of his football players into people. Coach Osborne always stressed to his players the importance of academics, respect and organization, and should be commended and remembered for the hundreds of fine men he introduced into the "real world."

Last and certainly not least, I would like to recognize the Nebraska football fans. Your loyalty and support for the Cornhuskers is the benchmark for college fans across the country. On many Saturdays in Lincoln during my career, I was enthused and inspired by "The Sea of Red" and for that, I am thankful.

Roger Craig

Derek Brown finished his three-year career at Nebraska in the top 10 among NU's career rushers with 2,699 yards. (Journal Star Library).

DEREK BROWN/STATS

LETTERED:	1990-92
HEIGHT:	5-10
WEIGHT:	185
HOMETOWN:	LA HABRA, CALIFORNIA
HONORS:	1991 ALL-BIG EIGHT
	1992 ALL-BIG EIGHT
PRO EXPERIENCE:	NEW ORLEANS SAINTS, 1993-97

NU'S BROWN SET TO START IF NEEDED

Injuries to Flowers, Baldwin cloud picture at I-back for Huskers

By Curt McKeever

September 20, 1990—Derek Brown never skimps when it comes to setting goals, but even he is bewildered by the fact that Saturday he could become the focal point of the Nebraska football team's offense.

Because of injuries to junior Leodis Flowers and sophomore Scott Baldwin, Brown finds himself in an enviable position. In just his second collegiate game, he could be the Cornhuskers' starting I-back.

"I didn't think it would be this soon," said Brown, a first-team high school All-American from La Habra, California. "I expected it not to happen until maybe a few more years.

"I know I'm ready. All this week I've had a real good practice, concentrating real hard on what I had to do."

While the 5-foot-10, 185-pound speedster is blessed with plenty of physical tools, his ability to learn Nebraska's system has vaulted him to his current position. "He knows his stuff," Nebraska Coach Tom Osborne said. "We thought he had the physical ability.

The thing you never know is how quickly somebody picks things up. He's really learned it very well." Brown attributes that to being a fast learner.

"It's just, basically, concentration," he said. "Once I go through things, they just come to me."

Brown showed that in his collegiate debut against Northern Illinois two weeks ago. On his first carry, he scored a touchdown, diving in from a yard out. Less than three minutes later, he took a pitch and raced down the sideline 59 yards for his second score.

For Brown, that game was quite a contrast to Nebraska's opener against Baylor. He didn't see action against the Bears.

"A couple of weeks ago it wasn't so fun," Brown said. "I just wasn't used to sitting out. It was real awkward to me and I didn't like that very much, but Coach (Frank) Solich spoke to me and we had a nice conversation."

Solich reiterated to Brown that he remain patient while waiting for his chance. Of course, no one knew that opportunity might come as

early as Saturday, when Nebraska plays host to Minnesota at 1:30 p.m. Brown said none of the Nebraska coaches has talked to him about starting, but when his roommate mentioned that possibility, Brown had a freshman-like reaction.

"I was nervous, so what I did was call my mother," Brown said. "She relaxes me and it made me feel better. Later on, I'm sure I'll still get a few jitters."

Brown guesses that Baldwin, who is battling a painful turf-toe injury, will get the starting nod against Minnesota, but he said he's ready for whatever role the Nebraska coaches want him to play. "I take the same attitude to every game," Brown said. "Even if I'm not going to play much, or if I'm starting, I'm going to be prepared."

Of course, Brown wouldn't mind starting, and he isn't shy about offering advice to Baldwin and Flowers, who strained a knee Tuesday and is questionable for Saturday's game.

"Those two should take the rest because we'll need them later on for the big games," he said.

BROWN LIFTS NU'S PLAY

Weight room ethic helps sophomore I-back Brown set records

By Ken Hambleton

October 1, 1991—Nebraska's Derek Brown celebrated his status as Big Eight offensive player of the week in the weight room after football practice.

Actually, he "celebrates" the same way every day. He's almost always the last one out of the weight room and there are times when he is chased out after someone turns off the lights.

"They call me 'weight room' and stuff like that because I'm always in there," Brown, a sophomore I-back, said after Monday's practice.

"I know it can all go so fast. Nothing is permanent. I could be behind someone—Calvin Jones, George Achola, Scott Baldwin, when he comes back—if they play better than me. So I have to be my best."

On Saturday, against Arizona State, Brown gained 135 yards on 25 carries to boost his average to 132.75 yards per game this year. He became the first Cornhusker to pass the 100-yard mark four straight games to open the season. He leads the Big Eight and is 17th nationally in all-purpose yards with an average of 146.5 per game.

Brown won a split vote over Oklahoma quarterback Cale Gundy and Kansas State receiver Michael Smith for the weekly offensive award.

"That's a nice deal to win, but I'm just getting warmed up," Brown said. "The first game of the year, I was impatient and I missed a lot of chances for more yards." He gained 175 yards against Utah State in the opener.

"The second game, I was a little better, but still too impatient for the holes to open," he said. He gained 122 yards and scored two touchdowns against Colorado State and appeared in USA Today's Heisman Watch list.

"By Washington, I was starting to feel comfortable and starting to get the timing down, although I got hit pretty hard in the shin and was in pain for a while," he said.

He gained 100 yards against Washington.

"The last game, I was starting to get the confidence to wait for my spot and take advantage of the blocking," he said. "I'm getting past the first man and now, I've got to work on getting past the last man.

"I'm trying to improve on the little things—getting better blocks, getting more yards in the open field and getting to the hole when it opens. I'm catching on."

Brown caught NU Coach Tom Osborne's attention.

"He ran very hard, and he's shown the last two weeks that he is a competitor," Osborne said. "These games help sort out those people who are competitors. If the games were easy, the competitors don't stand out from the rest.

"But Derek practices as hard as he plays in games, and he's shown he's a great game player."

Twenty-five carries in the 90-degree heat of the Arizona night didn't faze Brown.

Brown got hit by a facemask in his other shin against Arizona State and was rested through the second quarter. "But I came back in the second half and I felt so fresh, it felt like I was just starting the game again," he said. "I got enough carries to help the team out, and that's all I'm here for.

"If I get 5.4 yards a carry, like the other night, then it's because the offense is helping itself. I feel better getting more carries, but I've got to make sure it helps the team, too.

"This year, I'm just trying to let people know I'm still here at Nebraska because I kind of faded away last year. I'm still here and I want to help this team win the Big Eight."

I-BACK BROWN NOT LETTING UP

By Ken Hambleton

October 16, 1991—After rushing for 143 yards and three touchdowns in the Nebraska football team's 49-15 victory against Oklahoma State Saturday afternoon, Derek Brown said he was just trying to keep his job. Or words to that effect.

Brown, who's well on the way to rushing for 1,000 yards in his sophomore season, was being modest, as usual.

But there was also some truth in what he said.

Because of Nebraska's depth at I-back, a player at the position is only as good as his most recent performance. Brown can't let up. Redshirt freshman Calvin Jones and senior George Achola are right behind him, ready to take the starting job.

And both have the skills to do it, according to assistant head coach Frank Solich, who's in charge of the running backs.

Brown's success this season is the result of a proven system. "There's no question the competitiveness at the position has brought out the best in those players," Solich said.

A coach couldn't ask for a much better situation.

Five games into the season, Brown has proven to be not only Nebraska's best running back but also the best in the conference. He ranks seventh in the nation in rushing and has received mention from USA Today in its weekly Heisman Watch.

That was prior to Nebraska's 36-21 loss to Washington, however. For some inexplicable reason, Brown was dropped from the Heisman Watch the week after the Washington game, even though he rushed for 100 yards on 21 carries against the Huskies.

Brown had very little running room in that game. Washington's defense is such that few teams, much less individuals, are going to rush for 100 yards against it. Brown failed to get back to the line of scrimmage only twice in that game.

For the season, Brown has lost yardage on only three of his 102 carries— the total loss was 3 yards.

"Derek's had an outstanding season," Solich said. "He's played about as well as he could play of late."

Brown has shown big-play explosiveness. He broke touchdown runs of 61 and 40 yards against Oklahoma State, for example.

"People notice the long runs, but Derek is doing very well in the other phases of the game, too," Solich said.

Brown, a *Parade Magazine* All-American at Servite High in Anaheim, California, has played the way everyone expected.

Nebraska has a tradition of outstanding I-backs, and Brown has shown he's ready to be a part of it. But not just because of his considerable speed and strength. I-backs who are recruited by the Cornhuskers "know a lot is expected of them," Solich said. They have to be mentally tough, physically durable and extremely competitive.

If he remains healthy, Brown appears to be good enough to merit serious consideration for the Heisman Trophy at some point in his career. But his focus has to be keeping the No. 1 job, because until junior Scott Baldwin was injured in the early minutes of the season opener, Brown was Nebraska's No. 2 I-back.

Baldwin, who hasn't played since, might return to action Saturday, when the Cornhuskers play Kansas State in Memorial Stadium.

Baldwin is running the best

he's run since being injured, according to Solich, but he's still not quite full-speed.

Even so, "Scott feels he's ready to play," Solich said.

That's understandable. Baldwin, like the other I-backs, has seen how Nebraska's highly competitive system works. When one I-back doesn't perform to his potential or—in Baldwin's case—is sidelined by an injury, someone equally talented is waiting to step in.

As well as Brown has played, it's easy to forget he began the season on the second team. Brown, however, hasn't forgotten.

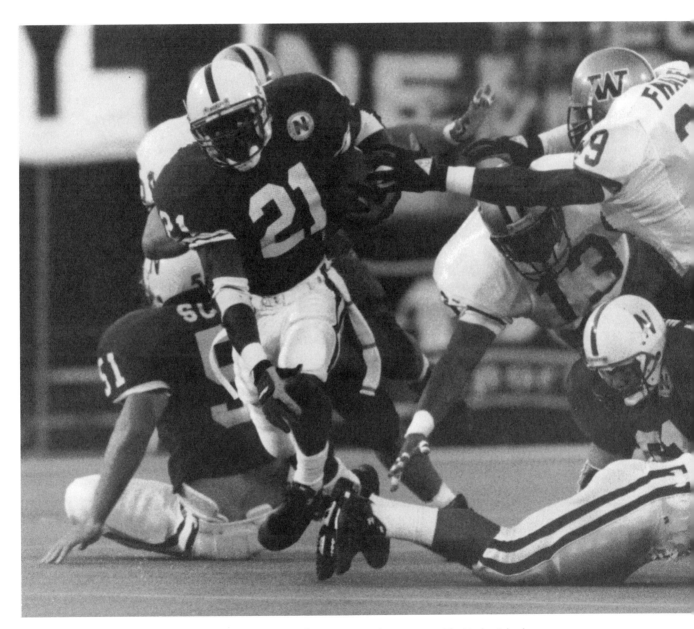

The Washington defense had trouble stopping NU's Derek Brown September 21, 1991. The Husker I-back rushed for 100 yards, but it wasn't enough, as the Huskies won 36-21. (Journal Star Library).

BROWN LEFT FOES BREATHLESS

By John Mabry

Derek Brown created a lot of excitement during his freshman year at Nebraska.

A little too much excitement.

While helping the Huskers put together a 9-3 season in 1990, Brown said he had a hard time catching his breath after each carry.

"I run hard and try to break every play," Brown said before starting his sophomore season. "That's no different than anybody else. But when game time comes, and I get in the game, I'm just a bit hyper.

"I guess all the excitement made me lose my breath."

Brown, who was born on April 15, 1971 in Banning, California, came to Lincoln after leaving opponents breathless in his senior season at Servite High School in Anaheim, California.

He set an Orange County record by rushing for 2,324 yards in 1988. He also had 27 touchdowns.

"He's as tough as nails and lets his feet do the talking," Servite Coach Jerry Person said. "We've never had a back like him, and we may never have another like him again."

With numbers like the ones Brown put up in high school, Nebraska Coach Tom Osborne knew there would be a lot of competition for Brown's services.

"Derek was a very highly recruited player out of high school," Osborne said.

He attracted interested from several schools, including Southern California, UCLA and Colorado.

But Brown really liked what he saw in Lincoln.

"It was an easy choice," Brown said after announcing his decision to accept a scholarship from Osborne. "The players, the coaches and even the fans seemed so close—like a family. I want to be a part of that. I think it's perfect."

Brown was not a perfect specimen for a running back. At 5-feet-10, he was smaller than the ideal NCAA Division I-A back.

His height did not turn out to be a problem.

"He had great quickness and acceleration through the hole," said Frank Solich, who was Nebraska's running backs coach for 15 seasons before becoming head coach in 1998. "He started off so well at the snap, he could get to the line very quickly and make a lot of yardage because he was able to use the blocking so well.

"He was built well (185 pounds) and was very durable."

Brown did not play for the Huskers in 1989 because he did not meet NCAA academic requirements, but he quickly made an impact in 1990.

He scored on his first college carry, a 1-yard run against Northern Illinois in the second game of the '90 season. And he took off for a 59-yard TD sprint in the fourth quarter of Nebraska's 60-14 victory over the Huskies.

Because of injuries to running backs Leodis Flowers and Scott Baldwin, Brown was called upon to start two weeks later when the Huskers took on Minnesota in Lincoln.

Brown led Nebraska to a 56-0 rout by rushing for 120 yards and two touchdowns. He also caught a 21-yard touchdown pass from quarterback Mickey Joseph in the game.

After suffering a separated shoulder in a mid-season game against Iowa State, Brown didn't see much action in the last three regular-season games of the year, but he did make some noise against Georgia Tech in the Florida Citrus Bowl.

Brown rushed for 99 yards,

including a 50-yard touchdown run late in the first half that helped the Huskers stay close. The Yellow Jackets pulled away in the second half and won 45-21.

Brown was No. 2 on the I-back depth chart when the Huskers began the 1991 season with a home game against Utah State. By the end of Nebraska's 59-28 rout of the Aggies, he was clearly the main man in the backfield.

Baldwin, the starter at I-back, suffered an ankle injury in the first quarter, leaving Brown as the top ball carrier. Brown carried the ball 23 times for 175 yards and later claimed that he "missed a lot of chances for more yards."

The Utah State game started a seven-game run of 100-yard efforts for Brown.

He broke off some big scoring runs during the stretch—36 yards against Colorado State, 27 yards against Washington, 61 and 40 yards against Oklahoma State.

In the game against the Cowboys, a 49-15 Husker victory, Brown had Oklahoma State Coach Pat Jones gasping for air.

"Brown knocked the breath completely out of me today," Jones said. "He might be the best back in this league."

As the season wound down, however, some started to wonder if Brown was even the best back in a Big Red uniform. Redshirt freshman Calvin Jones was also racking up big numbers.

When Jones ran for a school-record 294 yards against Kansas on Nov. 9, it was clear that Brown wasn't going to be a one-man show.

Before the start of the season, Brown said, "I know, like everybody else here, the day-to-day competition for the starting job will never, ever let up."

It never did let up for Brown.

Brown and Jones were no longer called I-backs. They were the Husker "We-backs."

Both finished the season with outstanding numbers. Only a handful of NU running backs have done better than Brown's total of 1,313 yards rushing in 1991. Jones ended up with 900.

For Osborne and Solich, picking a No. 1 back for the 1992 season was like trying to decide which World Trade Center tower was taller.

"Each wanted to be the featured back," Osborne recalled.

There was never really a No. 1 and a No. 2 that year, and it didn't really seem to matter which back had the ball.

"The good thing about the situation," Osborne said, "is that they'll both stay fresh. I hope they can accept that."

Whether they ever really accepted it or not, the results were remarkable. Brown rushed for 1,011 yards, and Jones had 1,210, making them the first 1,000-yard twosome in Nebraska football history.

The end of the "We-back" situation came early in 1993, when Brown decided he wouldn't be back for his senior season.

He said the battle for playing time with Jones was not a factor in his decision to enter the NFL draft.

"I wasn't unhappy with sharing time," Brown said. "Between the end of the Orange Bowl, getting back home to California and the time I had to myself, I decided it was time to turn pro."

Jones said he was sorry to see his backfield mate go.

"We shared some good times together as roommates on the road," Jones said. "Derek is a very competitive player, and I learned a lot from him."

The New Orleans Saints selected Brown in the fourth round of the draft, and he had a solid rookie season, leading the team in rushing with 705 yards.

He left Nebraska with 2,699 yards rushing, 13 100-yard games and no hard feelings.

"I have no ill feelings about Nebraska," Brown said. "It's a great school and a great program, and I will always appreciate all the help they gave me."

Derek Brown brought his 2-year-old son, Brennan, to watch the Huskers scrimmage April 10, 1993. Earlier that year, Brown announced that he was foregoing his senior season at Nebraska to make himself eligible for the NFL draft. (Ted Kirk/Lincoln Journal Star).

Lloyd Cardwell

LLOYD CARDWELL/STATS

LETTERED:	1934-36
HEIGHT:	6-3
WEIGHT:	200
HOMETOWN:	SEWARD, NEBRASKA
HONORS:	1934 ALL-BIG SIX
	1935 ALL-BIG SIX
	1936 ALL-BIG SIX
	NEBRASKA FOOTBALL HALL OF FAME
PRO	
EXPERIENCE:	DETROIT LIONS 1937-43

HUSKERS BLANK CYCLONES, 34 TO 0

Record crowd at stadium watches as Huskers run wild at times

By John Bentley

October 4, 1936—Nebraska ushered in the 1936 football season by playing a game of "forty yards or no count" against Iowa State's Cyclones and took the first step—and a definite step it was—toward the defense of its Big Six title by scoring a 34 to 0 victory before a crowd of close to 28,500. This set a new record for all-time opening-day assemblages here.

Three of the five Cornhusker touchdowns came on runs ranging from 37 to 97 yards. There were some ragged displays, fumbles at critical times costing the Cornhuskers. Iowa State also crossed up the reverses with an even-man line, but they couldn't stop Wild Hoss Cardwell, who snorted and pranced and roared around with that ball. Running either to the right or left this year, the big boy was sliding off tacklers and running over them when he couldn't elude them.

The game was nine minutes old when the first Husker score was rung up. Starting on their own 37-yard line, the Scarlet marched and passed the 63 yards to the first touchdown, the sustained march

being marked by Cardwell's 38-yard scamper on a hidden ball play and a forward, Johnny Howell to Game Captain McDonald, picking up 16 yards. It was a double lateral that

brought the touchdown, Sam Francis to Douglas to Cardwell, Cardy eluding two Iowa State tacklers who had a fine chance to nab him.

Lloyd "Wild Hoss" Cardwell earned all-conference honors three straight years (1934-36). (Journal Star Library).

'WILD HOSS' PRANCED ACROSS GRIDIRON

By Mike Babcock

December 25, 1978—He was called the "Wild Hoss."

At 6-foot-3 and 200 pounds, that was probably appropriate, even though Lloyd Cardwell doesn't agree. Size didn't have much to do with it, he claims.

"In those days that was pretty good size. Nowadays, it would be a midget," Cardwell said by phone from his home in Omaha.

Well, maybe not. That's still a good-sized running back.

"But I think it must have been the way I pranced; I ran with my knees a little high. That kind of came naturally from track, and it helped knock off the tacklers," he said.

Cardwell knows a little something about shedding tacklers. He knocked off enough of them in his years as a Nebraska Cornhusker.

From 1934 to 1936, defenders tried to corral the "Wild Hoss" on college football fields across the Midwest. Few succeeded.

In his three varsity seasons, Cardwell scored 120 points.

Sam Francis was the Husker fullback on those same teams, and

when Nebraska's offense attacked, it must have seemed like a mustang stampede.

Now 65 years old and retired, Lloyd Raymond Cardwell, the "Wild Hoss," is one of two new members in the *Lincoln Journal's* Nebraska Sports Hall of Fame.

Cardwell played football at Nebraska during the heart of the Depression. But the Cornhusker football program certainly wasn't left penniless under the coaching of the legendary Dana X. Bible, not when he had Cardwell and Francis to invest in his team's fortunes on Saturday afternoons.

"We had some real teamwork," Cardwell recalled. "The fellas all worked together because they all knew no one was getting any more than anyone else. We got nothing for it but fun."

There were no scholarships then . . . everyone was a walk-on.

"We played because we really wanted to, not because they gave us anything. We were all there because we loved Nebraska," Cardwell said.

"Another reason I went to Nebraska was because of coaches like

D.X. Bible, Ed Weir, H.F. Schulte, and W.H. Browne," he said. "You've got to mention those men, too."

The love of a state to which he moved as a child—he was born in Republic City, Kansas—has never waned.

Cardwell grew up in Seward, where he starred on the high school athletic teams.

Then he took his track and football talents to Nebraska.

True to his nickname, the "Wild Hoss" was tough. Most college football players in those days had to be, because their protective equipment was minimal.

"I could never have stood using a mouthpiece and something across my eyes (a facemask). It would have been a handicap, I think," Cardwell said.

"We didn't want a lot of added weight. We wanted as little (equipment) as possible if we were running the football.

"But maybe players are braver now because of those things. They'll stick their head right into a pile. Back when I played, we might have just stuck our shoulder in there."

Then, players were used both

on offense and defense. Cardwell held down a defensive halfback slot when he wasn't carrying the football or blocking for someone else.

"We played 60 minutes in those days," he said. "Of course, the games slowed down a little in the fourth quarter, but I think a boy misses a lot by not playing both ways.

"We had to get in real good shape. I was in sports practically the year around, so I didn't let myself get too far out of shape," Cardwell said.

At Nebraska he was All-Big Six, earning his name as a hard-running halfback. He scored a touchdown in his first varsity game, a 50-0 romp over Wyoming in Lincoln.

He capped his varsity career in the same way it began.

"I think the last time I carried the ball I scored a touchdown," he said.

The Cornhuskers defeated Oregon State 32-14 in Portland that day.

Cardwell played in the East-West Shrine Game, and the next summer, he and Francis helped the collegians defeat the Green Bay Packers, 6-0, in the 1937 College All-Star Game.

Just before that, Cardwell signed for a $250 bonus to play with the Detroit Lions of the National Football League.

He was married to Beth Horner, his high school sweetheart, on July 7, 1937, and used the bonus to pay for a short honeymoon—"they didn't cost much in those days," he said—which had to end in time for him to report to the College All-Star training camp.

Cardwell was an All-Pro in 1938 and 1939, and in 1946, four years after he retired he became head football coach at Omaha University.

His 1954 team was undefeated and won the Tangerine Bowl, defeating Eastern Kentucky 7-6.

"I'll cherish that the rest of my life," Cardwell said. "That also was a team of players with no scholarships. Those kids all just loved to play football.

"We never gave them anything."

Of course, Cardwell gave his players many things, things that can't be measured in scholarships or any other material medium. For 13 seasons—good and bad—he was the football coach at Omaha and also coached the Indian (now Maverick) track and cross country teams.

Cardwell retired last September as UNO track coach after 32 years in that job.

"Wild Hoss" he was called. Cornhusker fans remember Lloyd Raymond Cardwell that way.

GRAND MARSHALL ALL-NEBRASKAN

By Mike Babcock

July 16, 1993—Lloyd Cardwell's name isn't on the University of Nebraska's lengthy list of All-America football players, an omission that underscores the limitations of such recognition.

Cardwell, grand marshal for the 1993 Cornhusker State Games, was as good of a football player as ever represented Nebraska, according to Lincoln's Bill Pfeiff.

"If I were to pick my No. 1 football player, he'd be the one," Pfeiff said recently.

Cardwell was a Cornhusker back on Coach D.X. Bible's teams from 1934-1936, so I have to defer to another's opinion on his ability. And Pfeiff, the former coach, teacher and administrator at Lincoln High, certainly qualifies as a reliable source.

Pfeiff was a freshman football player at Nebraska in 1936, Cardwell's final season. That means Pfeiff was able to assess his ability firsthand, on the practice field as a member of the "meat squad." Cardwell and Sam Francis, the Cornhuskers' senior fullback, "made hamburger out of us," Pfeiff said.

Francis was voted an All-American in 1936 because of his considerable ability—and with an assist from Cardwell. The defensive middle was often a little softer for Francis because of the threat of Cardwell breaking a long run to the outside.

"As a coach, I would do a lot to try to stop 'Cardy' from going all the way and maybe give Sam 10 yards," Pfeiff said.

Cardwell had sprinter's speed. He was a multi-event performer on Coach Henry F. Schulte's Cornhusker track and field team.

Cardwell wasn't a sports car running back, though. He was more a customized pickup truck. He stood 6-foot-3, weighed 200 pounds and never tried to avoid a collision, according to Pfeiff.

To provide perspective, Nebraska had "big" football teams in the 1930s and Cornhusker linemen averaged 193 pounds in 1936. Cardwell was bigger than an average lineman. Yet, he was a back.

With room to run, defenders had difficulty catching him. And even if they caught him, they had problems tackling him.

"If you got him, it was usually only by one leg and you needed help," said Pfeiff, no wimp himself. "When 'Cardy' knew he was going to get hit, he'd just knock the tar out of you. We were worked over pretty good by Cardwell, Francis and those guys."

Among Cardwell's nicknames was "Wild Hoss of the Plains."

Horsepower seems an appropriate metaphor.

"Believe me, I would have wanted 'Cardy' playing for me. He was ahead of his time," Pfeiff said. "He was a great one."

After he and Francis helped the collegians defeat the Green Bay Packers 6-0 in the 1937 College All-Star Game, Cardwell played for the NFL's Detroit Lions from 1937 to 1943. He coached football and track and field at the University of Nebraska at Omaha (previously Omaha University) for 32 years, retiring in 1978.

In 1954, the Omaha University football team was undefeated and won the Tangerine Bowl under Cardwell's direction.

Cardwell is 80 years old now and lives in Omaha. He'll participate in the opening ceremonies of the State Games on Friday at Seacrest Field. The event is scheduled to begin at 8 p.m.

His is a fitting choice for such an honor. Cardwell, a Seward native, represents what it means to be a Nebraskan.

His personality was shaped by the Depression. He worked hard and competed hard. He was proud, yet always self-effacing, "as humble of a guy and as good of a guy as you'll find," Pfeiff said.

Nebraska has had numerous football All-Americans, including numerous running backs. Pfeiff has seen most of them, from Glenn Presnell and Clair Sloan to Mike Rozier and Calvin Jones.

Cardwell is at the top of his list.

FROM BEGINNING TO END, CARDWELL PLAYED HARD

By Ken Hambleton

There was a common explanation as to why Nebraska running back Lloyd Cardwell never was named an All-American.

"I think a lot of people geared their defenses to stop Sam Francis (who was an All-America fullback at Nebraska in 1936) at about 10 yards or so," said former Husker Bill Pfeiff. "That way, you could keep Cardwell from going all the way."

Of course, Francis was deserving. He was an All-American in both track and football. He finished second in the Heisman Trophy balloting and was a force in Nebraska's powerful teams in the last years of Coach Dana X. Bible's reign in Lincoln.

But the statistics support the case for Cardwell, too.

Cardwell scored 120 points from 1934-36. Although records were not kept, *Lincoln Journal* and The *Lincoln Star* files show that he scored at least 10 touchdowns on runs of more than 20 yards. He was often the end-sweep runner, the shovel-pass receiver and backfield receiver for passes from quarterback John Howell.

Sports writer Cy Sherman wrote in 1936: "Although Nebraska in the very nature of things will have

11 men on the field and perfect co-ordination will be necessary if the Huskers are to accomplish definite results in the department of scoring, it almost goes without saying that the Scarlet's chief threat will be the 'Wild Hoss', the same being Lloyd Cardwell.

"Shake the Seward snorter loose, giving him the aid of a block, first on the end and later on the halfback, 'Cardy' has the rare speed to go places against anybody's ball club."

On his last play as a collegian, he ran 65 yards off-tackle for a TD to lift the Huskers to a 7-2 record and a final No. 9 ranking in the first Associated Press poll.

On his first play as a Husker, Cardwell returned a punt 75 yards for a touchdown against Wyoming.

"He was the greatest competitor I ever saw," said Omaha World Herald Sports Editor Fredrick Ware.

Lincoln Journal Sports Editor John Bentley added, "The rangy Seward youth was in the end zone, unsullied by human hand, before anyone knew what had happened."

Fans had no trouble spotting Cardwell. Players didn't wear facemasks and were on the field most

of the time, playing both offense and defense.

Cardwell became a legend in Nebraska.

Nicknamed "Wild Hoss" at Seward High School, Cardwell set state high school records in the long jump (22 feet, $6^{1}/_{4}$ inches), 220-yard dash (21.8 seconds), 220 low hurdles (:25.9), 120 high hurdles (:16.1) and javelin (160-1).

He walked on at Nebraska to play for football Hall of Fame Coach Bible. "Of course, everybody was a walk-on," Cardwell said later. "I just wanted to play for Nebraska. Northwestern contacted me and said they'd give me some aid, but I didn't want to go there. And it wasn't until after I was at Nebraska that I found out players from Pittsburgh and Minnesota got scholarships."

Cardwell finally did cash in on football when he was picked by the Detroit Lions in the first round of the first NFL draft. He signed for a whopping $250 and earned up to $2,000 as an all-pro in his second year.

"I used the signing bonus for a honeymoon in Estes Park (Colorado)," he said in 1978. He quickly ended the honeymoon to play in the College All-Star Game that matched the top collegians against the defending NFL champion. The All-Stars beat the Green Bay Packers 6-0 and Cardwell played well.

Eventually, Cardwell was paid up to $175 a game as a pro, and he earned it, playing as he did in college, almost every minute. He survived a broken cheekbone, various knee injuries and bumps and bruises, but retired in 1943 after breaking a leg.

He worked in the off-season as a personnel director for a automobile parts manufacturer, and in 1945, assumed the same post with the Martin bomber plant near Omaha. In 1946, former teammate Virg Yelkin asked Cardwell if he would coach track and football at Omaha University.

He coached the Indians (later the Nebraska-Omaha Mavericks) to records of 10-0 and 8-1, with 16 wins in a row in 1954-55. Omaha U. even posted its first postseason victory with a win against Eastern Kentucky in the 1954 Tangerine Bowl.

"Lloyd Cardwell was as good a player as there ever was," said Pfeiff, his former teammate. "He played 60 minutes a game and was the guy who could break any play for a touchdown and stop any play with his speed and strength on defense. And he was a decent human being. He made us freshmen feel like we were just as important as anybody else on the team. He made all his players, when he was coaching, feel just as important as everyone else.

"It would be hard to find somebody better at just about anything."

Nebraska I-back Ken Clark breaks away from a Kansas defender for some of his 177 yards against the Jayhawks November 11, 1989. (Ted Kirk/Lincoln Journal Star)

KEN CLARK/STATS

LETTERED:	1987-89
HEIGHT:	5-10
WEIGHT:	200
HOMETOWN:	OMAHA (BRYAN HIGH SCHOOL)
HONORS:	1988 ALL-BIG EIGHT
	1989 ALL-BIG EIGHT
PRO EXPERIENCE:	INDIANAPOLIS COLTS 1990-92

ATTITUDE ADJUSTMENT

Now, Clark hopes to carry on NU's I-back tradition

By Mike Babcock

AUGUST 21, 1988—**The play wasn't exactly spectacular, an under-thrown screen pass from Mickey Joseph to Ken Clark.**

It probably wasn't worth mentioning in an account of the Nebraska football team's scrimmage Friday, the final full-scale contact prior to the season opener in the Kickoff Classic.

But the pass play illustrated a reason Clark has emerged as a clear-cut No. 1 at I-back, just as surely as his 57-yard touchdown run earlier in the scrimmage or his 117 rushing yards did.

Clark, a junior from Omaha, reached behind him, caught the ball one-handed and turned an apparent loss into a 13-yard gain. "It was quite an athletic move," said Frank Solich, the Cornhusker running backs coach.

George Darlington, the secondary coach, shook his head. "You'd better get him when you have the chance," he said of Clark, "If you don't..."

No need to complete the thought.

It was obvious from the 57-yard run that Clark has the acceleration and speed to go all the way.

Barring injury in practice be-

tween now and then, Clark will start against Texas A&M Saturday night at Giants Stadium in East Rutherford, N.J. He'll become the key figure in what has been college football's most successful I-formation program during the 1980s.

He'll try to establish himself in a tradition that has included, among others, Jarvis Redwine, Roger Craig, Jeff Smith, Doug DuBose, Keith Jones and, of course, Mike Rozier, who won the Heisman Trophy in 1983.

On occasion, Clark has been compared to Rozier, most recently after last Saturday's scrimmage, by Nebraska defensive coordinator Charlie McBride.

Such comparisons usually draw raised eyebrows from listeners, who don't have the ability to evaluate football players the way coaches do.

Ken Clark? Mike Rozier? Huh?

Part of the problem is Clark's athletic background. He's the first Omaha Bryan football player to receive a scholarship from Nebraska, and he got little recognition in a much-publicized Cornhusker recruiting class that included Steve Taylor, Broderick Thomas, LeRoy Etienne and Richard Bell.

There was some thought Clark might not even be an I-back, that

he might be tried at defensive back, instead.

Another part, maybe the most significant, was Clark's attitude—toward himself and, more importantly, toward football. He wasn't consistent. He didn't concentrate at times. He let seemingly minor injuries bother him.

And to make matters worse, he occasionally allowed his on-the-field frustrations to carry over off the field.

That's all in the past.

"My attitude has changed," Clark said after Friday night's scrimmage. "I wasn't really happy when I came here."

During his first year at Nebraska, Clark alternated at I-back on an undefeated freshman-junior varsity team, averaging nearly 6 yards per carry.

He was solid, but not spectacular.

Clark redshirted the next year. That, combined with nagging injuries, had him believing "this wasn't the place I was supposed to be. I got kind of negative. I missed practices. I missed meetings," he said. "I felt like I was in the Army or something and had to be here."

Clark persevered. He stayed with it, though exactly why he isn't sure. "There are lots of doors and exits out of this place. I could have left," he said.

But he didn't, even though a knee strain eight games into last season must have set him to wondering again.

Encouragement and support from Solich helped. But there was more to his personal turnaround than that.

"It has come from within," said Clark, who spent the summer in Lincoln running and lifting weights to prepare for his junior season.

Some days he arrived on campus at 9 a.m. and didn't go home until 8 p.m.

"I made it (playing football) my No. 1 priority," he said.

Clark's efforts haven't gone unnoticed. "He's really played well in the two major scrimmages," said Solich.

Senior Tyreese Knox has been sidelined by a sore hamstring and sophomore Terry Rodgers is still learning, after redshirting last season.

But Clark isn't No. 1 by default. "Ken's earned everything he's gotten," Solich said. "He's put in a lot of time, and his attitude's been great."

Those were the missing elements because Clark, apparently, has always had the athletic ability to be a successful I-back. You don't develop the skill to make a play like the one he made on the pass from Joseph in Friday night's scrimmage. That's God-given.

NU'S CLARK HAS PAID PRICE FOR CAREER RUSHING NUMBERS

By Ken Hambleton

OCTOBER 18, 1989—**It's not as bad as someone putting a "kick me," sign on your back, but building up good statistics can bring on some nasty reactions.**

"You get some yards, some touchdowns and a couple of good games and you're a marked man," Ken Clark said. "The defenses practice all week on how to stop you and how to make your job harder.

"You expect it. It doesn't mean you have to enjoy it," he said. "I like the challenge, but my body doesn't during halftimes when we sit around, or in between practices, when I have a chance to stiffen up."

Such is the life of Nebraska's starting I-back.

Clark, like so many other I-backs before him, has taken the limelight of the Nebraska offense. He has jumped from oblivion to No. 3 on Nebraska's all-time career rushing chart. He is in line for All-Big Eight, All-America and even Heisman Trophy consideration with his 2,589 career yards.

The senior from Omaha Bryan needs just 87 yards to become the top major college rusher from a Nebraska high school, passing Gale Sayers, who played at Kansas.

Despite ankle sprains, knee strains, back pulls and hip bruises, Clark has run for more than 100 yards in 11 of his last 16 games.

The yards have not been gifts. Clark has played behind a sometimes makeshift line that has been hampered by injuries. He has been the focus of defensive coordinators and in the gun sights of defensive players all season.

Naturally, he has tried to avoid getting creamed by outrunning, outdancing and outfoxing defenses.

That didn't last long.

Two games ago, Clark promised to avoid the "tip-toeing" he allowed himself earlier this season. "I will be more aggressive. Put my head down and break tackles. Every season I try finesse and playing hardnosed football seems to be the way I have to play to finish," he said.

The change has worked to the tune of 168 yards against Kansas State and 125 against Missouri with 22 and 17 carries, respectively. But there is a physical toll to pay to play that way.

"I'm pretty healthy," Clark said. "A little ache in my right knee, but otherwise great."

Clark said he is looking forward to playing at Oklahoma State this weekend. He had a career high of 256 yards against the Cowboys last year. But he knows that he's in for some pain, no matter how the game is resolved.

In other words, the bruises on Clark's legs and the soreness in his knees is not lessened by the fact Nebraska is playing lesser opponents.

NU'S CLARK PREFERS TO LET ACTIONS DO HIS TALKING

By Ken Hambleton

OCTOBER 25, 1988—In his silence, reporters and broadcasters have fumbled and been thrown for a loss to describe Nebraska I-back Ken Clark.

Clark spirited through the Oklahoma State and Kansas State defenses for 481 yards and four touchdowns and didn't stop to talk about it.

Nobody could stop him, not even the press corps after his last two impressive shows.

Clark gained 256 yards against Oklahoma State and 225 against Kansas State and is ninth in the country in rushing. His recent performances helped boost Nebraska to the national lead in rushing offense and the No. 2 spot in total offense.

But he wasn't talking to the press about the accomplishments. The problem was, as Clark said, "there just isn't much I have to say."

The junior from Omaha Bryan said he is happy with his last couple of games but he didn't want to get wrapped up in talking about the past. The best way to avoid that was to not talk about it at all.

"The Oklahoma State game was done. I was beat up, sitting in the training room and I had another game in seven days. The Kansas State game was done and I felt the same way," he said. "As for explanations, I'm still trying to put it all together myself."

Clark needs 38 yards against Missouri this weekend to become the 10th Cornhusker back to reach 1,000 yards in a season. If he maintains his current averages, he would be third on the all-time single season rushing chart behind former Heisman Trophy winner Mike Rozier, who has the top two single-season marks.

"A 1,000-yard season would mean a lot to me," Clark said. "I never got it in high school and I didn't know if I'd ever get the chance here. To get 1,000 this year would be something to build on for next year and something to celebrate this year."

Clark said the difference in his running is a matter of letting go of tensions, caution and concern about injury.

"I'm seeing the big picture and I've given up protecting myself," he said. "I'm starting to play the complete game as running back. I'm coming out of my shell.

"Best of all, I'm getting more carries. I can use my balance, work on keeping one guy from knocking me down, and make better decisions on where to cut and when to cut," he said.

Clark has paid a price with a sore ankle, sore forearm and sore ribs. He had a chance to become the first back in Big Eight history to have back-to-back 250-yards-plus games when he followed his performance against Oklahoma State with 225 yards in 20 carries against Kansas State. But Clark didn't play against Kansas State for most of the final two quarters. "I was hurting a bit and Coach Osborne said there was no need to risk more injuries," he said.

But unlike minor injuries in the past, this was different. The game was all but decided and Clark had proven himself.

The difference was evident when Clark broke free on a 73-yard touchdown run against Oklahoma State on Nebraska's first play of the game.

Coach Tom Osborne called it one of the greatest runs he'd ever seen.

Clark said it was a great run for him in that he had never done anything like it before.

"That run shocked me. Our guard (Andy Keeler) was downfield

knocking people down and I let go," Clark said. "I got hit a couple of times and kept going and people kept blocking for me."

Osborne said Clark was doing everything expected, but nothing special before that long run. Clark has blossomed since then. Playing a little hurt, breaking a couple of tackles and making the right moves were good signs, Osborne said.

It was as if he finally got some shoulder pads that weighed less than 150 pounds, Clark said.

"It meant a lot to get those yards against Oklahoma State on the same field with Barry Sanders (the OSU back who leads the nation in rushing and had 189 yards against Nebraska)," he said.

"I didn't want to get caught up in comparing myself to him. I saw what that kind of thinking can do to a back when Keith Jones talked about how he'd match up with Gaston Green last year."

Clark has had his disappointments this fall, but he put them behind him.

"I had taken a lot of fun out of the game because I was getting what the plays were designed for and not a lot else before that," Clark said. "The Kansas game was probably the worst."

"I needed to prove I could do more with more carries," he said.

The Nebraska coaching staff recognizes that, too. In each of the games he's had more than 20 carries, Clark has gained more than 100 yards and scored at least one touchdown.

"I'm getting more carries, more chances to get something going," Clark said. "You build some momentum and the defenses wear down. When you get to around 20 carries, the game changes. You are a lot more familiar with the way the defenses play, and personally, I feel a lot stronger the more I play."

Ken Clark was surrounded by fans at Nebraska's annual Media Day in 1989. The running back from Omaha Bryan rushed for more than 1,000 yards in 1988 and repeated the feat with 1,196 yards in 1989. He finished his NU career with 3,037 yards. (Harald Dreimanis/Lincoln Journal Star).

QUIET CLARK AVOIDED LIMELIGHT

By Steve Sipple

Ken Clark typically went about his business quietly. He performed so quietly, in fact, his name often is forgotten during discussions about Nebraska's elite running backs.

Former Nebraska head coach Tom Osborne understands why Clark tends to get overlooked.

"There wasn't anything about him that really grabbed your attention," Osborne said. "He wasn't overly fast or overly big. But he was there. He was a player. He had great balance, good instincts. He wasn't slow, but it wasn't like he ran 100 yards in 10.4 seconds or anything like that."

Clark's college statistics speak for themselves. In three seasons, 1987-89, the 5-foot-10, 200-pound Clark rushed for 3,037 yards, fourth on the school's all-time list. His best season was 1988, when he gained 1,497 yards, including back-to-back rushing performances of 256 yards against Oklahoma State and 225 against Kansas State.

After slipping tackle after tackle against the Cowboys and Wildcats, Clark slipped past the media on both occasions, declining interview requests. Such was his nature.

"A lot of great running backs like the limelight," said Tim Bond, Clark's coach at Bryan High in Omaha, Neb. "That's part of the reason some guys become running backs. I never, ever saw that in Ken. Ken wanted the ball because he saw it as a way to lead his team to victory."

"Ken pretty much stuck to himself," said Frank Solich, the former Nebraska running backs coach who is now the Huskers' head coach. "He was not a guy who would go with the crowd necessarily, and he is not a flamboyant guy."

In college, Clark avoided attention to the point of sometimes seeming aloof. "A lot of times, I don't have a lot to say," he said in 1989.

Clark's low-profile style probably helps to explain why he sometimes gets overlooked by Husker fans. There is more to it, though. The fact he played on three losing bowl teams didn't help his standing in Husker history. Nor did his running style; he was a blue-collar type of I-back who relied more on balance and instinct than eye-popping bursts of speed and amazing moves.

During Clark's junior year, Oklahoma State's Barry Sanders attracted the brunt of the national media attention, winning the Heisman Trophy after rushing for 2,628 yards and scoring 39 touchdowns, both NCAA records.

As a senior, Clark rushed for 1,196 yards and 12 touchdowns despite a slew of nagging injuries. Yet Gerry Gdowski's outstanding season at quarterback, after coming out of virtually nowhere, was a more compelling story.

Bryan Carpenter played fullback in the same backfield as Clark for three seasons. Carpenter now serves on the Huskers' film staff. He said younger running backs occasionally approach him with questions about former Nebraska big-name running backs.

"I always mention Ken, and they'll say, 'When did he play?'" Carpenter said. "I thought he was a great back. He was a tough guy, and he knew what it took to be good."

In his junior season, Clark finished second in the Big Eight Conference and fifth in the nation in rushing, averaging 6.5 yards per carry and 124.8 rushing yards per game. He outgained Sanders 256 to 189 in Nebraska's 63-42 victory in Lincoln, Neb.

Later that season, before the Oklahoma game, one Sooner assistant said if Nebraska had any one of Oklahoma's top four running backs, the Huskers would be stronger offensively. Sooners Coach Barry Switzer described Clark as a "hammer back"—not a disparaging remark but not exactly lavish praise. Clark hammered the Sooners for 167 yards on 24 carries in a 7-3 Husker triumph.

Clark gained 146 or more yards in five of seven conference games, and yet received first-team All-Big Eight recognition from only the Associated Press. Colorado's Eric Bieniemy received first-team honors from the league coaches and United Press International.

As a senior, Clark was a consensus All-Big Eight selection despite battling a swollen toe, a wrenched knee and a sprained thumb, among other injuries. He had five 100-yard games but was limited to 95 yards against Colorado and 91 against Oklahoma.

"We passed more against Oklahoma and Colorado, but the reasoning behind that was those teams were keying on Ken Clark," Osborne said at the time. "So, even when Ken didn't get the ball, he was effective for our offense."

Solich said the Nebraska coaches never overlook Clark when the best Husker I-backs are discussed.

"He was really a smooth running back," Solich said. "At the same time, he had excellent quickness and tremendous balance. He's the kind of guy who made the most out of all his plays.

"He had the ability to absorb a hit and, when you thought he was going to go down, he kept going.

He read blocks well and didn't rush things. His timing was good."

It took a few years for Clark to emerge at Nebraska. During his first year in Lincoln, he alternated at I-back with Tyreese Knox on the freshman-junior varsity team and averaged 6.0 yards per carry. He redshirted the next season. Then, in 1987, he and Knox shared time as the alternate varsity I-backs behind starter Keith Jones. Clark gained 344 yards on 64 carries, with all of his statistics coming during the first eight games, after which he was sidelined by a knee strain.

Nagging injuries would continue to haunt Clark. Solich, though, appreciated Clark's determination to play, and practice, with pain.

"There are guys who sometimes just want to take a week off and show up for games," Solich said. "I saw Ken as a guy who always wanted to work hard to get on the field."

Bond—the Omaha Bryan coach—said Clark's willingness to play when he was injured was the biggest adjustment he made from high school to college. "You couldn't get him out of a ball game (in college)," Bond said. "He realized the training room wasn't the place to be."

Clark spent his share of time in the training room during his senior year in high school, missing four games with a lower-leg injury. In 4 1/2 games, he rushed for 750 yards. After the four-game layoff, he came back to rush for 146 yards against Omaha Gross.

"He was a great athlete," Bond said. "He was an explosive blocker and a great defensive back and kick returner. He could throw the ball farther than anybody on the

team. He was by far our best athlete.

"Speed wasn't his greatest asset. His biggest asset was he was just one tough son of a gun. He would put his head down and run through people."

Even so, Osborne recalls, Clark "wasn't a guy who people knew a lot about" in high school. Osborne remembers attending an Omaha Central-Omaha Bryan game with Solich. The two coaches were on hand to scout a few Central prospects, but Clark kept catching their eye.

"We came away feeling like Ken was a legitimate prospect," Solich said.

Clark would prove the coaches were right in years to come, making a mark in college and, to a lesser degree, professional football. He was an eighth-round draft pick of the Indianapolis Colts, whose 1990 roster included Pro Bowl running back Eric Dickerson. But Dickerson was sidelined by a hamstring injury, leaving Clark, second-year player Ivy Joe Hunter and veteran Albert Bentley to compete for his spot.

Clark won the starting job for the opener after rushing 25 times for 86 yards in exhibition play. The honeymoon, however, didn't last long. Midway through October, Colts Coach Ron Meyer waived Clark to make room for Dickerson.

Clark, though, made the Colts' roster in 1991 and 1992. He enjoyed his best pro season in 1991, carrying 114 times for 366 yards and catching 33 passes for 245 yards. His final season was 1992, when he carried 40 times for 134 yards.

In 1981, Roger Craig rushed for 1,060 yards, including 234 against Florida State. In that game, he tied the NU record for longest TD run with a 94-yard burst. (Journal Star Library).

ROGER CRAIG/STATS

LETTERED: 1979-82
HEIGHT: 6-2
WEIGHT: 220
HOMETOWN: DAVENPORT, IOWA
HONORS: 1981 ALL-BIG EIGHT
NEBRASKA FOOTBALL HALL OF FAME
PRO
EXPERIENCE: SAN FRANCISCO 49ERS 1983-90
LOS ANGELES RAIDERS 1991
MINNESOTA VIKINGS 1992-93

CRAIG IGNORES EARLY TALK

By Randy York

April 26, 1981—Early All-American endorsements and spring game rushing records are nice, but neither are about to change Roger Craig's hat size.

Nebraska's junior I-back has two simple goals before he parades his talents September 12 at Iowa, his home state.

"All I want to do between now and then is work hard and keep my nose clean," Craig said Saturday after breaking Nebraska's 14-year-old spring game rushing record of 113 yards on only 11 carries.

Craig netted 126 yards and bolted for two first-quarter touchdowns in the Reds' 22-21 loss to the Whites.

His first touchdown, a 2-yard run around right end, gave the Reds a 7-0 lead $3^1/_2$ minutes into the game.

His second touchdown, a 61-yard gallop around left end $9^1/_2$ minutes later, had 25,431 Memorial Stadium fans believing what they had been reading—that Craig is a bona fide preseason All-America candidate.

"It's a little hard putting me in that class," Craig said. "I think of myself as an average player going out and getting the job done the best way I can.

"My personal goals, other than to stay healthy, are team goals," he said. "I just want to win the Big Eight and hopefully, the national championship."

With Craig in the backfield, such ideas are not out of line.

"As far as I'm concerned, he can hang with any back in the country," quarterback Mark Mauer said. "I don't mind handing off to him or pitching to him. Rog has a knack for finding the right place and getting the yards."

More importantly, Mauer said, Craig "has great character. He has such an influence on this whole team. He's always in the weight room, working out. He's a leader on and off the field."

Craig is so busy worrying about the team, he never even thought about a 100-yard afternoon until he rehashed the game with reporters. He said breaking Ben Gregory's 1967 rushing record was "shocking."

"I thought I had about 80 yards or something like that," Craig said. "That long run did it."

Craig's 61-yard touchdown should have been stamped and sent as a postcard. The play was executed on the AstroTurf like Tom Osborne diagrams it on the blackboard.

All blocks were delivered, especially tackle Dan Hurley's.

"That's the one that sprung me loose," Craig said. "I set it up for him when I dipped inside. Once he took out the defensive back and I turned the corner, I knew I was gone."

At that point, Craig had 98 yards rushing on only seven carries. He broke the record with a 16-yard burst on his eighth carry, but lost 5 yards on his next attempt.

Craig then waited until the third quarter to set the record again, on an 8-yard gain. That run also erased his worst experience of the game—running the wrong way and watching Mauer pitch out to an invisible man who promptly fumbled.

"The offensive line did a great job. I owe everything to them," Craig said. "They're patting each other on the back and keeping each other going."

Craig was happy to contribute his part, especially since his mother, a brother and two sisters had driven from Iowa to watch him play.

Jack Leabo, Craig's high school running back coach from Davenport, also saw him play for the first time in a college uniform.

"He'd seen me on TV, but not live," Craig said. "I kind of wanted to give him a show."

HUSKERS' CRAIG HARDWORKING

By Mike Babcock

September 20, 1981—Superman, you say?

Not really.

Roger Craig wasn't more powerful than a locomotive Saturday afternoon, even though he did run over some Florida State football players when they got in his way.

He didn't leap tall buildings at a single bound, though Nebraska's junior I-back did hurdle a few Seminole defenders when he was left with no other choice.

And Craig certainly wasn't faster than a speeding bullet, even when he ran away from FSU defensive backs Harvey Clayton and James Harris on his school record-tying 94-yard touchdown.

No, the 234 yards Craig gained on 20 carries Saturday in Memorial Stadium weren't evidence that he's superhuman. Rather, they showed what hard work and good blocking can do.

"I'm not surprised by what Roger Craig did today," said NU fullback Phil Bates, one of the

people responsible for the blocking. "I just hope we can get him out in the open more often."

Craig wasted no time getting into the open Saturday afternoon. The first time he carried the ball, on Nebraska's first play from scrimmage, he hurdled over the right side of the line and ran for 10 yards. The second time he carried, Craig went through the line behind a Bates block and then took off on his own, breaking two tackles before being brought down after a 37-yard run.

By halftime, he had carried 10 times and gained 104 yards.

Craig prepared for Saturday "by running stadium steps and lifting weights (to strengthen his legs) three times (days) last week." Those are exercises he wouldn't ordinarily do, but "I knew I had to be ready," he said.

Craig's motivation was what he considered an unsatisfactory effort in last week's season opener at Iowa. Craig gained a respectable 74 yards in 19 carries, but he had fumble problems and, more

importantly, Nebraska lost.

Craig attributed his success against Florida State to the blocking of Nebraska's offensive line and Bates' lead blocking. Bates also opened the way on Craig's 94-yard run, taking out a linebacker who, by then, "was trying to hide. The (FSU) linebackers got a little tired as the game went along because if I wasn't beating on them, our guards were," Bates said.

According to Craig, both of his long runs were on "iso(lation)" plays designed to go up the middle, the key strategy in Nebraska's offensive game plan. "We wanted to run straight at them, run it right down their throat," he said.

Craig's record-tying touchdown run came only seconds after an embarrassing attempt at a kickoff return on which he stepped out-of-bounds at the Nebraska 6-yard line. As it turned out, Craig set himself up with the opportunity to tie the Nebraska school record set by Craig Johnson against Kansas two years ago in Lincoln.

On the first play from scrimmage, quarterback Mark Mauer handed the ball to Craig, who "was just concentrating on getting us out of there. I didn't expect it to break like that," he said.

BIG HAND FOR ROGER

By Mike Babcock

November 1, 1982—In the closing seconds of Nebraska's 52-0 victory over Kansas on Saturday, center Dave Rimington helped an injured Roger Craig to the Cornhusker locker room. The applause began as the two moved past a section of Nebraska fans, one of whom jumped over the wall to get Craig's autograph.

Craig is as popular as ever. His efforts have not gone unnoticed, which is as it should be. He deserves the recognition.

This football season has been full of disappointment for Craig, the senior running back from Davenport, Iowa. Last fall, he was Nebraska's leading rusher as an I-back sharing time with Mike Rozier, but he began this year dividing time between I-back and fullback.

Craig didn't complain; he became a fullback in order to help the team. No Cornhusker wants to win more than Roger Craig wants to win. Not one. And no Cornhusker is willing to sacrifice more than Roger Craig to achieve that goal.

Unfortunately, learning a second position has been the least of Craig's problems this season. His frustrations have been the result of injuries, first a severe thigh bruise that kept him home from Penn State, then an ankle sprain that continues to bother him.

Craig has finished only two games this season—the opener against Iowa and Colorado.

Saturday at Kansas, with Rozier less than 100 percent, Craig

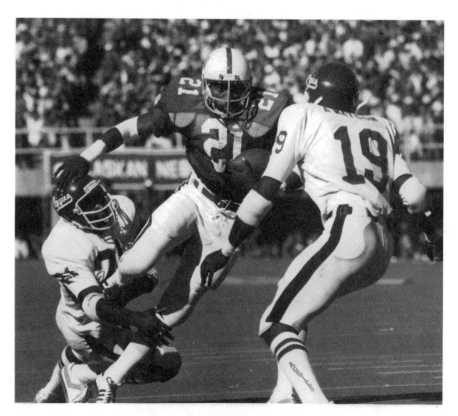

Roger Craig, who went on to star for the San Francisco 49ers in the NFL, saw action as a freshman at Nebraska in 1979. (Journal Star Library).

opened at I-back. For a half, he ran better than he's run in a long time, carrying 13 times for 67 yards. On his first carry in the second half, Craig bolted for 15 yards, a costly gain considering he had to be helped to his feet and off the field following the play.

According to Craig, the injury was more than a twisted ankle. "My Achilles' tendon, the ligaments there were real tight, and I felt it twist," he said.

Actually, Craig had reinjured his ankle "earlier in the game. I just didn't tell anybody." He played with the pain until he twisted the leg in the second half. "Usually, I can get up," said Craig. That time, however, he couldn't.

Craig's 82 rushing yards against Kansas were a personal, single-game high this season. By comparison, in 12 games last year,

he rushed for fewer than 82 yards only four times, going over 100 in four games, with a career high of 234 against Florida State.

Despite his disappointments, Craig remains as positive as ever. His injuries will clear up "sooner or later," he said, adding: "I can't get down or start feeling sorry for myself. I've got to keep my head up."

The training room report on NU Coach Tom Osborne's desk Sunday afternoon listed Craig as questionable for this Saturday's game against Oklahoma State, but Craig's own evaluation of his physical status differed. "I'm certainly not going to count myself out," said Craig. "I'm going to give it a shot."

He'll continue to listen to NU head trainer and physical therapist George Sullivan, "who's been doing a great job; I do whatever he tells me." That means more whirl-

pools, both hot and cold, and ultrasound treatments.

His ankle and lower leg "are going to stay a little sore because the ligaments are so weak. It's just one of those injuries where you have to bite down and keep going," Craig said.

Craig isn't looking for sympathy, and doesn't expect the recognition that he surely deserves. His attitude is best expressed by cliches that take on substantive meaning when applied to Roger Craig.

Losing his identity in the interests of the team "doesn't bother me as long as we win the games," he said. "I just perform the best I can. I've tried to give my best effort and be a team player since the first day I came here."

Anyone who follows Nebraska football closely enough knows that. It almost goes without saying.

A wide-eyed Roger Craig squirts through a hole against Colorado October 9, 1982. (Journal Star Library).

Roger Craig's great field vision and high-stepping style helped him rush for 2,446 yards during his Husker career (1979-82). (Journal Star Library).

CRAIG SET STANDARD FOR NU RUNNING BACKS

By Curt McKeever

Always easy-going and accommodating, Roger Craig was a sweet dream to his family, the coaches he played for, his teammates, adoring fans, even members of the media.

But to anyone who got in the way of his desire to win and become the most complete running back in the game, Craig was nothing but a nightmare.

"I think of him coming around the corner with his knees up in the air and driving," said Frank Solich, who joined the NU coaching staff in 1979, the same year Craig came to the Cornhuskers after earning All-America honors at Davenport (Iowa) Central High School.

In 15 years as Nebraska's running backs coach, Solich developed a trademark of demanding durable, tough-minded players. Craig, who was the featured back on Solich's 1979 junior varsity team, set the standard.

He was "a very determined guy, who the moment he was hit would take off," Solich recalled. "He'd look like he was going down, and get 30 yards."

Craig exploded out of his stance like a bull who'd just caught sight of a red cape, with knees pumping high. If would-be tacklers caught a glimpse of his wide-eyed, maniacal look, they might have thought twice about trying to take him down.

"The reason why my eyes are wide-open is I'm looking for spaces, so I'm really focused," said Craig, who went on to have the most illustrious NFL career of any Cornhusker from the Tom Osborne era. "The high-knee action comes from natural running. I developed that. I don't think defenders like to tackle you when you have knee action like that.

"I ripped through it pretty nice. When linebackers come low, I just connect under their chin and knock them out."

Craig, whose older brother Curtis was a standout wingback at NU from 1975-77, lowered the boom and provided an accurate barometer of things to come in his jayvee debut with the Cornhuskers on September 10, 1979, in Laramie, Wyoming. On the fourth play from scrimmage, he took a handoff from quarterback Nate Mason and ran 69 yards for a TD. He finished with 196 yards on 12 carries.

During the game, Craig also had a 70-yard burst to the Wyoming 17, but, running 5 yards ahead of his closest pursuer, was denied a TD when he fumbled out-of-bounds.

"I got too excited on my run, and the ball hit my facemask," Craig said that afternoon. "When I fumbled, I thought it was the end of the world."

Actually, it was just the beginning.

Craig had responded from his first major setback (he missed his junior season at Davenport Central when he broke his leg in the opener) by rushing for 1,565 yards and scoring 27 touchdowns as a senior in high school.

For Solich's junior varsity team, he averaged nearly a first down per carry—9.3 yards. The next season, Craig was rightfully dubbed the best third-string running back in the country, rushing for 769 yards and finishing sixth in the NCAA in scoring with 15 touchdowns.

Roger The Dodger was just starting to get heated up, though.

As a junior in 1981, while sharing time with up-and-coming sophomore Mike Rozier, he gained another 1,060 yards on the ground.

Against Florida State in the second game, Craig torched the Seminoles for 234 yards—the fourth-best single-game rushing total in Nebraska history. He was named second-team All-Big Eight, but after Rozier earned first-team honors, the Cornhusker coaching staff suddenly had a dilemma to ponder during the off-season.

Craig, however, provided an easy and early solution when he agreed to a request by Osborne prior to the start of spring practice to line up as a fullback in the same backfield with Rozier.

Three years later, Craig was playing fullback and helping San Francisco win the first of three Super Bowl championships during his eight seasons with the 49ers.

"When I finish, I want people to think that Roger Craig was a hard worker—a dedicated athlete to the team—that he would sell out all the time to the team as far as winning," he said in October of 1985.

Craig's team-first attitude inspired Nebraska into becoming a national championship-caliber squad in 1982. But with Craig hampered most the season, first with a bruised thigh and then with an ankle sprain, the Cornhuskers fell just short of the title.

Not surprisingly, NU's only loss of the season, at Penn State, came with Craig not in uniform for the first time in his college career.

Thereafter, because of his injuries, Craig (who finished the season with barely half the total yardage he produced in 1981 and finished as the school's fourth-leading rusher) was usually out of games before the fourth quarter. Publicly, he never showed signs of disappointment, and that temperament paid off, because the 49ers used their first pick to select Craig in the second round of the 1983 NFL draft

"The one thing that carried me through my senior year was attitude," Craig said. "I never missed a practice. Scouts would see that, and teammates and coaches would see that, and they would say, 'He's still giving his best.'"

But Craig's best was yet to come.

He was San Francisco's starting fullback as a rookie, scoring 12 touchdowns. He capped his second year by scoring a Super Bowl-record three touchdowns and totaling 135 yards of offense in the 49ers' victory against Miami.

"I was so ready when I left Nebraska and went to that high-tech offense because I was used to studying, watching film, and the plays weren't too complicated for me that I couldn't catch on," Craig said. "Some guys can't catch on."

Craig caught on partly because of his ability to catch passes.

Although he seldom was a receiving target at Nebraska (16 catches in his career), Craig grabbed 48 passes his rookie season at San Francisco.

"Roger was so easy to get along with, I can't remember ever having to tell him anything twice," said Craig's high school coach, Jim Fox. "He was a very bright kid, and he worked so hard and tried so hard, we expected a lot of good things from him."

In 1986, just his third season in the league, Craig became the first NFL back to gain 1,000 yards both rushing and receiving. On the day he accomplished the feat, Craig said, "This record means more to me today because we made the playoffs."

The most-rounded back in the game moved to halfback during the 1987 season, and a year later was the league's Offensive Player of the Year after rushing for 1,502 yards and 9 touchdowns, and catching 76 passes for 534 yards and one TD.

Craig celebrated that season, and the next, by adding two more Super Bowl championship rings to his collection.

A knee injury slowed Craig in 1990, and San Francisco opted to let him test free agency after the season. Craig then led the Los Angeles Raiders in rushing in 1991, tested free agency again and played for Minnesota for two years.

The 49ers, in a classy show of appreciation, allowed Craig to sign with them in August of 1994 and officially retire as a 49er. In 11 seasons in the NFL, he rushed for 8,189 yards and 56 touchdowns, had another 4,911 yards and 17

scores on receptions, and was named to the Pro Bowl five times.

"If I stood up here for two hours, I couldn't tell you what Roger Craig has meant to our franchise over the years," owner Eddie DeBartolo said at the time. "Roger and I became good friends. Sometimes that's not good when you own a sports franchise. This is very bittersweet. But it makes me proud that somebody who has meant so much to us also wants to come back and mean something for the future, and retire as a 49er."

Craig, who married his high school sweetheart, Vernessia, and has five children (Damesha, Rometra, Rogdrick, Alexander and Nai-jai), remains busy in the San Francisco area managing his foundation for at-risk youth and working in marketing. He also owns a sports bar in Davenport and has an annual golf benefit for the United Way.

It's the perfect schedule for Craig—one that requires him to keep that wide-eyed look and his knees up in the air and driving.

"He is the epitome of a guy who works harder than anyone and got more from the work," Brock Olivo, the all-time leading rusher at Missouri who patterned his running style and workout ethic after Craig, said in 1996. "I finally met him, and told him he was my idol when it came to running."

Olivo needn't have qualified his statement. As anyone who ever ran across his path would know, Craig had the total package.

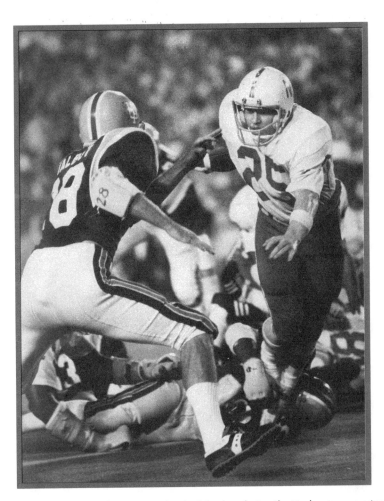

Nebraska's Tony Davis takes on two Florida defenders during the Huskers' game-winning drive in the 1974 Sugar Bowl. Davis rushed for 126 yards and was named the game's outstanding offensive player in NU's 13-10 victory against the Gators. He finished his career with an NU fullback-record 2,153 yards. (Journal Star Library).

TONY DAVIS/STATS

LETTERED: 1973-75
HEIGHT: 5-11
WEIGHT: 214
HOMETOWN: TECUMSEH, NEBRASKA
HONORS: NEBRASKA FOOTBALL HALL OF FAME
PRO
EXPERIENCE: CINCINNATI BENGALS 1976-78
TAMPA BAY BUCCANEERS 1979-81
BOSTON BREAKERS (USFL) 1983

KIDS TAG TOUGH TONY 'OUR FRIEND' AFTER VISIT

By Jim Cunningham

October 22, 1975—The way he slashes and crashes and bolts and jolts his way around a football field, it's no wonder that Tony Davis has been the subject of some unique descriptions.

During his slam-bang grid career, he's been variously referred to as "Tony the Terror", "The Tecumseh Tornado" and, most famously no doubt, "Tough Tony."

Last Friday, prior to departing for Stillwater, Oklahoma and a confrontation with some hostile Oklahoma State Cowboys, "Tough Tony" received another title. This one was the result of activity away from the gridiron.

The title was bestowed by the 70 students who attend Lincoln's Hayward School. The NU star entered the school as Tony Davis, football player. He left an hour later as Tony Davis, "Our Friend."

Hayward School, located a short distance from Memorial Stadium, is the home of Training for Occupational Proficiency, a program for mentally retarded young people, ages 13-18. Friday was Tony Davis Day at the school and the Husker's visit marked a special occasion out of which a special relationship grew.

At a full school assembly, Davis patiently and explicitly answered questions for perhaps 20 minutes before the effect of Tough Tony's presence was suddenly but clearly expressed.

Fourteen-year-old Jill spontaneously jumped up among her schoolmates and chirped: "Tony Davis is the best football player and he's my friend."

With that, the entire group clapped and cheered in agreement.

Davis' visit also included an autograph session. Every student wanted one. Some got two. Davis signed the school's two footballs. He even autographed the underside of a pet turtle.

Posters had been prepared, saluting the Big Red fullback and Nebraska football in general. Most of the signs were mounted on the gymnasium walls but one received special attention. It was made by 15-year-old Mark.

Mark was on the building's second floor when Davis arrived but spotted the gridder from the stairway.

"Hey Tough Tony," he yelled, charging down the steps. "I've got something for you."

He presented Davis with his poster and recited its message:

"Tony Davis, I trust you to win for Nebraska."

Davis earned the new friendship tag. He took charge of the affair and showed a remarkable ability to understand the gist of the many questions asked of him. In turn, his questioners showed a keen knowledge of football.

"Are you going to play pro football?," one youngster asked.

"I sure would like to," Davis replied.

"How come you don't wear stripes anymore?"

"We changed uniforms this year," Davis explained. "We now wear what are called mesh jerseys. They're cooler. The other jerseys were just too hot."

"Which is the best football team in the whole United States?"

"I think Nebraska is."

That answer brought a round of cheers.

Hayward students are trained in vocational skills, so it wasn't unusual for one youngster to ask: "Tony Davis, do you have a boss?"

"Oh yes, I sure do. His name is Tom Osborne and he's over at that big stadium, not too far from here."

"What position do you play?"

"I play fullback. Do you know what a fullback is?"

Some nodded affirmatively. Others weren't so sure.

"A fullback runs with the ball, but he also does more blocking. Do you know what blocking is?"

Again the reactions varied.

"Blocking is when you run into someone real hard."

Not all responses came in the form of questions. Another student had a more personal observation.

"I bet Tony Davis is embarrassed to have all of those muscles under his shirt," the young man whispered to his teacher. "I bet he never takes his shirt off."

Davis, whose sister Jeannine teaches special education in New Jersey, exhibited a special sensitivity, different from the physical toughness he shows on the field.

"This is the kind of situation that makes you realize just how many gifts you have and that you have to use those gifts in the best possible way," he said after signing his name over and over.

"These kids really have a lot of love to share and they want to spread it around. I think it's important to show them that you care."

While Davis has become famous for the impact he can create on the playing field, he can also make an impact off the field.

Twenty minutes after the assembly had ended and Tony had gone, it was discovered that 14-year-old Julie was not in her classroom.

She was quickly located. When found she was clutching her Tony Davis autograph and crying. An instructor asked her why.

"I'm just so happy, I can't stop," she replied.

That's what having a friend can mean.

DAVIS GOES FOR THE RECORD

By Bob Owens

NOVEMBER 8, 1975—Senior Tony Davis should be assigned No. 62 and his position should be called "guard-back" in Nebraska's football terminology.

Guards, who are required to wear numbers in the sixties, also are required to do a lot of blocking. They don't have to carry the football (unless Coach Tom Osborne has dreamed up a guard-around play).

Well, Tony Davis does both and does well at either assignment. Just take a few minutes the next time you watch the Huskers to see what No. 25 does on a few plays. You'll see he gets his yards the hard way, just as he gets his blocks—by sticking his head in the hole and driving or by sticking his head into an opponent and driving to create the hole.

That's why the Tecumseh flash is sometimes called "Tough Tony" out of respect for the job he does on a football field. Barring injury in the remaining three regular-season games and the bowl game—wherever it is—Davis probably will end his collegiate career as Nebraska's all-time leading rusher.

Davis goes into Saturday's Big Eight battle against Kansas State needing just 11 yards to tie Bobby Reynolds' career rushing record of 2,196 yards, which is second-best in NU history.

Davis should pass that milestone on the second or third carry against the Wildcats—maybe even the first—and then set his sights on becoming No. 1. That mark is 2,420 yards, held by Jeff Kinney, now a tough running back in the NFL for Kansas City. Tony is just 236 yards short of Kinney's record.

Coach Tom Osborne said Davis, who is a mere 5-11, 214-pounder, is "as valuable a player as we have" in more ways than as a runner and blocker.

"Tony doesn't get many calls where he has a lot of running room and he's as good a receiver as we have," Osborne said. Davis so far this year has rushed 97 times for 419 yards for a 4.3-yard average per attempt. He also has caught nine passes for 107 yards and one touchdown.

"He's also a tremendous leader," Osborne added. "He talks to the team before every game. The most important thing in Tony's mind is Nebraska winning. That's not the way it always is with seniors, especially ones who have had some previous success. By then, they usually start thinking about personal goals."

Davis showed his "team" spirit a year ago when he accepted a switch from I-back, where he gained 1,158 yards as a sophomore, to fullback, where blocking is just as important (if not more so) than carrying the ball.

Will his size keep him from making it as a pro? Not if Tony has anything to say about it. "There are a lot of pro backs smaller than me," he remarked to Big Eight Skywriters before the start of this season. "As a for instance, I'm bigger than Walt Garrison or Jim Kiick and I can block better than all of them"

EMOTIONS MELT 'TOUGH TONY'

By Randy York

JANUARY 1, 1975 – Tony Davis overwhelmed? Tough Tony, the kind of guy who would ask Gerald Ford if he really was that good a football player at Michigan?

Yes, Tony was overwhelmed Tuesday night after busting his way to 114 yards rushing in the second half to power Nebraska to a come-from-behind 13-10 win over Florida in the Sugar Bowl.

The gutty performance earned Davis the game's outstanding player award after having won a similar honor as a sophomore in the Cotton Bowl win over Texas.

In the locker room after the triumph over the Gators, Davis wasn't his usually talkative self. He had consumed five Cokes in less than 10 minutes and dressed hurriedly "because I thought I was going to vomit."

Tony, however, took time out at the Fountainbleau Motor Hotel early Wednesday morning to reflect on the Cornhuskers' and his own courageous comeback.

"I guess I was just so overwhelmed by the victory that I retreated into a shell. A lot of guys, myself included, were crying after the game," Tony observed.

"The team drew so close together—as close as I've ever seen," added Davis. "The coaches and

Tony Davis celebrates after scoring the game's only touchdown on a 4-yard run in the third quarter of Nebraska's 7-3 victory against Oklahoma State November 26, 1974. (Journal Star Library)

players were hugging each other. Terry Luck and I cried on each other. I was just emotionally spent and it all hadn't soaked in yet."

"We pulled down together— dug down as deep as we could and I want to stress we," Tony offered.

"Most people on this football team, with the possible exception of Dave Humm, have had to work for everything they've gotten.

"I've had to fight for everything I've gotten. I'm not from a rich family. My motto has always been never to quit under any circumstances. It's a characteristic I must have gotten from my parents," Davis says.

While Nebraska struggled in the first half, Davis carried only five times for 12 yards.

But when the Huskers revamped their strategy as Humm gave way to Luck at quarterback midway through the third quarter, Davis was the foremost beneficiary.

His sizable chunks of yardage came when the Cornhuskers needed them most. In fact, in Nebraska's time-consuming 99-yard scoring drive, Davis accounted for 54 of them on seven carries.

One was a 12-yard gallop on a draw play. He also scooted for 13 yards around right end and 11 yards up the middle to the Florida 13-yard line in the same drive.

Tony's most important run to daylight was a 40-yard scamper down the right sideline to the Florida 29 to set up Mike Coyle's game-winning field goal four plays later with 1:46 remaining.

"It was a 19 take, fake 49-pitch play," Davis said of the 40-yarder. "My path is inside. The guard pulls like it's a sweep and the strongside linebacker goes for him. Doak and Bonness had already taken their people out and Hegener just cut down the weakside linebacker.

"We were just as tired as Florida was at that point, but we all reached down for that something extra," according to Davis.

The Tecumseh fullback cherishes the Sugar Bowl award more than the Cotton Bowl trophy he received last year.

"First, we beat a better football team and second, this came after a more disappointing personal season for me," Davis reasoned.

"I don't feel I was used as effectively as maybe I could have been used this season," Tony offered. "But Coach Osborne and Coach Corgan have stuck with me even when I've looked down. I owed them something.

"You can't compete in anything unless you feel you can be the best. I've always felt I could play as well as anyone," Davis continued.

"Sure, I'd like to have gotten my hands on the ball more this season (he averaged 5 yards a carry)," Tony admits. "But maybe we just didn't play the way we should have played when we needed it most.

"Champions never let down,"

Davis believes. "Oklahoma never let down this season. Ohio State did. We did. But we were champions tonight and there's going to be more champions on this team in the next few years. Don't ever count us out of anything.

"I'm going to have to fight my tail off again just to keep my job next year. It's going to be a real dogfight with guys like Gary Higgs, Monte Anthony, Jason Justice, and Lindsay Kucera back," according to Davis.

"We push each other so hard. It's helped all of us," he adds. "The payoff was there tonight."

DAVIS WINS, BREAKS TROPHY

NEW ORLEANS, LA. – Nebraska fullback Tony Davis earned the Most Valuable Player trophy in Tuesday night's Sugar Bowl clash with Florida.

But Davis' crowd-crashing tactics, which earned him the honor, failed him once – after the game.

Davis tried to plow through a crowd of well-wishers to gain entrance to the NU dressing room after the game and broke the football player statue off the top of his new trophy.

Tecumseh, Nebraska, native Tony Davis earned the nickname Tough Tony with runs such as this one against Oklahoma State October 18, 1975. (Journal Star Library)

SWITCH TO FULLBACK CHANGED DAVIS' DESTINY

By Ron Powell

As a sophomore in 1973, Tony Davis appeared destined to become one of Nebraska's greatest I-backs. In Tom Osborne's first game as head coach, Davis rushed for 147 yards and two touchdowns in Nebraska's 40-13 win against UCLA.

He finished the regular season with 1,008 yards rushing, then added 109 yards in earning MVP honors as Nebraska defeated Texas 19-3 in the Cotton Bowl.

It turned out to be his final season at I-back. Before spring practice began in 1974, Osborne approached Davis about the prospect of playing fullback, a move that would mean few carries and less glory and honor.

"When he (Osborne) calls me in for this meeting, I thought I was in trouble or something," Davis said. "He told me that we were in a predicament, that we didn't have a fullback and that we had all these I-backs with John O'Leary and Monte Anthony. He wondered what I would think about moving. I told him I would have no problem with that, and I remember that it kind of surprised him."

Tough Tony, the nickname his

brothers gave him growing up in Tecumseh, Nebraska, saw his rushing attempts drop from 282 as a sophomore I-back to 113 as a junior and 158 as a senior. Davis, who finished with 2,445 career yards, gained 652 yards his junior season and picked up another 679 as a senior. When he finished, Davis stood as the all-time leading rusher in school history.

The move to fullback, however, probably cost him another 600 yards, which would've put him at more than 3,000 in his career.

Looking back, Davis has no regrets about the position change. He says it probably boosted his professional career, which consisted of three seasons with the Cincinnati Bengals (1976-78), three more with the Tampa Bay Buccaneers (1979-81) and one year ('83) with the Boston Breakers of the United States Football League.

"It benefited me down the road and made me much better at the pro level because I learned how to run between the tackles and I became a tougher runner," Davis said. "People might not understand this, but it saved me physically. Man, I took a beating when I was an I-back. At fullback, it's the other

way around, I was the one giving out the punishment."

Davis was a highly recruited high school player from Tecumseh. He considered Oklahoma, Notre Dame, Minnesota and UCLA before deciding to become a Husker.

After a year on the freshman team (freshmen were ineligible for varsity football then), Davis appeared ready to crack the starting lineup in 1972 and contribute to Nebraska's run for a third straight national championship. But a knee injury knocked him out for the entire season.

Davis showed what Coach Bob Devaney missed out on in the '73 opener, an NU win that avenged a loss at UCLA to start the 1972 season that ended Nebraska's 32-game unbeaten streak. Davis rushed for 25 yards in Nebraska's 56-yard scoring drive midway through the first quarter. A 39-yard run by Davis set up NU's third touchdown, 10-yard pass from Steve Runty to Frosty Anderson that gave the Huskers a 20-6 lead with 13:36 left in the first half.

An 80-yard drive in 15 plays to open the third quarter put the Huskers in control. Davis capped the march with his first Nebraska

TD—a 1-yard run on fourth down that epitomized the kind of player he was. He shed three UCLA defenders on his way to the end zone.

Davis added his second TD on a 43-yard run early in the fourth quarter that he celebrated by punching the fence just off the corner of the end zone in front of cheering fans.

"The funny thing about that game is that I remember the first touchdown clearly, but I can't recall what happened on the second one," Davis said. "When I see it on film, I can't remember it."

After the game, Davis said his performance "doesn't quite equal the 327 yards I gained in one high school game, but I'll do that some other day."

Davis also remembers Runty's play in the UCLA win. Runty, the backup quarterback that season, earned the start because of a leg injury to David Humm. Runty, a senior from Ogallala, Nebraska, completed 9 of 11 passes for 105 yards.

"Steve is not only the best second-string quarterback in the country, he's the best first-stringer around," Davis proclaimed after the game.

Davis went on to post four more 100-yard games during the regular season—106 against North Carolina State, 109 in a 13-12 loss at Missouri (Osborne's first defeat as coach), 111 in a 17-17 tie against Oklahoma State (one of only three

ties in Osborne's career) and 111 against Kansas State.

Against Texas in the Cotton Bowl, Nebraska broke from a 3-3 tie with 16 unanswered points in the second half behind another relief job from Runty, who replaced an ineffective Humm at halftime. Davis scored on a 3-yard TD run late in the third quarter.

Davis appeared to have won the individual battle against Texas' highly regarded running back, Roosevelt Leaks, who picked up just 48 yards.

"But I didn't really win because he wasn't at full-speed, so the whole thing didn't count," Davis said.

"We just moved better in the second half. We went out and went to work."

After he moved to fullback, Davis recorded only one more 100-yard performance, rallying Nebraska to a 13-10 Sugar Bowl victory against Florida to end the 1974 season. Davis smashed the Gators' defense for 126 yards on 17 carries on his way to the MVP award.

Nebraska trailed 10-0 at halftime in what Davis recalled as a miserable first half that drew the ire of Osborne in the locker room.

"Before the game when we were taking still pictures for TV, the Florida defense started talking smack to us and that stirred me up a little bit," said Davis.

"Then we came out and

played so poorly. Coach Osborne was very upset. It's the only time I've ever heard him swear. He told us we had to go out there and knock the hell out of them."

And that's what Davis did. He had runs of 11, 12 and 13 yards during a 99-yard scoring drive capped by a 2-yard TD run by Anthony that cut Florida's lead to 10-7 with 13:24 left. Mike Coyle kicked a 37-yard field goal to tie the game at 10 with 7:12 left. On Nebraska's next possession, a 40-yard run by Davis to the Gator 29 set up Coyle's game-winning 39-yard field goal with 1:46 remaining.

A picture of Davis was taped to the wall of the Florida locker room before the game with the words "Stop Him!" written across it in blue ink. The Gators failed to deliver.

"All I know is that Tony Davis is the toughest competitor I've ever faced on a football field," said Florida All-America linebacker Ralph Ortega. "He fought for his extra yards and now he has his reward."

Davis is now a stockbroker in Loveland, Colorado, who also serves as the Loveland High School offensive coordinator in the fall. Starting in 1999, he will once again have a connection to Nebraska football, as his son, I-back Josh Davis, made an oral commitment to the Huskers in the summer of 1998.

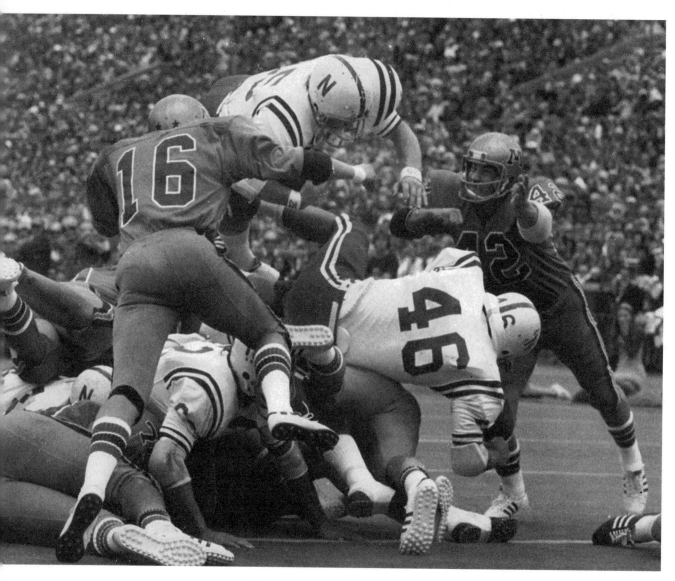

With Maury Damkroger (46) leading the way, Tony Davis goes over the top of the Minnesota defense to score October 7, 1973. Davis rushed for more than 1,000 yards and scored 13 touchdowns while playing I-back his sophomore season in 1973. He later switched to fullback. (Journal Star Library)

As a junior, NU's Doug DuBose rushed for 1,161 yards and eight touchdowns to lead the Huskers. (Harald Dreimanis/Lincoln Journal Star).

DOUG DUBOSE/STATS

LETTERED:	1984-85
HEIGHT:	5-11
WEIGHT:	185
HOMETOWN:	UNCASVILLE, CONNECTICUT
HONORS:	1984 ALL-BIG EIGHT
	1985 ALL-BIG EIGHT
PRO EXPERIENCE:	SAN FRANCISCO 49ERS 1987-88
	SACRAMENTO SURGE (WLAF) 1992

SUB DUBOSE COMES OFF BENCH TO GIVE NU EMOTIONAL BOOST

By Mike Babcock

January 2, 1985—Doug DuBose took matters into his own hands Tuesday night, during Nebraska's 28-10 victory over Louisiana State in the 51st annual Sugar Bowl football game at the Louisiana Superdome.

Cornhusker teammate Craig Sundberg took home the trophy as the game's most valuable player, but it was DuBose who provided the emotional boost when Nebraska needed it.

The sophomore I-back from Uncasville, Connecticut, didn't start the game, but he helped finish it.

His numbers told part of the story. DuBose carried 20 times for 102 yards and scored one touchdown, the Cornhuskers' first.

Less than three minutes after LSU took a 10-0 lead with 13:11 remaining in the first, DuBose converted a Sundberg screen pass into a 31-yard touchdown play. That was the spark Nebraska needed.

The Cornhuskers' first scoring drive covered 70 yards in six plays, including runs of 10 and 12 yards by DuBose. On a second-and-10, Sundberg dropped back, faked a pass to his left, then lobbed the ball to DuBose.

"We tried to get everybody to flow to the left, and I kinda snuck out in the flat to the right side," DuBose said. "Once I caught the ball, it was wide open."

A wall of blockers was about the only thing between him and the end zone.

"There was a whole lot of guys out there," DuBose said. "I was happy to see that."

DuBose caught the ball at the 38-yard line, some 7 yards behind the line of scrimmage and turned up-field. LSU defensive back Liffort Hobley had an angle and got to DuBose inside the 5-yard line but couldn't stop him.

Nebraska put in the screen pass especially for LSU.

"We had watched films and knew how well they pursued, so we thought something like that would work. They've got a pretty quick defense," said DuBose, a 5-11, 185-pounder.

"Doug may be slight of build, but he's not lacking in guts and determination. He can make runs Mike Rozier style," Cornhusker offensive guard Harry Grimminger said.

Because of LSU's quickness on defense, Nebraska's plan was to "run more options and spread 'em out to make the inside game work," said DuBose.

Senior Jeff Smith started at I-back and gained 84 yards on 17 carries. Both he and DuBose "can be slashing-type runners," Grimminger said.

Nebraska, which rushed for only 19 yards in the first quarter, finished with 280 yards on the ground.

As the game progressed, the Cornhuskers' strength in the offensive line began to wear on LSU. "By the end of the third quarter and the start of the fourth, the holes were getting bigger," said DuBose.

The interior of Nebraska's starting offensive line is comprised entirely of seniors—Mark Behning and Tom Morrow at tackles, Grimminger and Greg Orton at guards, and All-American Mark Traynowicz at center.

At halftime, "we got together and told each other this was our last game, so we'd better get after it," Traynowicz said.

The linemen decided to take matters into their own hands, and everyone benefited, particularly DuBose. "There were good holes in there, and all I had to do was read the blocks," he said.

DuBose made it sound simple.

HEISMAN HYPE JUST AROUND CORNER FOR DUBOSE

By Mike Babcock

July 31, 1985—Frank Solich is conservative in his praise of Doug DuBose. He has to be, of course, because he coaches DuBose.

Solich, the offensive backs coach for the Nebraska football team, is in no position to play favorites.

He's got to be objective.

Even so, Solich doesn't mind other people being subjective about DuBose, who'll be a junior this fall.

Solich doesn't even care if someone else includes "DuBose" and "Heisman Trophy" in the same sentence.

He just doesn't think it would be appropriate for him to do so.

"People can talk all they want about how they feel a player's ability is," Solich said recently. "You can ask different people around here, and they'll give you different answers about who should be starting in our backfield."

Solich would back a DuBose for Heisman campaign because "I think Doug has the ability to be that type of player," he said. But "so many things have to happen to a young back for him to be considered for the Heisman."

DuBose can be a legitimate Heisman Trophy candidate a year from now.

But the odds are against his being in the running to succeed Doug Flutie (a quarterback) this season because of the running backs with whom he will have to compete for national headlines—Ohio State's Keith Byars, Washington State's Rueben Mayes and Texas Christian's Kenneth Davis, for starters.

Those three were consensus All-Americans last fall.

In addition, Auburn's Bo Jackson returns after a season on the sidelines, as does Napoleon McCallum, Navy's first redshirt. Jackson and McCallum were consensus All-Americans in 1983.

Notre Dame's designated Heisman candidate is Allen Pinkett.

LSU has Dalton Hilliard; Southern Methodist has Reggie Dupard, and Southern Cal has Fred Crutcher.

Their abilities may be comparable; but because they're all seniors, they've got running starts on DuBose in the Heisman hype department.

Byars, for example, drew considerable attention last season by leading the nation in rushing, scoring and all-purpose running. Davis, who rushed for more than 1,600 yards, led the nation in yards per carry, averaging 7.6.

DuBose was second in that category among the top 25 returnees, averaging 6.7 yards per carry. He led the Big Eight and ranked 20th in the nation in rushing.

Still, there's too much ground . . .

Nebraska's offense isn't designed to showcase individuals. The Cornhuskers have always used more than one I-back.

"But if we have a back who stands out from the rest, we use him extensively," Solich said. Mike Rozier was handed the ball 300 times during his Heisman Trophy-winning, senior season.

Besides, "even if time gets split, we run the ball so much that the first I-back can get 20-some carries a game and the second-team I-back still has a chance to prove himself," said Solich.

"I think our system is great for an I-back to get recognition."

DuBose goes into the season as the best running back in the Big Eight.

Ideally, he'll perform well enough to draw some All-American attention and earn a few votes for the Heisman Trophy. That way he'll go into his senior season as a viable Heisman candidate.

Right now, however, "Doug's not thinking about that and neither am I," Solich said. "He's the type of guy who will go about his business."

A year from now that business might include the Heisman Trophy. Solich doesn't dismiss the possibility.

Conservative or not, "there's a chance that down the road things might fall into place for Doug," he said.

Such talk must begin now.

Doug DuBose injured his knee during fall practice and missed the entire 1986 season. (Journal Star Library).

DUBOSE DELIVERS WITH MOM THERE

By Virgil Parker

September 27, 1985—Nebraska's Doug DuBose is regarded as one of the nation's premier running backs. He's also well-known for the gold chains he wears around his neck.

But DuBose won't be wearing them for good luck when the Cornhuskers host the Oregon Ducks at Memorial Stadium Saturday afternoon. His good luck charm will be in the stands.

"My folks came out last weekend for the Illinois game," the Uncasville, Connecticut, native said. "My dad had to go back, but Mom has stayed to watch the Oregon game. She's my good luck charm. It seems like every time she watches me play, I have a real good game. I'd like to keep her here all season."

With his folks absent, DuBose gained 129 yards—not exactly a bad day—against Florida State in the Nebraska opener. But the Huskers lost 17-13.

But with his parents on hand for last Saturday's Illinois game, DuBose gained an average of 7.4 yards every time he touched the ball, piling up 191 yards as Nebraska romped to a 52-25 victory.

The gold chain collection began because of Walter Payton's nickname. The Chicago Bear running back is DuBose's idol.

"One day, a couple of Walter's teammates said his running style was kind of sweet. That's how his nickname of 'Sweetness' got started," DuBose said.

"When I was in high school, a lot of the guys on my team, knowing I idolized Payton, started calling me 'Sweetness.' Later on, my mom bought me a gold chain with a nameplate that says 'Sweetness' on it."

DuBose said Payton has been his hero since childhood.

"I figure if there is a guy to idolize, Walter should be the one," DuBose said. "He's the all-time leading rusher in the NFL and certainly one of the greatest running backs to ever play the game."

Another in DuBose's chain collection, one that refers to his jersey number, also has become a favorite. The charm hanging from it reads "22 is No. 1."

DuBose was No. 1 last season. Although starting just one game as a sophomore—against Syracuse when senior Jeff Smith was sidelined by injuries—DuBose earned All-Big Eight honors after leading the league with 1,040 rushing yards.

After two games this fall, DuBose is well ahead of last season's 94.5 yards-per-game average.

"I really don't keep track of stuff like that," DuBose insisted. "I just go out each game and try to help the team win. If I only carried the ball one or two times and we won, that wouldn't bother me. I try to put stats, goals and stuff like that out of my mind."

Does that mean DuBose doesn't have aspirations of becoming a Heisman Trophy winner? Not really.

"It would be nice to get more votes than any other junior in the Heisman voting this year and be able to say I am the highest man coming back next season," he admits.

"But, right now, if I think about winning the Heisman, I don't think I would get anything accomplished. If the team goes out and we have a great season, I think all of those things will take care of themselves."

Has DuBose studied Payton's running style and tried to imitate it?

In two seasons at NU, Doug DuBose rushed for 2,201 yards. (Harald Dreimanis/Lincoln Journal Star).

"You can't copy another runner's style," he answered. "My style is completely different than Walter's.

"I have tried to pick up things from him like running into the defenders, attacking people, not letting the tackler get into your body. But each person's running style has to come naturally. You just do things on instinct."

The Cornhusker I-back thinks the weight he added since last season "has helped me run a little bit tougher. I gained about 10 or 11 pounds. I think that has given me more confidence and more punch when I run inside. I'm learning how to make those extra yards after contact."

at 194.

"I still have the same speed," he said, "and I feel good. I've gained a lot of strength since I came here. When I first came to Nebraska I was known as an outside, breakaway-type runner. Now, people consider me an inside runner and I can go in there and get some tough yards."

Nebraska Coach Tom Osborne calls DuBose "a running back with great instincts, great balance and excellent speed.

"It's hard to compare Doug to the other fine backs we've had in the past because he is only a junior. The others played three full seasons, or four, as in the case of some, like Andra Franklin. But at this point, Doug compares very well. If

he stays healthy and keeps going, he can have as good a career as anybody we've ever had."

DuBose called last week's win over Illinois "a big game for us after coming off a loss. If we had dropped that game, we'd have been 0-2. It's hard to come back from two straight losses."

What about Oregon this Saturday?

"We've watched the films on them," he said. "they've given up a lot of points, but you can never tell what a team like that will do against us. They might stack the line and make us throw the ball.

"They've got a very good offense, and I'm sure their defense will be ready for us."

DUBOSE'S CAREER A STORY OF WHAT-MIGHT-HAVE-BEEN

By Mark Derowitsch

Doug DuBose's final act as a Cornhusker wasn't played out in the spotlight, but rather on the sideline. He spent what should have been his senior season at Nebraska away from the action, on the sideline resting his weight on a pair of crutches because of a severe knee injury that occurred just two weeks before the 1986 season began.

Maybe it was fitting.

After all, DuBose's career at Nebraska could fit in the what-might-have-been category.

Throughout his stay in Lincoln, DuBose was hampered by leg injuries. It still didn't stop him from becoming the first running back in Nebraska history to rush for at least 1,000 yards in each of his sophomore and junior seasons.

But the comparisons to Mike Rozier, the Heisman Trophy-winning Husker who set an all-time school record for most yards in a season (2,148 yards in 1983) and career (4,780 from 1981-1983), were constantly being made from the moment DuBose emerged as a candidate to replace Rozier as the Huskers' No. 1 I-back.

DuBose even got into the act. During spring football practice in April 1984, Rozier came back to Nebraska to check on the group of running backs who were fighting to replace him. DuBose was then listed third on the depth chart.

Rozier teased him with biting remarks.

"He told me I'd never be another Mike Rozier," DuBose said. "I told him I'd be better."

He wasn't, but to those who watched him practice day after day and play on Saturdays, DuBose was the next best thing.

As a sophomore in 1984, DuBose gained 1,040 yards on just 156 carries. He followed that up with a 1,161-yard rushing season as a junior. He was everything Nebraska wanted in an I-back: a tough, hard-nosed runner who could be called upon in short-yardage situations but possessed the speed necessary to out run opposing defensive backs.

"When Mike Rozier graduated, we wondered if we could find a back that good at everything," said Husker Coach Frank Solich, who was the running backs coach under Tom Osborne when DuBose played for the Huskers.

"Doug was close. He had excellent balance and great instinctiveness and could get a lot out of any play. You'd think he was going down and he'd come back up and get a bunch more yards."

DuBose made sure his name would be included among the Heisman hopefuls in the future with a solid performance during Nebraska's 28-10 win against Louisiana State in the Sugar Bowl following the 1984 season.

He was given the ball 20 times against the Tigers and rushed for 102 yards. But it was a pass play—

a screen that the Huskers put in their offense especially for LSU—that got DuBose noticed. Trailing 10-0, DuBose caught a pass from quarterback Craig Sundberg and sprinted 31 yards into the end zone.

The 5-foot-11, 190-pound DuBose was a play-maker.

"Doug may be slight of build, but he's not lacking in guts and determination," said Harry Grimminger, an offensive guard on the 1985 team. "He can make runs Mike Rozier-style."

DuBose used the 1984 and '85 seasons to build up his resume. In the third game of his sophomore year, DuBose rushed for 104 yards on just eight carries in a 42-3 win against UCLA. He earned the starting nod the following week and rushed for 107 yards on 23 tries, but the Huskers were upset by Syracuse. He finished the year with six games with at least 100 yards rushing, including a season-high 162 against Missouri.

He won the starting job for good in 1985, and came through with seven games with at least 100 yards on the ground. His 199-yard effort against Missouri was his career single-game best.

DuBose opened the year by rushing for 129 yards against Florida State, 191 against Illinois and 27 first-quarter yards against Oregon before a knee injury sidelined him for the rest of the contest and the game against New Mexico the following week.

He came back and finished the year with 1,161 yards and eight touchdowns.

"Doug started out running about as well as any I-back we've had through the first three games," Osborne said. "I thought he was just tremendous. But he got hurt and missed the better part of a game and three-quarters, and then he played the next two or three games subpar. I don't know if he ever rebounded to where he was. He's played well the last three games or so, but I don't know if he's ever gotten back to where he was the first three games of the year."

DuBose's Heisman hopes were dashed before he took the field in the fall of 1986. Fourteen days before the season began, DuBose tore the anterior cruciate ligament in his left knee during a preseason scrimmage. His injured knee was the same one he sprained the previous season.

"He had a legitimate chance—he was one of the top two or three—at the Heisman," Osborne said of DuBose at the time of the injury. "With the line we have and our ability to run, we had a good chance for him to have a great year."

Without DuBose, the Huskers won their first seven games before losing to Colorado. Nebraska fin-ished the regular season 9-2 before beating Louisiana State in the Sugar Bowl.

If DuBose had been in the lineup, at least one member of the '86 squad feels Nebraska would have been in the running for a national championship.

"That's what I think of when I think about Doug," said Steve Taylor, who was Nebraska's starting quarterback that season. "If he didn't get hurt, I think we would have had a special team that year. He probably would have made a big difference for us because we lost two close ball games. The knee injury probably cost us a shot at a national championship."

DuBose was just as sorry.

"It was real sad watching my teammates, knowing I was sup-posed to be out there," he said.

What followed is something DuBose wishes never happened, too. The Huskers were put on pro-bation because of a 1985 Nissan 300 ZX that was leased to DuBose. The NCAA ruled the Husker re-ceived "extra benefits," a claim DuBose disputed.

He then went undrafted, and spent the next couple of years try-ing to hang on in the NFL. He was signed by San Francisco, and played sparingly in 1988 because of a knee injury, but was waived in the spring of 1989.

He was banned from the NFL for one year after he tested posi-tive for drugs for a third time. He attempted to make a comeback in 1992, with Sacramento of the World League of American Football, but he failed to make it back to the NFL.

Still, it's hard to dispute what DuBose did on the field while he was at Nebraska, even if injuries forced him to use only a little of his seemingly endless potential.

"Doug was a great running back," Taylor said. "I know things didn't turn out like he had hoped. When he was at Nebraska, I don't think people realized what a spe-cial player he really was."

Harrison 'Sam' Francis competed for the United States in the shot put at the 1936 Olympics in Berlin. (Journal Star Library).

HARRISON 'SAM' FRANCIS

HARRISON 'SAM' FRANCIS/STATS

LETTERED:	1934-36
HEIGHT:	6-1
WEIGHT:	200
HOMETOWN:	OBERLIN, KANSAS
HONORS:	1935 ALL-BIG SIX
	1936 ALL-BIG SIX
	1936 ALL-AMERICAN
	NATIONAL FOOTBALL HALL OF FAME
	NEBRASKA FOOTBALL HALL OF FAME
PRO EXPERIENCE:	CHICAGO BEARS 1937-38
	PITTSBURGH STEELERS 1939
	BROOKLYN DODGERS 1939-40

TWO-SPORT ALL-AMERICAN FRANCIS RECEIVES HONOR

By Virgil Parker

December 25, 1974—Harrison 'Sam' Francis, one of the few athletes ever to achieve All-America status in two sports, today is honored as the newest member of the *Lincoln Journal* Nebraska Sports Hall of Fame.

Francis, an All-America football player as a Cornhusker fullback in the mid-30s, was also a member of the 1936 U.S. Olympic track team as a shot putter.

Following a long and distinguished military career from which he retired as a colonel, Francis now lives in Springfield, Missouri.

Francis is one of a select group of just three or four athletes—the legendary Jim Thorpe and more recently Ollie Matson are two—who gained All-America recognition in both football and track.

The 6-1, 200-pounder was a three-year letterman in both sports at Nebraska (1934-36). He was an All-Big Six Conference football choice at fullback his last two seasons. Francis led the league in scoring his junior year and following his senior season, was a consensus All-American and finished second in the Heisman Trophy balloting to Yale's Larry Kelley.

As a shot putter for the NU track team, Francis pulled off a 'Triple Crown' by winning his specialty at the Texas, Kansas, and Drake relays in both 1936 and '37.

After capturing the Big Six shot put title in the spring of 1936, Francis went to Randall Island, N.Y., where he won the Olympic Trials and earned the right to represent the United States in the Games at Berlin that summer.

"The funny thing," Francis now recalls, "is that all through high school (at Oberlin, Kansas), I thought my strongest sports were basketball and baseball. I always figured my least chance for success at the college level were in football and track."

Francis was recruited by Phog Allen to go to Kansas as a basketball player.

"It was just a last-minute thing that I ever wound up at Nebraska," Sam remembers. "I was already on the Kansas campus and moved into a dorm. But I knew deep down that I felt more comfortable around the Nebraska people, so I moved out without telling anybody and went up to Lincoln."

Francis, who was born near Nebraska City (Dunbar), had met Nebraska track coach Henry Schulte the spring of his senior year in high school.

"I qualified for the national interscholastic meet at the 1933 Chicago World's Fair," Francis says. "I think it was the last year such a national meet for high school kids was ever held. I won the shot put. I remember Jesse Owens was there. He was also a high school senior. Owens won the same events he later won at the Olympics in Berlin. Anyway, Schulte and I became well acquainted and he had a great bearing on my wanting to come to Nebraska.

Francis is well remembered for his kicking exploits as a Nebraska gridder.

"The newspaper reports claimed one of my kicks against Pittsburgh went 84 yards in the air," Francis says. "But the most fuss I recall over a punt was when we were practicing for the East-West game after my senior season.

"We worked out on the Stanford campus and Stanford track coach Dink Templeton and football coach Tiny Thornhill got in an argument over how far I could kick one. They measured it that time at 87 yards."

In addition to playing in the

Bob Devaney (left) and National Football Hall of Fame member Fred Singleton (right) recognize Sam Francis (center) for his induction into the National Hall of Fame in 1977. Francis was an All-America fullback in 1936 for Nebraska. (Journal Star Library).

East-West game, Francis led the fans' voting for selection to the 1937 College All-Star Game in Chicago—the fans voted to select the team in those days—and he played on the college team that defeated the Green Bay Packers.

"Having been on the Olympic team the summer before didn't hurt me any," Francis admits. "I met some of the eastern sports writers and their support was very important in gaining All-America status as a football player the next fall."

Following his senior season, Sam remembers that he signed a pro contract with the Chicago Bears "a little early. Things weren't quite as supervised in those days," he admits, "and I suppose I was already a pro before the track season of my senior year."

Francis played two seasons with the Bears, then two with the Brooklyn Dodgers. He had signed with the Dodgers for a third season, but went home to find a letter from another Sam . . . Uncle.

"I had taken advanced ROTC in college and had a commission in the infantry. I reported for active duty in March of 1941, nine months before Pearl Harbor," Sam recalls.

Francis took a brief fling at still another career in 1947 when he resigned his commission as a Lt. Colonel to become the head football coach at Kansas State.

Though his Wildcats were 0-10 on the season, six of those 10 losses were by two touchdowns or less.

Francis resigned a three-year contract to return to the service, from which he retired in 1966.

Has football changed much since he played 40 years ago?

"If a college team passed four or five times a game in those days that was a lot," Sam recalls. "As far as the pros are concerned, the big change is money. A lot of fine players—mostly linemen—were getting 50 bucks a game in those days. And that was on a game-to-game basis, as long as they stayed healthy.

"To my knowledge, I was only the third player—Red Grange and Bronko Nagurski were the first two—who received a regular season-long contract."

The Bears management had to keep the amount—a little over $7,000 for the year—a secret to prevent a mutiny by other team members.

"I've never been resentful that I played in the days before the big money," Sam says. "But I am terribly disappointed that the hot shots of today, who are making all that money, have never voted the early players—who pioneered pro football and made all this possible—into their pension plan.

"I don't need the money, but there are those who do," Francis continued. "And there are so few old-timers still around who would qualify that it wouldn't amount to peanuts in comparison to the size of fund they have. It wouldn't hurt them to show a little compassion to their fellow man."

KANSAN FRANCIS LED CORNHUSKERS INTO PROMINENCE IN THE 1930S

By Curt McKeever

September 29, 1989—Harrison 'Sam' Francis must have been a Nebraskan at heart, for it was a rare thing in the early 1930s to have someone from outside the Cornhusker state come play football for the university in Lincoln.

Even rarer was it when a Nebraska coach would venture across the state border to take a look at a prospect.

But in Oberlin, a small community tucked away in the north-central portion of Kansas, just south of McCook, plenty of folks were taking notice of Francis.

Four years later, many others were probably wishing they had, as Francis' name was synonymous with the Cornhusker football team emerging into national prominence. Francis also received accolades in track, and in the 1936 Olympics at Berlin he finished fourth in the shot put.

"The funny thing is that all through high school I thought my strongest sports were basketball and baseball," said Francis, a retired Army lieutenant colonel now residing in Springfield, Missouri. "I always figured my least chance for success at the college level were in football and track."

In 1932, Nebraska track coach Henry Schulte and football coach D.X. Bible were not of that belief. Both were after Francis' talents, but Kansas' legendary basketball coach, Phog Allen, beat them to Francis' door and convinced him to become a Jayhawk . . . at least for a short time.

"I was on the campus at KU for about two weeks just before school started," Francis recalled. "But the guys I was around were big-city boys and I was just a simple little old town guy and didn't feel real comfortable."

So without telling anyone at Kansas, Francis, the seventh of 10 children, born in Dunbar, Nebraska, packed and left for Lincoln.

"I was a little afraid and everything, but I'll never forget my first day of school," Francis said. "The first guy I met was Johnny Howell, a big guy from Omaha who was a quarterback. We hit it up and that gave me a little bit of confidence."

Three years later, the two were helping Nebraska win its sixth Big Six Conference championship in eight years under Bible, a coach of deep integrity who became known as the little colonel.

"He was firm and a good disciplinarian," Francis said. "But it didn't reflect that way. He was like a dad to me—he was one of the grandest of guys."

One who could get a team to do incredible things. Like in 1936, when no conference team scored against Nebraska.

Four seasons earlier, Francis and his freshmen teammates showed that kind of ability against the Cornhusker varsity.

Freshmen weren't allowed to play with the varsity in those days, so "we scrimmaged the varsity all year and got beat on," Francis said.

But not always.

"D.X. had a helluva team, but we had to quit playing against them because in one of the big scrimmages about the second or third week of the season they couldn't score against us."

The next three years, Nebraska opponents had trouble keeping Francis, and running mate Lloyd Cardwell out of the end zone, as they combined for 32 touchdowns and 222 points. Francis led the league in scoring his senior season (he had an added incentive . . . the owner of Bob's Coffee Shop offered meal tickets for certain accomplishments) and finished a close second to Yale end Larry Kelley in the Heisman Trophy voting. In a poll of 1,498 players, he led the nation with an efficiency rating of 97.85 percent. Of 127 opposing players, all but one called him the best they had faced.

Francis was a first-round draft choice of the Chicago Bears and played with them for two seasons before going to the Brooklyn Dodgers of the National Professional League. He was all ready to play a third season when he was drafted again . . . into the U.S. Army.

"Everyone took military classes for two years, but I took advanced military after that because you'd get paid $30 every month or so," Francis recalled. "I really hadn't planned on making a career out of the military and here I am one of the first ones ordered in."

Francis left the service in 1947 to take the head football coaching job at Kansas State. But after an 0-10 season, one in which K-State lost six times by two touchdowns or less, Francis rejoined the forces when offered a regular commission.

NEBRASKA WAS HOME TO FRANCIS

By John Mabry

Most college kids go home and try to find a job during summer vacation.

Sam Francis went to Berlin to compete in the Olympics.

In 1936, Francis qualified for the Summer Games in the shot put. At the time, he was only the second University of Nebraska track and field athlete to participate in the Olympics. He just missed winning a medal.

"I got all excited and fouled a couple of times," Francis said. "I finished fourth."

The overseas trip was not a bust. He rebounded by winning several international competitions later that summer.

The European vacation came to an end when Francis got a phone call from southeast Nebraska. On the other end of the line was Nebraska football coach Dana X. Bible.

"He said 'Get the heck back here,'" Francis recalled. "'We've got to get ready for football.'"

Oh, yeah. Football.

So back to Nebraska he went to get ready for his senior season.

Harrison "Sam" Francis was born on October 26, 1913, in Dunbar, Nebraska, which is about 30 miles southeast of Lincoln, but his route to NU took a detour through Kansas.

When Francis was in first grade, his mother and father, Viscount and Ella Francis, moved the family to Oberlin, Kansas. Sam was part of a big team at the time. He had six sisters and three brothers.

Francis excelled in several sports, and his high school achievements made him popular with several coaches at the University of Kansas in Lawrence. Jayhawk basketball coach Phog Allen had his eyes on Francis, and the football and track coaches also wanted him.

Francis made the trip to Lawrence to begin his freshman year. In no time, he knew something wasn't right. Francis was a small-town boy trying to fit in with a bunch of big-city kids from Kansas City.

"I was on the campus for about a week and a half," Francis said. "I just picked up and came up to Lincoln. I felt better there."

A good move for Francis. A great move for the Nebraska athletic department, specifically Bible and track coach Henry Schulte.

In football, Francis was an All-Big Six selection after both his junior and senior seasons. He was a consensus All-America pick in '36 and was runner-up to Yale end Larry Kelley in the Heisman Trophy balloting that year.

Francis spent his junior and senior springs helping Schulte win Big Six track titles. Francis was the top collegiate shot putter in the nation as a senior after finishing second in the country the year before. He also was one of the best discus throwers in the nation.

Had he received permission to play, Francis probably would have excelled for the NU basketball team as well. Schulte, however, didn't want his star performer messing around on the hardwood.

But Francis could sure play football.

There are no official statistics from that chapter in Nebraska football history, but there is little doubt that Francis and backfield mate Lloyd Cardwell did a lot of damage while playing together in 1935 and 1936.

Bill Pfeiff was a freshman guard on the '36 team. He said Francis and Cardwell made it rough work being on the defensive side of the ball during practice.

"We got battered around a bit," Pfeiff said. "We were kind of the cannon fodder."

Pfeiff said Cardwell was the quicker runner of the two. Francis was the bulldog.

"He was more of a power runner," Pfeiff said. "He would run the short-yardage stuff and the traps.

"He and Cardwell made quite a combination."

Paul Amen, an end on the Francis-Cardwell teams, said it was extremely difficult for defenders to know which back to follow.

"Cardwell could run the outside plays and that would open up the inside for Sam," Amen said.

Francis, who was 6-foot-1 and 200 pounds during his playing days, admitted that he wasn't the fastest player ever to take the field, but he could move when he had to.

"I would start pretty fast and break away once in a while," he said.

Cardwell once described Francis as "big, powerful inside runner who just exploded through a hole, and if he got into the clear, he ran away from people. If he didn't get into the clear, he'd run over tacklers."

Francis was not a one-dimensional player. He was an outstanding punter—one of his practice kicks was measured at 87 yards—and also threw a pass now and then.

"He had a play," Amen said, "where he would run out to the flanks, get the defenders to come up, and then he would throw the ball."

When asked to recall his most memorable game as a Husker,

Francis brought up a 1936 home contest against Indiana.

The Huskers were down 9-0 at halftime, and Francis was out because of a leg injury.

"I had my leg wrapped, taped up to the knee," Francis said. "Coach made me sit."

During his halftime speech, Bible made an offer to the team: The first 11 players to race onto the field would start the second half.

That group included Francis.

"The timing was off in our offense (in the first half)," Francis said. "We seemed to get it going when I was in there. I ran well. Cardy ran well. (Ron) Douglas ran well."

The offense ran well.

With Francis in the game, the Huskers put together a rally. Francis had a 22-yard run that set up the game-winning touchdown in a 13-9 victory.

He showed his versatility in the final game of the season, throwing two touchdown passes in a 32-14 victory over Oregon State in Portland. Nebraska finished the year 7-2 overall and 5-0 in the Big Six.

Francis was picked by the last-place Philadelphia Eagles in the first round of the pro draft, but the thought of playing for a cellar-dwellar didn't appeal to him. The Chicago Bears were interested in Francis and made a deal with the Eagles.

After a couple of seasons with Chicago, Francis went to the Brooklyn Dodgers. Although he didn't know it at the time, Francis' last game was against the New York Giants at the Polo Grounds in 1940.

His contract called for him to return for the 1941 season, but Uncle Sam had another plan. When he returned to Warrensburg, Missouri—where he and his wife, Lyneve, lived at the time—Francis found a letter from the U.S. Army asking that he report for duty.

"I went all through the Pacific," Francis said. "Then word came out that the war was over."

After leaving the service in 1947, he tried his hand at coaching when Kansas State offered him a job. Francis inherited a bunch of Wildcats who weren't quite as talented as the teams he had been associated with at Nebraska.

"We were getting our tail beat," Francis said.

The military called again to offer Francis a regular commission, and after an 0-10 season in Manhattan, the deal sounded pretty good.

Francis stayed in the Army until 1966. He was inducted into the Nebraska Football Hall of Fame in 1972 and the National Football Hall of Fame in 1977.

Atop the Capitol in Lincoln, just a mile or so from the fields of competition where Francis made his mark, stands a statue of a farmer sowing seeds. The statue looks a lot like a discus thrower.

Francis said some people used to look up at the Capitol and say, "Hey, there's Sam."

A phrase not to be confused with "Hey, there goes Sam." That's what Nebraska football fans used to say.

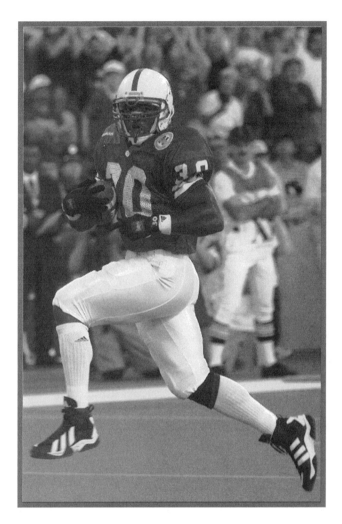

Ahman Green, who left Nebraska after his junior season, rushed for 3,880 yards in three years, second-best on NU's all-time career rushing chart. (Journal Star Library).

AHMAN GREEN/STATS

LETTERED:	1995-97
HEIGHT:	6-0
WEIGHT:	215
HOMETOWN:	OMAHA (CENTRAL HIGH SCHOOL)
HONORS:	1995 ALL-BIG EIGHT
	1997 ALL-BIG EIGHT

GREEN HAS CAREER DAY

Back from Omaha scores 4 TDs

By Jeff Korbelik

October 5, 1997—The name and number on the jersey were the same, but the running back who ran around the Kansas State defense Saturday looked a lot different than the one who punished Washington two weeks earlier in Seattle.

Ahman Green, Nebraska's junior I-back from Omaha, broke three uncharacteristically long touchdown runs and added one more to help propel the No. 3-ranked Cornhuskers to a 56-26 win over No. 17 Kansas State at Memorial Stadium.

The four touchdowns were a career best for Green. The feat hadn't been achieved by a Husker running back since Lawrence Phillips did it against Michigan State in 1995. Green also gained 193 yards on 20 carries for a 9.6 average.

"It's not a matter of me getting 200 (yards) or me getting 300," Green said. "It's a matter of me moving the ball up and down the field and getting it into the end zone like we did today."

How Green did that was what made it so interesting. Two weeks ago, he ran between the tackles to forge 129 yards on 29 carries. He scored once against the Huskies.

Against Kansas State, Green used his 4.34-second speed in the 40-yard dash to turn the corner and break three long touchdown runs.

His first was a 25-yarder with 9:56 left in the first quarter to give Nebraska a 7-0 lead. He then exploded for three touchdowns in the third quarter. The first was a 7-yard scamper to put Nebraska ahead 26-7. Then came the back-to-back 59 and 50-yard runs that left Kansas State defenders gasping for air.

"Against Washington, we were pleased with Ahman's running," Nebraska running backs coach Frank Solich said. "This was a different style of game. He had the opportunity for the long runs. It was no accident that he ran well tonight."

Green hadn't ripped off a significant long run since a 45-yard touchdown jaunt against Akron in the opener. He said it was just a matter of time.

"Our line was obviously putting an effort out there," Green said. "It's been one tackle here and there. A shoestring tackle would get me. I was just waiting for a big run to burst, and it just happened today."

After the 59-yard score, Green stopped in the end zone and stared into the north stands in a mild celebration. He said it was his way to give something to the fans and acknowledge his offensive linemen.

"It's something that the team came up with because the rules of college football won't let you do much," Green said. "It's something decent, something subtle, nothing flamboyant. We get into the end zone and we give it to our crowd because they are there supporting us."

Green moved into seventh on Nebraska's career rushing list with his 193-yard effort. He moved behind Derek Brown and passed Roger Craig, Rick Berns and Keith Jones. Green has 2,537 yards in two-plus seasons.

He quashed any Heisman Trophy talk after the game.

"That's not a big thing in my mind," Green said. "I'm just worried about Monday's practice, Tuesday's practice, Wednesday's practice..."

GREEN INTENT ON PROVING HE'S RETURNED TO FORM

By Curt McKeever

October 10, 1997—After having the finest season by a Nebraska freshman I-back, Ahman Green became human last year. But it's not like he disappeared.

Despite a turf toe injury that forced him to miss one game and severely limited his ability to make quick or sharp cuts during the final six regular-season games of 1996, Green rushed for 917 yards.

Even so, some people questioned his toughness because his production fell off from 1995, when he had an NU freshman-record 1,086 yards and 13 touchdowns.

"I don't get angry, but it makes me wonder what are people watching, because I know when I'm out on that field I'm running as hard as I can," Green said. "And I still had close to 1,000 yards with the injury. You don't pick up 1,000 yards running soft."

The past two games in particular, Green looked intent on driving that point home. At Washington September 20, he took repeated shots running up the middle, but also dished some out en route to gaining 129 yards. Against Kansas State Saturday, he displayed breakaway speed, ripping off touch-down runs of 25, 59 and 50 yards on the way to a four-TD, 193-yard effort.

"I think, to a degree, he wanted to prove a point against Washington," NU running backs coach Frank Solich said of Green, who is entering Saturday's game at Baylor eighth nationally with a 133.5-yard rushing average.

"He was healthy. He was ready to go. He wanted to get back to the same type of style and get some things done like he did as a freshman.

"I think he knows he's a tough back. He knows he can be a power back when it's needed, can be a breakaway back when it's needed, and maybe he felt there were some people out there that didn't feel that way, and he felt like he had to prove something. He certainly didn't to me because I knew when he was healthy he had the potential to have a great year, and I expected him to play extremely well."

Green's last two performances followed a 113-yard day against Central Florida and a 99-yard outing against Akron that was cut short after one half because his back tightened up.

But with that problem cleared up, Green has gotten a full work load. He had 25 carries against Central Florida, 29 against Washington and 20 against Kansas State.

"There were times as a freshman that he showed the things that he showed in these last two games, but I think he's matured in that he's able to take the 25 to 30 snaps per game, and I think his durability has increased a great deal," Solich said.

"And I've got to believe his confidence level has also increased. As a true freshman, even if you're rushing for over 1,000 yards like he did, when you're an experienced guy you've been through it in games and enough plays in practice it's just going to make you a more confident player no matter who you are."

Green agrees.

"When I say I feel like my freshman year, (I mean) I was healthy then," Green said. "I really haven't added nothing to my package. The only thing that's added on is the years I've been here and the experience I have on the field.

"My freshman year, I was young in terms of learning the system, and last year I knew the system, it's just I got injured, so I had to come back off of that. Right now,

I'm fine. No injuries, and I know what I'm doing. I know my plays right off the bat. It's just a growing process coming from my freshman year to now."

Of course, that process also involves Nebraska opponents paying more attention to Green. But that's just fine with the 6-foot, 210-pounder, who's shed 12 pounds from last year in order to better handle a heavier load.

"With the two games I had against Washington and K-State, I'm going to be expecting that and just keep doing my same ol' running," Green said. "It makes you want to run harder when you know people are coming after you. It's basically what football is about—you're out there with your 11 and they're out there with their 11, and they're trying to stop the person with the ball. Half the time, that person is myself."

Thus far, the more Green has carried the ball, the further he's put last season behind him.

"Mentally, he's in great shape right now," Solich said. "He's ready to take as many handoffs as we want to give him, and we can get him the ball so many different ways. And given his snaps, all things being equal, he's going to make some big plays."

Ahman Green accounted for 178 yards on the ground against Texas Tech in 1997. (Journal Star Library).

HUSKER FANS LUCKY GREEN STAYED HOME

By John Mabry

Nebraska football fans can be thankful Ahman Green wanted to limit his serious traveling to long trips down the field.

He could have gone to Michigan. He could have gone to Penn State. He could have gone to Arizona.

As it got closer to decision time, the standout from Omaha Central High School narrowed his choices to Nebraska and Notre Dame. You don't need to be a geography whiz to know that Lincoln, Nebraska, is a little closer to Omaha than South Bend, Indiana.

"The deciding factor was being close to home," Green said.

The decision worked out pretty well.

In three seasons, Green helped the Cornhuskers win two national championships—in 1995 and 1997.

Green decided to turn pro after his junior season. When he was drafted by the Seattle Seahawks in the third round of the 1998 NFL draft, he left Nebraska with some amazing statistics:

A career total of 3,880 yards rushing (No. 2 in school history).

A career total of 42 rushing touchdowns (No. 2 in school history).

A career total of 19 100-yard games, including three games with 200 yards or more. And that doesn't include his 206-yard performance in the 1998 Orange Bowl.

A career average of 6.76 yards per carry.

Green wasn't thinking about numbers as a kid, but he did realize early on that he felt comfortable on a football field.

He was born in Omaha on Feb. 16, 1977, and spent some of his childhood in California before moving back to Nebraska. While playing flag football in Los Angeles, he had the older kids grabbing air.

"I found out I could run with the ball and make people miss me," Green said. "I was 9 and playing against 15- and 16-year-olds, and I was making them miss me or running over them."

After announcing his plans to attend Nebraska, Green said he was hoping to get some significant playing time as a freshman despite some stiff competition in the backfield.

"I'm hoping to compete for a job on the field," he said. "I know Damon Benning and Clinton Childs, and I know Lawrence Phillips is very good. But I think if I keep working hard, I can give it a try."

Not only did Green give it a try, he had the best freshman season by a running back in Nebraska history.

Phillips had been suspended, and Childs and Benning were battling injuries, so Green was shoved into the spotlight right away. Running backs coach Frank Solich said early in the season that it was a tough spot for a freshman.

"He came in under very difficult situations—maybe as highly recruited a running back as there was in the country, with already some great running backs here—with the people not only in the state but really around the country wondering how he was going to do.

"That's a tremendous amount of pressure on a young player, but he really responded well."

Solich made those comments about a week before Green's breakthrough performance.

On Sept. 30, 1995, he rushed for 176 yards on 13 carries, leading the second-ranked Huskers to a 35-21 victory over Washington State.

"Benning came out of the game," Green said. "Once I got in there, I knew I was toting the rock for the Huskers.

"Pound-for-pound it was the toughest game I've played."

Green finished the season with 1,086 yards rushing and 13 touchdowns. Before that, no Nebraska freshman had ever run for more than 900 yards in a year.

With Phillips back in the lineup and quarterback Tommie Frazier running wild, Green did not play a major role in Nebraska's 62-24 victory over Florida in the Fiesta Bowl.

He rushed for 68 yards and a touchdown against the Gators. But more important, he already had what he came to Lincoln for—a national championship.

The 1996 season was a painful one for Green because of foot injuries. Still, he managed to rack up 917 yards and seven touchdowns.

He would more than double those figures as a junior.

Green opened the 1997 season with a 99-yard performance against Akron that included touchdown runs of 7 and 45 yards. That would be his only game with less than 100 yards all year.

Green helped Nebraska get past Central Florida and Washington in the second and third games of the season. Then it was time for Kansas State to visit Lincoln.

Because the Huskers had faced a tough opponent the game before in Washington, there was some concern that the 17th-ranked Wildcats might have a shot at pulling off the upset.

It wasn't even close.

Green rushed for 193 yards and four touchdowns as Nebraska cruised to a 56-26 victory. In the third quarter, Green helped the Huskers pull away with TD runs of 7, 59 and 50 yards.

"Everyone was thinking we would be down," he said. "Everyone was in a zone. That game, we just could not be stopped."

The Huskers were not stopped by anyone in Green's junior season.

They finished the regular season 12-0, and Green finished second in the nation in rushing with 1,877 yards. It was the second-highest total in Husker history.

Green came flying down the stretch in 1997 with games of 189 yards (at Missouri), 209 yards (Iowa State), 202 yards (at Colorado) and 179 yards (Texas A&M).

There was no secret to Green's success. When you're strong, and you can fly, defenders are going to have a hard time stopping you.

"He was a powerful back with tremendous speed," said Solich, who was without Green's services when he took over as Nebraska's head coach in 1998. "He could hit the creases and run on the angles very well.

"He became a guy who could stay on the field with 30 carries or more in a game and still look good—a style runner."

The capper to Green's collegiate career was a record-setting performance against Tennessee in the 1998 Orange Bowl.

He rushed for an Orange Bowl-record 206 yards and two touchdowns in the Huskers' 42-17 victory. With Green racking up 149 yards, Nebraska put the game away with three touchdowns in the third quarter.

Husker fullback Joel Makovicka said there was no way Green was going to rest in that game. Not with a shot at a national championship on the line.

"He was really tired," Makovicka said, "but he couldn't come out of that game."

Green was selected as the most valuable player in the Orange Bowl, and a couple of hours after it was over, the ESPN/USA Today coaches' poll was released with Nebraska on top.

Three seasons, two national championships.

"A lot of players don't get one national title," Green said. "I had two."

I.M. Hipp pulls away from Kansas defenders October 8, 1977. (Journal Star Library).

I.M. HIPP

ISAIAH MOSES HIPP/STATS

LETTERED: 1977-79
HEIGHT: 6-0
WEIGHT: 200
HOMETOWN: CHAPIN, S.C.
HONORS: 1977 ALL-BIG EIGHT
NEBRASKA FOOTBALL HALL OF FAME
PRO EXPERIENCE: ATLANTA FALCONS 1980
OAKLAND RAIDERS 1980
DENVER BRONCOS 1981
PHILADELPHIA EAGLES 1982

HUSKERS FIND ISAIAH 'HIPP' FELLOW

By Dave Sittler

September 20, 1977—Isaiah Hipp personally has more moves and almost as many names as you would find on some entire football teams.

In the moves department, Hipp demonstrated last Saturday that he has a bag full, as he sidestepped, juked, hurdled, bulled, twisted and flat-out ran past Alabama defenders to the delight of the Nebraska fans in the packed house at Memorial Stadium.

A sophomore from Chapin, South Carolina, Hipp isn't about to give away any of his backfield moves. But he wouldn't mind shedding a few of the names.

The 6-0, 200-pound I-back is referred to as I.M. Hipp in the Nebraska press guide. The I.M. stands for Isaiah Moses and the reason for using the initials is obvious—publicity. After all, it didn't hurt a fellow named Orenthal James Simpson to go by O.J.

But Hipp, who idolizes Simpson and wears No. 32 like O.J., says he would rather be called Isaiah. He recalls that he has been called a number of different names, including: Zeke, Ike, and Ezekiel in addition to the obvious one of Moses, I.M., Isaiah and Hipp.

"I've never really told anyone this before," Hipp said, "but my entire name is Isaiah Moses Walter Hipp."

Hipp said Nebraska weight coach Boyd Epley started the I.M. Hipp fad. Husker backfield coach Mike Corgan came up with Ezekiel and Zeke and most of his NU teammates call him I.M.

"In high school, my teachers called me Isaiah, but I didn't like the way they would drag it out when they said it, so I told them to just call me Hipp." Isaiah said. "So almost everyone back home calls me Hipp. But, I've always liked Isaiah, so that's what I prefer."

The way he performed in the Huskers' 31-24 win over the Crimson Tide, Hipp's name is a household word in most Nebraska homes this week.

Relieving starting I-back Rick Berns, who also had a brilliant afternoon against Alabama, Hipp had a 53-yard pass reception and a bolting 13-yard run on back-to-back second-quarter plays that pulled Nebraska back into a 17-14 lead.

While that series was impressive, the most important play as far as Hipp was concerned came the series prior to the touchdown drive. He carried the ball just one time in that series, when he gained 9 yards on a pitch.

That play was the first action Hipp had seen since the season opener against Washington State. In the loss to the Cougars, Hipp replaced Berns and on his first ball-carrying attempt, he fumbled to halt a Nebraska drive on the Washington State 2-yard line. It was the last bit of playing time he saw that afternoon.

"All I was thinking about on that first play against Alabama was hanging onto the ball," Hipp said. "The fumble against Washington State wasn't really my fault, but it bothered me. But I put it out of my mind a few days after the game."

While most running backs might prefer to run some type of quick-hitting, up-the-middle style of play on their first carry to get a feel for the action, Hipp said he preferred the pitch.

"A pitch seems to give more time to get limber or loosen up," Hipp explained.

Playing against Alabama and legendary Coach Paul "Bear" Bryant was a thrill for many of the Nebraska players. It was doubly exciting for Hipp.

It was after watching Nebraska and Alabama play in the 1972 Orange Bowl, that Hipp decided he wanted to be a Husker. He had sided with Nebraska when he watched the titanic Nebraska-Oklahoma struggle on the tube in 1971.

When a shoulder injury slowed him his senior year of high school, the college recruiters backed off. With no scholarship offers coming in, Hipp took matters into his own hands and wrote Nebraska asking for a chance to walk on.

The Husker coaches wrote back saying they would love to have him. Being a pure walk-on who was not actively recruited, Hipp qualifies for a Basic Equal Opportunity Grant (BEOG), which is a federal

grant for needy students. So he is not counted against Nebraska's 30 scholarship limit.

"I always wanted to get away from home when I went to college," Hipp said. "I was just pleased Nebraska wrote back and invited me to come out. I'm really enjoying myself."

Redshirted last season, Hipp demonstrated he was going to give Berns a strong run for the I-back slot this fall when he continually ripped the defenses while playing with the scout team.

"I could feel things coming along when I was on the scout team," Hipp said.

A speedster with 4.5 40-yard dash speed and one of Nebraska's strongest players, Hipp admitted he was "down" for awhile when he didn't get a second chance against Washington State.

"But then Coach Corgan came to me and explained that Richard (Berns) was having such a good day so that's why they left him in," Hipp said. "I appreciated him talking to me about it."

With the talented Berns playing ahead of him, Hipp must patiently bide his time. It's a situation he says he doesn't really mind.

"I just want to contribute," Hipp said. "I just want to do whatever is good for this team."

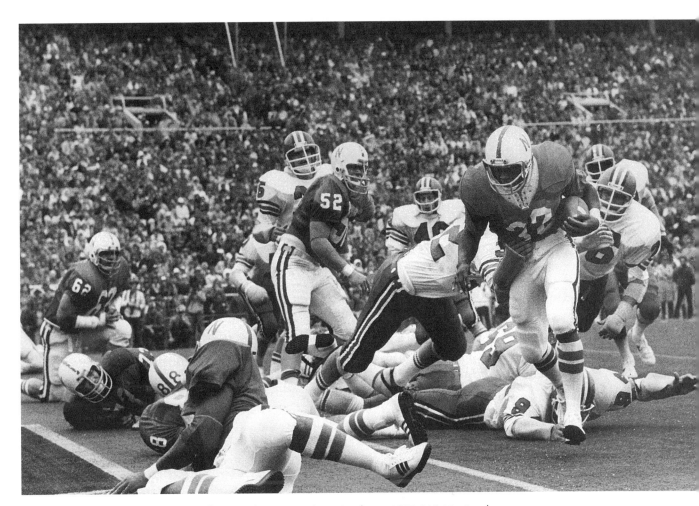

Despite rushing for an NU-record 254 yards against Indiana October 1, 1977, I.M. Hipp's only points came on this two-point conversion. NU ripped Indiana 31-13. (Journal Star Library).

HUSKERS ENJOY SAME OLD SONG

By Dave Sittler

October 9, 1977—If this story sounds like a broken record, there's a simple explanation— Isaiah Hipp keeps breaking records.

Hipp, Nebraska's sterling I-back who grabbed local and national headlines the past two weeks while filling sports pages with the news of his running feats, was up to his crafty tricks Saturday afternoon against Kansas State.

It was like the same song second verse. While no other Husker cracked the magic 200-yard rushing barrier more than once in their Nebraska careers, Hipp did it in back-to-back games.

After romping to a Husker single-game record of 254 yards last week against Indiana. Hipp ripped K-State for 207 more to lead Nebraska to a 26-9 victory over the Wildcats.

Hipp, who has amassed a staggering 583 yards in just three games—which certainly must be another Nebraska record—added a new twist to his latest performance by scoring a couple of touchdowns.

Held to just a two-point conversion against Indiana, Hipp hit paydirt twice against the Cats with cross-country scoring jaunts of 66 and 82 yards.

"It's called a 41-pitch," Hipp said of the play that saw him take a pitch from the quarterback and swing to the right side of the Nebraska line much like the old Missouri student-body play of yesteryear.

"It (the 41-pitch) is designed to break inside or outside," Hipp said. "I just take the ball and follow my blockers and make a decision which way to go."

Running toward the South portion of KSU Stadium on both home run scoring punches, Hipp made the correct decision both times, much to the delight of red-clad Husker fans seated in the south end zone.

Aided by the downfield blocking of tight end Ken Spaeth on both scores, Hipp said he was elated with the 82-yarder, which became the second-longest scoring run in Husker history.

"I was happy on that one because a guy had me and I was lucky enough to get away from him," Hipp said of the run that was 2 yards shy of former Husker John Edwards' 84-yard touchdown against Oregon State in 1954.

Hipp's run did better former Nebraska fullback Frank Solich's 80-yarder against Air Force in 1965.

After his 66-yarder on the first play of the second quarter perked up Nebraska's sputtering offense and gave the Huskers a 7-3 lead, Hipp was rumored to have come off the field and said: "I 'Hipp-notized' 'em'."

"I didn't say that," Hipp said after the game, spoiling a great story. "Someone on the sidelines came up to me and said it. It is kind of funny, I like it."

Disgusted over his scoring drought a week ago, the Chapin, South Carolina native, who—believe it or not—is a walk-on, expressed his pleasure over the two touchdowns.

"When I go on the field, the only thing that matters to me is getting the ball across the goal line," Hipp said. "Yards are fine for me, but I want to get the ball over for the whole team."

Holding an ice pack over a badly swollen left hand that has bothered him since it was stepped on in the Baylor game, Hipp was asked how he would compare himself to Oklahoma State's Heisman Trophy candidate Terry Miller.

"I've only seen him (Miller) play once," Hipp said. 'I'd say on a given day I could be better than him. But he's got all the moves and good speed and balance."

When a Kansas writer informed Hipp that he was going to call him the best back in the Big Eight in his game story, Hipp replied, "You can say that, but I wouldn't. I'm not a braggart. I just try to do my job."

He's been doing his job so well the past three weeks, he's overshadowed Nebraska's other fine running back, Rich Berns. Hipp explained to reporters his relationship with Berns, who has been hampered by injuries the past three games.

"Richard and I don't really talk much," Hipp said in reference to both of their quiet-type personalities.

"But we get along fine. I don't go around talking behind his back and I don't think he talks behind mine. Richard is a very good person."

Berns, who lost his starting job to Hipp when he was injured in the Baylor contest, suffered another rough afternoon against Kansas State.

The Wichita Falls, Texas, junior sat out much of the first half after getting his "bell rung."

"I have no recall of the first half," Berns said. "I can't remember a thing that happened.

Following the Baylor game in which he gained 122 yards, Hipp had suggested that maybe the Nebraska coaches should find a way to play him and Berns at the same time.

Asked if he still felt that way, Hipp—who was chided by Husker Coach Tom Osborne for his coaching suggestions—said he preferred not to discuss the subject.

"I just want to do my job," said the powerfully built, 200-pound Hipp who also goes by his initials—I.M. Hipp. "If that means getting 100 yards or 200 yards, I don't care as long as we win."

While 200-yard days and outstanding efforts by the Hipp-express might get to sound like a broken record, it's sweet music to Nebraska fans.

I.M. Hipp became one of the most heralded walk-ons in history. (Journal Star Library).

'DIFFERENCES' AIDING NEBRASKA'S HIPP

By Mike Babcock

November 15, 1978 – Why run around what he could just as well run over?

Isaiah Hipp vowed that he wouldn't take as much punishment this season as he did a year ago.

This fall, the Nebraska I-back was determined to deliver more blows than he received when he carried the football. The set of his jaw and his well-muscled body provide ample evidence that such determination could be more than idle talk.

He has the strength to back up such a resolution.

So instead of using his customary deft fakes, Hipp chose the bowling ball approach.

"There are times when I succeeded in that, and times where I should have used a move and gotten more out of a run," Hipp said.

One such time occurred in the Colorado game when he collided head-on with Buffalo defensive back Mark Haynes. The ball, which Isaiah was supposed to be advancing at the time, became secondary to the excitement of the impact.

It was after that game that Hipp re-evaluated his philosophy of running with a football.

"After Colorado I thought about it," he said. "I realized that being a back, you've got to be physical, but you've also got to use your best running ability.

"I thought about how I was trying to punish people instead of putting on moves until I got to where there were no more yards and then using my physical force," Hipp said.

That was revelation No. 1 for the quiet Husker junior from Chapin, South Carolina.

Hipp's second revelation came after an Oklahoma State game in which he fumbled the football three times.

The Huskers slipped past the Cowboys 22-14, but Hipp sat in dejection in the locker room after the game. No one felt worse than Isaiah did that day.

"I was down," he said. "When I fumbled those three times, that was the lowest point of the whole season for me.

"But that's all straightened around now. Fumbling is all a state of mind...concentration. There was nothing I could do except put it in my mind that it wasn't going to happen again," Hipp said.

Hipp is a reflective young man, who still uses the head-on approach when it comes to dealing with his problems. He doesn't resort to the shifty moves then.

"I'm not saying I like to be alone," he said. "But I do like to sit down and read sometimes.

"I try to forget what other people say and read the Bible because it sorta helps me find myself. It helps me find my personality...my father taught me that," Hipp said.

One season ago he burst onto the college football scene as the most famous walk-on in the country.

He set a Nebraska single-season rushing record of 1,353 yards though not becoming a starter until the Huskers' third game. Six times he went over 100 yards and established a single-game record of 254 yards against Indiana.

Talk this fall was that Hipp would pursue a 2,000-yard season and become Nebraska's all-time leading career rusher before he even began his senior year.

But for an encore to last season, he has gained yardage at a lesser rate, had only three 100-yard games, and suffered through the two-game stretch in which he was plagued by fumbles.

Yet Isaiah remains optimistic and stands second only to Oklahoma's Billy Sims among Big Eight rushers with 908 yards...a super season by most standards.

"For some people it might be an adjustment; they might be ticked that they didn't have what they had last year," Hipp said after practice Tuesday.

"But I'm pleased with what I've done. We're playing as a team. We're right where we want to be," he said. "Our goals are almost complete."

Hipp's goal is to win a national championship, and it's no revelation to him that such things are achieved by teams, not by individuals. He contributed an 8-yard touchdown run to Saturday's victory over Oklahoma...the highlight of the season for him.

"If everybody played as individuals, we wouldn't be where we are right now," he said.

Isaiah Hipp is doing just fine. He vowed things would be different this season...and they have been.

WHATEVER YOU CALL HIM, I.M. HIPP WAS GOOD

By Steve Sipple

When he signs his name, it is always "Isaiah M. Hipp." People invariably pause and do a double-take. Then it hits them. They realize that before them stands I.M. Hipp, the former star running back at Nebraska, one of the most famous walk-ons in the history of college football.

"It makes me feel wonderful that people remember," said Isaiah Moses Walter Hipp. "You're talking about 20-some years ago and you're still remembered by people your age and even younger. It makes me feel blessed."

Hipp, 42, lives in Irmo, South Carolina (population 11,280), in the central part of the state, about 15 miles from his hometown of Chapin, which is too small to be listed in the 1998 Rand McNally Road Atlas.

More than a few Nebraska fans remember Hipp's story—how he borrowed $96 from a girlfriend so he could fly to Lincoln, Nebraska, and pursue his dream of playing big-time college football.

Hipp's start on the Nebraska campus in 1975 was inauspicious, according to the October 24, 1977 issue of *Sports Illustrated*. After sev-

eral days of practice, Cornhusker head coach Tom Osborne inquired, "Who is that little guy over there?" Nobody knew. "Where's he from?" Osborne asked. Same response.

But Hipp, 6-foot and 200 pounds, made a name for himself, earning a spot on the roster in his first year in Lincoln. In 1976, he struggled with academics and redshirted. His breakthrough season occurred in 1977, when Hipp surprised the nation by rushing for 254 yards against Indiana in the fourth game. He finished the season with 1,301 rushing yards and 10 touchdowns.

In 1978, Hipp gained 936 yards, and in 1979, was poised for a huge senior season. But he suffered a turf-toe injury early in the year and saw his final numbers sink to 585 yards on 128 carries with four TDs.

Nevertheless, Hipp who is now a property manager in Irmo, speaks with unyielding enthusiasm and gratitude about his college playing days. He has no regrets about the courageous decision he made to leave Chapin and travel to the Plains, even though he had never ventured west of Atlanta and never ridden in an airplane.

The fact Hipp was bypassed by major colleges in the recruiting process is somewhat puzzling. He was a prep All-American at Chapin High, gaining 2,889 yards on 541 carries (5.3 yards per carry). By all accounts, he was a physical player, and perhaps most importantly, he ran the 100-yard dash in 9.9 seconds.

During Hipp's senior season at Chapin, however, he suffered a collarbone injury that sidelined him for five games. He still managed to gain 880 yards and score 14 touchdowns for a team that finished 14-0. To this day, he feels the injury scared away recruiters.

Others have suggested his size—he weighed about 185 pounds in high school—was a handicap, or that there was an abundance of talented running backs in the area.

Whatever the reason(s), Hipp retained his confidence. He said he derived his high self-esteem from his great-grandmother, the late Cora Osby, who raised Hipp and his sister Bessie in a three-room cabin following the separation of their parents.

"She instilled in me the importance of always believing in

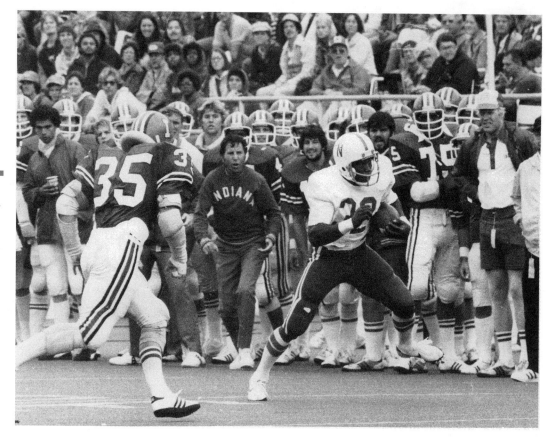

With Indiana Coach Lee Corso watching from the sideline, NU's I.M. Hipp breaks away against the Hoosiers September 30, 1978. Hipp scored four TDs and gained 123 yards in NU's 69-17 win. (Journal Star Library).

yourself and trusting the heavenly father," Hipp said. "I carry that with me today."

Hipp's great-grandmother supported his decision to attend Nebraska. She knew he always cheered for Nebraska when the family gathered to watch the epic Nebraska-Oklahoma battles in the early 1970s. She understood his desire to play for a major-college program.

"I had to go to a school that was recognized as a top program because I regarded myself as a No. 1 player," Hipp recalls. "I wanted to be at a school that highlighted my ability. I looked at it as a challenge. It gave my great-granny something to be proud of."

Hipp carefully avoids in-depth discussion about the racial tension that existed in South Carolina during the 1970s. But he now acknowledges it was one of the

major reasons he decided to leave the area.

"I just wanted to get out," Hipp said. "I knew there was much more than the South. I needed to leave because of the unchangeable environment (in South Carolina). There was still that problem (tension between races). We were getting better, but we were struggling.

"I felt I was doing what I needed to do."

Some Nebraska fans might remember Hipp as much for his idiosyncrasies as for his stellar career. For instance, he wore yellow-and-blue running shoes in practice—size 8 for size 10 feet.

"Some people call it cramped, but I call it comfortable," Hipp told the Lincoln Journal. "I like to have them tight on my feet. Having shoes too loose might cause blisters because you're slipping and sliding."

Then there were his thermal

underwear shirts that he wore under his pads. He cut off the shirts just below the rib cage and clipped the sleeves. He got the idea from watching a man in Chapin who everyone called "Uncle Jim." When "Uncle Jim" worked outdoors, Hipp said, he typically wore a thermal shirt, even if it was 100 degrees. Hipp maintains that thermal shirts can keep you cool, an assertion most people would question.

When Hipp's college career ended, National Football League scouts were naturally puzzled. Before his senior season, Coach Osborne had mentioned Hipp as a possible 1980 first-round draft choice. Then came the turf-toe injury, which led to a relatively disappointing senior season, especially when compared to his sophomore year.

"You see Hipp on film as a sophomore and he's sensational,"

Bobby Beathard, then the general manager of the Washington Redskins, told the *Lincoln Journal* before the 1980 NFL draft. "But Hipp looks different his last two years. Maybe it was (the toe injury). Maybe the offense didn't suit him anymore. Maybe they used him wrong."

Hipp got his chance when the Atlanta Falcons selected him with the 23rd choice of the fourth round. He rushed for 139 yards and scored two touchdowns in a preseason game against the Pittsburgh Steelers.

That performance turned out to be the highlight of his pro career. He bounced around the league the next few years, playing for three more teams: the Oakland Raiders, Denver Broncos and Philadelphia Eagles. According to NFL records,

however, Hipp never carried the ball in a regular-season game.

It was difficult to move ahead of veterans, Hipp said, because many of them had no-cut contracts.

"But after four teams in three years, you have to face the realization there are a lot of talented players out there," Hipp said.

Hipp said the discipline he picked up at Nebraska helped him during his pro career as well as during life after football. He still follows the Huskers closely and stays in contact with Osborne. In fact, Hipp said, he sent Osborne a photograph of his three-year-old daughter, Isabella Marie, shortly after she was born. Osborne wrote back, "I can see she's a very beautiful young lady—much prettier than you," Hipp recalls, laughing.

Hipp appreciates the way Ne-

braska coaches treated him during his playing career. He recalls frequent visits to his dormitory room from Osborne and some of his assistants.

"They wanted me to feel at home, even though I was so far away from home," Hipp said. "When I'd be having homesick moments, they would visit me.

"They were a positive force. If you don't have a positive force in your life, sometimes you can get sidetracked. They wouldn't let you get sidetracked.

"It is an honor and privilege to be associated with that era of Nebraska football. Not many players can say they were taught by, and remain a good friend of, a person like Tom Osborne. It's been a privilege to sit back and watch him be a positive force in many, many lives."

Nebraska's offensive line opened up big holes for I.M. Hipp in 1978. He rushed for 936 yards that year. (Journal Star Library).

I.M. scampered for 154 yards against California in 1978. (Journal Star Library).

A native of Omaha, Calvin Jones finished his career as Nebraska's second-leading all-time rusher with 3,153 yards. He also scored 40 touchdowns from 1991-93. (Journal Star Library).

CALVIN JONES/STATS

LETTERED: 1991-93

HEIGHT: 5-11

WEIGHT: 210

HOMETOWN: OMAHA (CENTRAL HIGH SCHOOL)

HONORS: 1991 ALL-BIG EIGHT

1993 ALL-BIG EIGHT

PRO
EXPERIENCE: LA/OAKLAND RAIDERS 1994-95

GREEN BAY PACKERS 1996

NOW IT'S TIME FOR OTHERS TO KEEP UP WITH JONES

By Mike Babcock

December 26, 1991—Some Nebraska football fans will tell you that the Cornhuskers would have beaten Colorado if Calvin Jones had played. Such is the respect Jones has earned in his first varsity season.

The redshirt freshman from Omaha rushed for 900 yards, a school record for a freshman, and led the Big Eight in scoring with 14 touchdowns. He achieved those totals playing in 10 of the Cornhuskers' 11 games.

Jones didn't play a single down in Nebraska's tie with Colorado, which you'd figure had to be the low point in an otherwise remarkable season that included his being chosen conference offensive newcomer of the year.

Jones, however, doesn't seem to have any complaints about the Colorado game. "The coaches know more about it than I do," he said.

Cornhusker sophomore Derek Brown played the entire Colorado game at I-back, rushing for 96 yards and a touchdown on 30 carries.

"I didn't see any reason for Derek not to be in there," said Jones, who spent the game encouraging Brown from the sideline. "If my job is to cheer, that's what I'll do."

And if his job is to carry the ball, Jones will do that, too. One week later, he turned in his record-setting performance against Kansas, rushing for 294 yards and scoring six touchdowns.

In the last three games of the regular season, Jones rushed for a combined 533 yards and scored nine touchdowns, including the dramatic game-winner against Oklahoma, after setting it up with a crucial first-down carry on fourth-and-1 at the Sooner 19.

Despite his strong finish, however, Jones remains No. 2 behind Brown, a role he readily accepts. Jones has genuine respect for the I-backs who have been in the program longer than he, Brown, junior Scott Baldwin and senior George Achola.

"You can't take away what Scott, Derek and George have done," Jones said. "Those guys have already been where I want to go."

Jones' attitude is typical of what you'll find on a Nebraska team preparing to play No. 1-ranked Miami in the Orange Bowl game on New Year's night. To understand his attitude is to understand the basis for the Cornhuskers' success.

At the beginning of the season there was considerable emphasis on team unity, facilitated by a unity council. The team orientation shown by Jones is evidence that unity exists.

Achieving unity is difficult because of the diverse personalities that make up a team. Most players on college teams have been successful in high school, and it can be difficult to accept a reserve's role.

Jones is an exception. Even though he was a prep All-American at Omaha Central, he learned patience. Kelly Yancey and Sherman Williams played at Central, and "coming out of junior high, I knew they'd be there until my senior year," Jones said.

Both now are playing in the Big Eight, Yancey at Oklahoma State and Williams at Iowa State.

Jones respected their abilities and used their success as motivation to improve his own skills, just as he had done when he was younger. Actually, his patience "probably came from my neighborhood," he said.

"There were always guys who could run faster or play basketball better than I could. And I always wanted to beat those guys."

Now, there are few, if any, in the neighborhood to challenge Jones. "Finally, I can go back and beat them," he said.

'PARTICIPANT' JONES DESERVING OF ODD OPPORTUNITY

By Mike Babcock

September 26, 1993—Two seasons ago, Calvin Jones watched the Colorado-Nebraska football game from the sidelines.

Jones, a redshirted freshman, was healthy that day in Boulder, Colorado, and could have played. But he didn't, even though he had been alternating with Derek Brown as the Cornhusker I-back.

Even so, Jones never complained. He was as upbeat as always. The next week against Kansas, he rushed for 294 yards, a Nebraska record, and scored six touchdowns, a Big Eight record.

That bit of history might help explain why Jones was at I-back on the Cornhuskers' first play from scrimmage Saturday.

Jones is recovering from a knee strain, suffered in the opening game, and wasn't supposed to play against Colorado State. Friday afternoon, in fact, Tom Osborne said he wouldn't play.

Jones didn't play on Saturday, according to Osborne, whose skill in semantics is exceeded only by his skill in coaching.

Jones "participated," as opposed to played, Osborne said.

For one snap, he participated. Then freshman Lawrence Phillips replaced him. Jones removed his pads and watched as the Cornhuskers completed non-conference play with a 48-13 victory.

Jones' per-game rushing average dropped from 124 yards to 62 because of the participation.

"Things happen," he said with a smile.

That's what he had wanted. In order to qualify for NCAA and conference statistics, a player must participate in at least 75 percent of his team's games. Since Jones already has missed two of Nebraska's 11 regular-season games, he can't miss another and qualify.

The Cornhusker sports information office brought that to the attention of Frank Solich, Nebraska's assistant head coach and running backs coach. Solich conferred with Osborne, who agreed to leave the decision to Jones. He could have one play and out.

"It made sense to both of us," Solich said.

It also made sense to Jones, who appreciated the chance to play. "It shows a lot of character by Coach Osborne," he said. "In a different situation, a coach might have said, 'Hey, he's not going to play at all. We're going to do what's best for the team.' But he gave me that opportunity, and I thank him for it."

Fullback Cory Schlesinger would carry the ball. Jones would be a decoy. And quarterback Tommie Frazier would not audible.

Jones wore dry-weather shoes and was instructed "not to worry about carrying out the fake," Solich said. "We had the bases covered."

Osborne and Solich probably wouldn't have allowed just any player to participate in a game for individual, statistical purposes.

Jones is special, and not only because of his athletic ability, which placed him among the preseason candidates for the Heisman Trophy.

The Colorado game two years ago illustrates how special.

"Anything Calvin can earn, we want," Solich said. "He's been a delight to coach since the day he stepped on campus. He's never come to me with a selfish request. Even when he was hurt, when a lot of guys would fade, drown themselves in sorrow, he did what he could.

"I'm sure Calvin's hurting inside, sometimes. All people are that way."

But Jones never shows the personal hurt, Solich said.

His focus has always been the team, according to Solich, just the way it was that bitterly cold night in Boulder.

Jones joked with the coaches about encouraging Frazier to audible so that he could carry the ball Saturday. "I was nervous," he said.

The play went smoothly. Frazier handed to Schlesinger, who ran off-right guard. Jones avoided contact and remained healthy.

That wasn't his only concern, though. The play on which he participated "gained a few yards," Jones said.

Schlesinger picked up 4, to be exact.

If the play hadn't been successful, Jones wouldn't have been quite as happy. For him, there's always a team consideration.

"Too good to be true? He's true," Solich said. "I hope he stays that way. Sometimes, athletics can change you."

Not Calvin Jones. Not so far, anyway.

NOW EVERYONE WANTS TO KEEP UP WITH JONES

August 22, 1993—It wasn't that long ago that Calvin Jones was just a regular guy.

"I could walk down the street, into a restaurant and talk with friends," he said. "I could go home, and maybe my mom would call. Maybe a friend would call.

"I was a regular guy, playing some football. Going to class. I enjoyed myself."

Now, seven different unlisted phone numbers, a few disguises and a sheltered life later, Jones is preparing for a leap into Nebraska football history.

Entering his junior year, Jones may be the most famous and most promising Nebraska I-back in at least 10 years and possibly ever.

It's been 10 years since Mike Rozier won the Heisman Trophy at Nebraska. Since then, Cornhusker fans have been delighted by the running of I-backs Derek Brown, Ken Clark, Keith Jones, Doug DuBose, Leodis Flowers and Jeff Smith, among others.

Brown and Jones shared time in the backfield the last two years. Brown had the edge in playing time because he had an edge in experience. But last December, in Tokyo,

with Brown in Lincoln nursing an injury, Jones finally got his chance to take the I-back role by himself.

Soon after the Orange Bowl game on New Year's night, Brown announced he was turning pro, and Jones was thrust into the limelight for at least the next season and possibly one more year.

"It was changing last year, when I started playing more," said Jones, an Omaha Central graduate. "Then when Derek said he was going pro, a lot more people started paying attention to me.

"Suddenly, people are talking about the Heisman Trophy and gaining 2,000 yards in a season and all kinds of wild dreams. People want to talk to me, mostly agent types, and the media seems to want a lot more from me."

The public reaction is logical. Jones rushed for 1,210 yards last year and was named All-Big Eight and Big Eight Offensive Player of the Year. With Brown gone, Jones could figure on getting 10 to 15 more carries a game than his 15-per-game average last year.

Magazines have tabbed Jones as a preseason All-American and possibly the best running back in Nebraska history.

"That's a lot to say without playing a game," Jones said. "I have high expectations and big dreams. But they involve the other guys on the offense and defense, too.

"People may be cheering for me, but that's because our offensive line blocked, our quarterback called the play and everything worked right, including the fact I didn't screw something up."

Jones said he still is trying to learn the system. He is still trying to be the hardest practice player he can be. He is still working on his classes and working in the weight room.

"I see the guys (offensive linemen) Zach Wiegert and Brenden Stai and Lance Lundberg and Rob Zatechka and Ken Mehlin, all working their butts off in practice and in the weight room," Jones said. "Am I supposed to relax because somebody said I was good? No way. That would be the biggest mistake I could make."

Jones has always had great ability. He was the Sunday Journal-Star Prep Athlete of the Year as a senior at Central. He was a high school All-American and one of the top recruits in the country. As a freshman he rushed for 533 yards

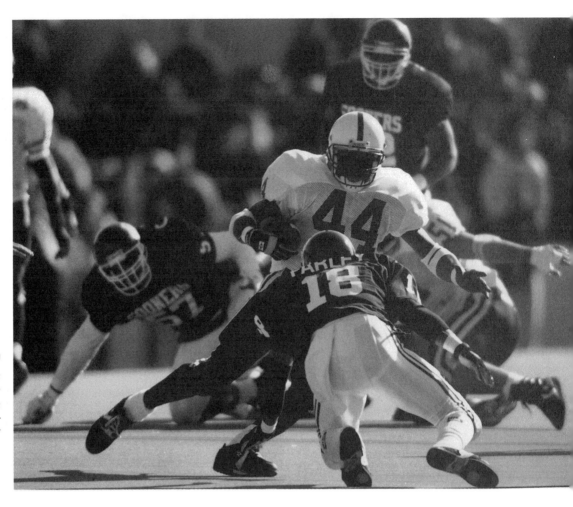

Calvin Jones prepares to juke an Oklahoma defender during NU's 33-9 victory November 27, 1992. (Ted Kirk/ Lincoln Journal Star).

in the final three games of the regular. That season, against Kansas, Jones rushed for an incredible 294 yards and six touchdowns after Brown was hurt in the second quarter.

Last year, he was steady. Improving on his blocking, receiving and running, Jones averaged 110 yards a game in helping Nebraska gain its 10th national rushing title. He was the first player to lead the Big Eight in scoring as a freshman and sophomore.

"The guys ahead of me never let up," he said. "I don't see any point to relaxing because of what happened in the past. I know I'm the only tailback with much experience here this year. But that doesn't keep the other guys from coming on and taking the job.

"You have to look at reality. Nebraska is going to do well because everybody works at it. Iowa State didn't care that we beat Colorado and Kansas back-to-back last year. And nobody is going to care about what Nebraska or Calvin Jones is supposed to do this year. You've got to do it each time you go out on the field."

As for the future, Jones isn't about to make any predictions. Will he follow Brown and leave school for the NFL a year before his eligibility is expired?

"You never know what's going to happen five months from now," he said. "I want to stay injury free, and I want to be a part of a national championship here at Nebraska.

"I am not going to think about the pros. I'm not going to talk about it much either. And it wouldn't be fair to my teammates to do anything but give 100 percent to Nebraska in time and effort."

Not even the lure of millions of dollars will make Jones look ahead.

"You can make a lot of money in the pros, and if you don't have a degree or some plan for life after football, you can be broke, bored and have nowhere to go," he said. "That's the big picture. That's reality. Education outweighs everything, and football is just icing on the cake. You can be happy playing football, but it's not fulfillment."

NU'S JONES BROKE LOOSE

By Ron Powell

Up until the Kansas game on November 9, 1991, Calvin Jones was having a quiet season.

The redshirt freshman had been patiently waiting his turn behind starting I-back Derek Brown. In the first seven games that season, Jones gained 367 yards and scored five touchdowns. In Nebraska's two biggest games to that point, Jones had been a non-factor. He carried the ball just three times for 29 yards in a 36-21 loss to Washington in September. Jones didn't play at all in the Huskers' 19-19 tie at Colorado on Nov. 2.

A week later, on a brisk afternoon in Lawrence, Kansas, the 5-foot-11, 210-pound Jones finally got his chance to make some noise. It turned out to be an explosion.

With Brown sidelined with blurred vision from a shot he took early in the second quarter, Jones rushed for a school-record 294 yards on 27 carries and scored a Big Eight-record six touchdowns in Nebraska's 59-23 victory. The fact Nebraska trailed 17-0 when Jones entered the contest made the performance even more impressive.

"I can't believe it worked out this way," Jones said. "I'll look back,

and the rest of us will, and say, 'Wow, we did that?'"

Jones scored Nebraska's first touchdown on a 3-yard run early in the second period and later tied the game at 17 with a 47-yard TD run with 5:09 left before halftime.

In the second half, Jones ran wild. He capped an 80-yard drive with a 9-yard TD run midway through the third quarter that put Nebraska in front to stay. Jones rushed for 55 yards in that drive alone.

Jones added a 1-yard TD run later in the third quarter and reeled off scoring jaunts of 68 and 12 yards in the first 4:19 of the fourth quarter.

"Credit the other 10 guys on offense, not me. They threw the blocks," Jones said. "Keithen McCant made the reads on the option, and he had guys all over him and got me the ball and I was open. With our offensive line and play-calling, anything was possible. I didn't feel I'd be able to do anything like this until I was a senior."

Jones' display even caused Nebraska Coach Tom Osborne to do something out of character. With Nebraska in command with less than seven minutes left, Osborne

sent Jones back into the game for two more carries of 6 yards each to eclipse the school record of 285 yards by Mike Rozier, set also against Kansas, in 1983.

"He (Osborne) told me 'Look, you only need a yard or so for the record. So when you go in there, you get it,'" Jones said.

Said Osborne: "We don't normally make concessions to records, but this was special."

And it was the start of what turned out to be a special career for Jones. By the time he left the Husker program for early entry into the NFL draft after the 1993 season, Jones had rushed for 3,153 yards (No. 2 all-time at Nebraska) and 40 touchdowns. He eclipsed the 100-yard mark 16 times in his college career.

Jones gained 533 yards and scored nine TDs in the final three games of the 1991 season. He contributed mightily down the stretch of another come-from-behind Nebraska win, a 19-14 conquest of Oklahoma that nailed down the Huskers' Orange Bowl berth.

On a cold rainy day at Memorial Stadium, Oklahoma jumped to a 14-0 lead in the first 12 minutes. Nebraska battled back and cut the difference to 14-13 on a 33-yard field goal by Byron Bennett with 12:20 left in the game.

The Huskers put together an 80-yard, 10-play fourth-quarter drive to complete the comeback. Jones contributed 78 yards on nine carries in the drive.

On fourth-and-1 at the Oklahoma 19-yard line with 3:08 left, Nebraska passed up a chance at a go-ahead field goal and decided to go for the first down. Jones picked up 4 yards on a pitch play to the left from McCant. On the next play, Jones busted loose on a draw play over left guard for a 15-yard TD run that proved to be the difference. Jones finished with 118 yards on 17 carries.

On the fourth-down play, "I had the run, but it wasn't me, I had no choice (but to get the first down) the way our line was blocking," Jones said. "On the touchdown, the linemen blocked a hole that I could have driven a garbage truck through."

Often, Jones ran like a garbage truck with a revved-up engine. He combined size and speed as well as any running back in Nebraska football history.

"A big back with excellent speed," recalled Frank Solich, the NU running backs coach when Jones played and now the Huskers' head coach.

"He had some really tremendous days, those two over 200 yards, and could have that type of afternoon almost any day. As a freshman, he stepped right in and showed his ability. He generally made a lot of things happen when he got the ball."

Jones, one of a long line of outstanding backs to come out of Omaha Central High School, came to Nebraska as one of most highly recruited backs in the nation in

1990. Jones rushed for what was then a Class A-record 2,210 yards his senior season. He finished with 3,965 yards in his high school career. Jones broke the Class A single-game rushing record with 367 yards against Omaha Benson his senior season.

Jones spurned offers from Tennessee, Louisiana State, Nevada-Las Vegas, Oklahoma, Iowa and Colorado.

"It was simple," Jones said of his decision to go to Nebraska. "I was born and raised in Nebraska and I wanted a chance to play for the Cornhuskers."

The end of the 1991 season proved to be the beginning of the 'We-Backs' with Jones and Brown sharing both the carries and the glory. In 1992, both Jones and Brown rushed for more than 1,000 yards, combining for 2,221 yards and 18 touchdowns. Jones accounted for 1,210 of those yards and 14 TDs.

Jones gained over 100 yards in seven games in 1992, including an astounding 176 yards on just seven carries against Oklahoma State when he recorded a career-long 90-yard TD run. He was a second-team All-American according to Football News that season and the coaches' Big Eight Offensive Player of the Year.

"People, fans and media have talked about what it would be like if we didn't have to share the running, but I never gave it a thought," Jones said.

Neither did Solich, who liked hitting opponents with the shifty Brown and the more powerful Jones.

"Together, I don't think you're going to get more effective than what they've been," Solich said. "If one of them played full-time, their stats would be at the top and there'd be a possibility of Heisman

and All-American."

And that's what Jones was looking at in 1993 after Brown left school early and was drafted by the NFL New Orleans Saints. Brown separated his shoulder late in the third quarter of NU's 33-9 win at Oklahoma November 27, making Jones the starter in Nebraska's final regular-season game against Kansas State in Tokyo. Jones responded by picking up 186 yards on 30 carries and led the Huskers to a 38-24 victory.

Jones' Heisman hopes were dashed by a knee injury in the '93 season opener against North Texas. Jones had 124 yards before going to the sidelines, but he then missed games against Texas Tech and UCLA and did not carry the ball against Colorado State.

When Oklahoma State Coach Pat Jones heard Calvin Jones planned to return for the Huskers' game against the Cowboys on October 9, it was not good news.

"Their young guys are good, but Calvin is one of the best ever," the OSU coach said. "He hits the hole quicker. He finds the hole quicker and overall, because of his knowledge of the game, he's much more dangerous than the new guys."

Jones' 136-yard performance against the Cowboys started a string of six straight 100-yard games, concluding with 208 yards against Iowa State. A week before the Iowa State game, he picked up 195 yards and set up Nebraska's winning TD in a 21-20 scare at Kansas. He rushed for a tough 82 yards on 25 carries and scored the clinching TD in NU's 21-7 regular-season finale victory against Oklahoma that gave the Huskers an 11-0 record and an opportunity to play Florida State for the national championship in the Orange Bowl.

Despite the knee injury, Jones still broke the 1,000-yard barrier (1,043) and scored 12 TDs.

Disappointment struck again, however, in Nebraska's 18-16 loss to the Seminoles in the Orange Bowl. Not only did the Huskers lose the game that determined the national championship, Jones injured his shoulder in the first half and was unable to return.

A week after the bowl game, Jones declared himself eligible for the NFL draft, bypassing his senior season.

"I needed something more, and I think I can find that in pro football," Jones said a month after deciding to go pro. "I value the chance to take the next step more than I value records or trophies."

Jones ended up being a third-round draft choice of the Los Angeles Raiders and stayed there for two seasons before becoming a member of the Green Bay Packers in their Super Bowl championship season in 1996. He's also embarked on a broadcasting career, working on a state-wide radio talk show in 1997 and '98.

So far, his professional football career has resembled his early days in Nebraska, with sparse playing time. But remember the Kansas game and know that Jones could break loose anytime.

Husker I-back Calvin Jones took time out to participate in a youth camp at Lincoln's Woods Park in July 1993. (Journal Star Library).

Senior I-back Calvin Jones dives into the end zone for a score in Nebraska's 49-7 victory against Missouri October 23, 1993. (Journal Star Library).

KEITH JONES

Keith Jones cruises on a 69-yard touchdown run during NU's 42-3 victory against Iowa State November 7, 1987. (Journal Star Library).

KEITH JONES/STATS

LETTERED:	1984-87
HEIGHT:	5-10
WEIGHT:	180
HOMETOWN:	OMAHA (CENTRAL HIGH SCHOOL)
HONORS:	1986 ALL-BIG EIGHT
	1987 ALL-BIG EIGHT
PRO EXPERIENCE:	LOS ANGELES RAMS 1988
	CLEVELAND BROWNS 1989
	DALLAS COWBOYS 1990-91

SYMBOLS OF SWEAT

I-back Jones' fashions on field are functional

By Mike Babcock

September 24, 1986—A little flair. A lot of work.

Keith Jones forgot to tie the red bandanna around his neck and put on the red headband as he prepared for a recent Nebraska football practice.

On the field, "I felt kind of naked," said Jones, the Cornhuskers' starting I-back. "So I asked one of the equipment guys to get them for me."

Only then could he concentrate.

The bandanna and headband are fast becoming Jones' trademarks, their bright color underscoring the special zest with which the junior from Omaha plays the game. They complement his No. 6 jersey (six points, touchdown) and his nickname—E.Z., "End Zone."

Without a doubt, Jones is unique. His personality isn't defined by the inevitable comparisons to Gale Sayers, the former Kansas All-American and Pro Football Hall of Fame running back who preceded him at Central High.

But Jones doesn't wear the headband and the bandanna to assert his individuality over the team. Both served a purpose during the summer, when he began wearing them during workouts.

The headband kept sweat out of his eyes, and the bandanna protected his neck from the sun. Without it, "I'd break out in a heat rash," Jones said.

Function has since been joined by symbolism. The headband and the bandanna have become reminders "of how hard I worked this past summer. I spent a lot of time in the weight room," Jones said. "It was hard work, no playing in there. And it's all paid off."

The payoff has been subtle. For example, it wasn't apparent when Jones ran 78 yards for a touchdown in Nebraska's 59-14 victory over Illinois Saturday. Husker fans know he's the fastest football player in school history.

The former Big Eight sprint champion has been timed, electronically, at :04:33 in the 40-yard dash. Jones always has been a threat to break long runs.

"We've always known Keith could make the big play if he had the blocks," Nebraska Coach Tom Osborne said.

But this season, "he's made some first downs, third-and-2, after he's been hit in the backfield and kind of gathered himself, gotten another surge," Osborne said. "Those are the kind of runs, sometimes, that

are more impressive to me than out-running everybody."

Those are the kind of runs that have been the result of Jones' hard work last summer, the work that the headband and the bandanna represent.

Now, Osborne can say without hesitation: "Keith's a guy who can run inside with authority. Maybe early on, that was our biggest concern about him."

The concern was understandable.

Jones, who's listed at 5-foot-10, "probably weighed 175 pounds when he came in as a freshman," Osborne said.

Jones never doubted his ability to run inside, "but I know for a matter of fact that the fans, and maybe some of my teammates, had doubts," he said. "Is he capable of running up in the middle?"

Frank Solich, who coaches the Cornhusker offensive backs, knew Jones could develop into an effective inside runner because "he's never been afraid of contact."

"It's been just a matter of knowing when and how to use his speed and the fact that he's getting stronger and feeling more confident," said Solich, who weighed about 150 pounds when he played fullback at Nebraska.

Jones, who now weighs 190, can bench press more than 300 pounds.

But running inside requires more than upper-body strength. It takes balance because "you're going to get hit from different angles, and a good share of the time, you don't see it coming," Solich said. "Breaking tackles requires a good deal of leg strength, too."

Like all sprinters, Jones has exceptional strength in his legs.

He also has a sprinter's confidence, which has been enhanced by his 168-yard rushing performance against Illinois.

Like every running back, Jones has had to deal with defenders' attempts to intimidate him. Florida State's linebackers were particularly talkative.

"Things like that don't bother me," Jones said. "I'm not trying to be cocky, but I'm not intimidated by any defense. It's a challenge. To be a great running back, no defense should intimidate you. When you go up against a good defense, that's when you should have your best games. That's one of my goals."

To achieve that goal, Jones worked hard over the summer. His red bandanna and red headband are reminders.

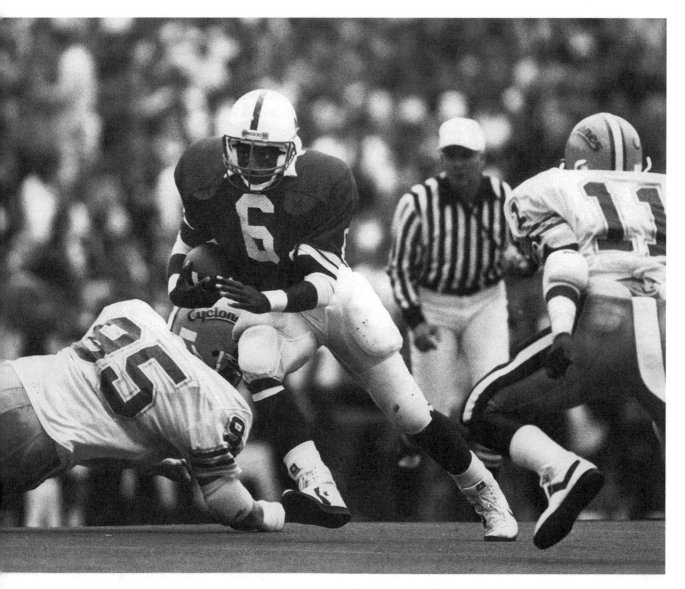

Using his great cutback ability, Keith Jones evades Iowa State defenders in the first half of the November 7, 1987 game. Jones rushed for 240 yards on 15 attempts in the game. (Journal Star Library).

I-BACK JONES READY FOR HIS OWN PRIME-TIME SHOW

By Mike Babcock

April 24, 1987—Finally, Keith Jones can concentrate on carrying the football instead of the burden of Doug DuBose. He can be himself instead of the replacement for a Heisman Trophy candidate.

That's why Jones is ready to "come into his own," said Frank Solich, Nebraska's offensive backs coach.

That's why Jones is eager for his senior season to begin.

"Now, it's my time," he said.

Actually, his time came last season, though it never really seemed that way. Jones became the No. 1 I-back after DuBose suffered a knee injury in the first major scrimmage of fall camp.

DuBose was a two-time Big Eight rushing leader and a top Heisman Trophy and All-America candidate.

Obviously, replacing him was difficult. "I said there wasn't any pressure, but there was," Jones said.

And it lasted all season.

"I fought it. I really had to dig deep," said Jones. "I worked extra hard to show the coaches I was able to step in."

He also had to prove himself to Cornhusker fans, who "were used to seeing Doug at I-back. You're concerned about what people say about you," Jones said.

What they said was he wasn't DuBose, an attitude that seemed to ignore Jones' considerable accomplishments.

Jones was first-team All-Big Eight, and he led the conference in rushing average and touchdowns, gaining 830 yards and scoring 14 touchdowns in 10 regular-season games. He missed one game because of a broken thumb and played in another with a cast.

Still, because he tried to meet other people's expectations, Jones didn't have the confidence he has now.

"I'm the starting I-back," he said. "I'm not expected to do what anyone else did, just what Keith Jones can do."

The burden has lifted.

"Definitely," Jones said.

His first real opportunity to show what that means will come Saturday in the Red-White intrasquad game at Memorial Stadium. Kickoff is 1:30 p.m.

The Red-White Game is important to Jones. He doesn't intend to just go through the motions. "It gives you a chance to display what the spring has done for you, the lifting, conditioning, learning the offense," he said.

Whether it's what spring practice has done for him or a year's maturity, "Keith has really come up a level in his play this spring," Solich said.

"I've really been pleased."

Jones, the fastest football player in Nebraska history, "is making quicker decisions. With his speed and quickness, if he doesn't hesitate on decisions, just makes them and goes with them, he's going to be a lot better off. I see that happening now," said Solich.

"A lot of it is confidence."

Solich wasn't disappointed with Jones' play last season. "I thought Keith handled things very well," Solich said. "He expected to play behind Doug (DuBose) and gain experience that way, and then, bam, he was thrown right in.

"Because of his speed and quickness and all the hype coming in, people expected instant success."

And unlike DuBose, "Keith didn't have the advantage of a redshirt. He's gone through without that," said Solich.

Jones is excited about the prospect of playing in the Red-White Spring Game. The former Omaha Central Super-Stater would like to make it a positive lead-in to his final season as a Cornhusker.

"Before I came to school here, I looked at all the I-backs in the past and tried to place myself, see if I fit in with those guys," Jones said.

Any doubts he might have had seemed to have disappeared this spring.

"I'm pretty confident in myself," he said. "I can do the job."

NU'S JONES FINDS RIGHT ANSWERS

By Ken Hambleton

December 13, 1987 – It's not surprising that Keith Jones didn't get All-America recognition this year.

A slow start this season was the main reason the Nebraska senior I-back was not an All-American along with Oklahoma State's Thurman Thomas or Michigan State's Lorenzo White.

Jones's 7.2 yards per carry average was better than any of the seven NCAA Division I-A running backs who finished the 1987 regular season with more yards. If Jones had as many carries as national rushing champ Everett Woods of Nevada-Las Vegas, the former Super-Stater from Omaha Central would have won the title by almost 200 yards.

"We think he showed he was in with the best," Nebraska running backs coach Frank Solich said. "He showed everything a running back needs when he made that fourth down-and-13 run against Colorado. He ran into the pile, lost and regained his balance, put a move on two players and then outran everybody else to the outside. Speed, balance and agility."

At 7.2 yards per carry, Jones, a two-time All-Big Eight back, would have easily won his second straight Big Eight rushing title. His 170 carries for 1,232 yards and 13 touchdowns are still significant. He became the third all-time leading rusher behind only Heisman Trophy winner Mike Rozier and All-Big Eight back I.M. Hipp.

Nebraska's famous pitch play averaged more yards per attempt with Jones than with any other Nebraska running back in the last 10 years, Cornhusker offensive line coach Milt Tenopir said.

"Keith probably improved as much as any back we've ever had, from the time he came here until now," NU head coach Tom Osborne said. "He probably came back from injury better than any back we've had. He probably was as effective a runner as we've ever had when he was healthy, too."

Jones finished the season with a flurry. He rushed for 584 yards on 56 carries in the final three games, for 10.4 yards-per-carry average against Iowa State, Oklahoma, and Colorado. His 248 yards on 26 carries, including touchdown runs of 50 and 44 yards, against Colorado was his best game as a Cornhusker.

"Keith's season finish was a sign of his getting well as much as anything," Osborne said.

Tenopir said it was also a sign of the chemistry between Jones and the offensive line. "In the games he did well, the line did well too," he said. "Keith read the blocks off-tackle so well, the whole running game came together."

There were struggles throughout his career, especially this season, both Osborne and Tenopir said.

Jones suffered through the UCLA game, gaining just 18 yards on six carries. Two of those runs ended with the ball in the hands of UCLA defensive players and Jones finished the last two quarters on the bench.

"I learned after the UCLA game, when I felt my career could have gone under, that it was something I had to earn, but not push for and not try to make happen sooner than it could," he said.

"It was hard. Nothing like that had ever happened to me in my whole life in anything.

"I pretended to be myself around the guys, but by myself, my mind was going 1,000 mph. I had tried to be something I wasn't and suddenly I wasn't the No. 1 I-back and things looked pretty bad."

Jones had long talks with Osborne and Solich and resolved the problems.

Osborne said that Jones

reached the solution by himself. "He didn't sulk and he recognized the problem and came to the right answers by himself," he said.

Jones recovered with a standout game against Arizona State and the next game he was Big Eight offensive player of the week with a 129-yard effort against South Carolina. He turned his ankle in the game in the third quarter and still managed to score a pair of touchdowns in the fourth quarter to lead Nebraska's comeback.

For the next four weeks, Jones would be able to practice on the first three days of the week, but the swelling in his ankle would keep him from working out on Thursday and Friday.

"He kept bouncing back," Solich said. "Day in and day out, you knew what he was going to be like. You knew he'd give everything and never slow down. I think with his speed, his endurance, his ability to play hurt and his aggressiveness will help him get a pro contract."

An Iowa State defender can't keep NU's Keith Jones from scoring during the teams' 1985 game. (Journal Star Library).

KEITH 'END ZONE' JONES LIVED UP TO HIS NICKNAME

By Curt McKeever

"End Zone."
It was a catchy little nickname that Keith Jones made stick.

The first time the speedster from Omaha Central High School carried the ball for Nebraska, in the closing seconds of NU's 17-3 win against Oklahoma State in 1984, he raced 10 yards into the end zone. The play was whistled dead because of an illegal-procedure penalty, but still served as Jones' calling card.

By the time his career ended, Jones had dialed up end zone territory 32 times, been named a first-team All-Big Eight Conference running back his junior and senior seasons and moved into third place on the Cornhuskers' all-time rushing chart with 2,488 yards.

Appropriately, Jones wore No. 6. That's six, as in touchdown, six points, end zone.

"He was not a big back, but could make a big play for you because of his speed and mobility," said Nebraska Coach Frank Solich, who was the running backs coach during Jones' career, which lasted from 1984-87. "He was just about gone on so many plays because he could break away from a lot of people in a flash."

That's also about how quickly Jones wound up in the spotlight.

After breaking Gale Sayers' rushing records at Omaha Central, the 5-foot-10, 175-pounder spent his first two years at Nebraska improving his strength and watching Doug DuBose post back-to-back 1,000-yard seasons. Jones, who recorded the fastest electronically timed 40-yard dash in NU football history (4.33 seconds), also figured on being a stand-in during 1986. That's because DuBose was primed to make a serious run for the Heisman Trophy.

But in the first scrimmage that fall, DuBose suffered a career-ending knee injury and Jones, who had missed the spring Red-White Game after having arthroscopic knee surgery, was thrust into the thick of the battle.

Jones—who once compared his playing availability to being in the Army ("If they need me, I'm ready. If they don't, I still prepare just as hard.")—proved to be a trustworthy soldier.

Ironically, his original intention upon graduating from high school was to join one of the armed services.

"When I was being recruited by all these colleges for football, I

had the Marines coming to my house," said Jones, now a manager for a well-known Italian restaurant in Omaha, Nebraska. "I remember one evening Coach (Tom) Osborne had just been to my house and as he was leaving a (Marine) recruiter was just coming by. Coach called me back the next day. He was pretty influential in me becoming a Cornhusker."

To land Jones, Osborne also had to win a tense recruiting battle with the University of Washington.

"I'm going to tell you, people don't really know how close I was to becoming a Husky," said Jones, who watched a couple of highly touted high school teammates (Larry Station and Tom Stawniak) go to schools other than NU. "Out of all the schools I visited, Washington was the only one comparable to Nebraska. In '84, they were a competitive team, and Coach (Don) James pretty much told me, 'Keith, we're looking to win the national championship this year and if you want to be a part of it, we'd love to have you.'"

Jones weighed his options, then decided the benefits of staying close to home were too great to pass up. Becoming a Cornhusker also gave him the opportunity to play on the same team as his older brother, Lee, who had attended Omaha Benson High School.

It turned out to be the right decision.

In Nebraska's second game of the 1986 season, Jones rushed for 168 yards and two touchdowns. By the end of the season, he was no longer the replacement for a Heisman Trophy candidate. Of course, that's what happens when one leads the Big Eight in rushing and scores 14 touchdowns.

"We've always known Keith could make the big play if he had the blocks," Osborne said in 1986.

Although speed was Jones' forte, it became evident that the man who wore a red bandanna around his neck and red headband during practice also was a pretty tough hombre.

In early November of 1986, Jones tore ligaments in a thumb and was expected to miss five weeks after having surgery. He sat out one game, then, wearing a specially designed cast, returned against Kansas to rush for 93 yards and two touchdowns. And that was just in the first quarter.

In 1987, Jones rebounded from a miserable performance against UCLA (6 carries, 18 yards, 2 fumbles) to rally the Cornhuskers past South Carolina. Despite suffering a hairline ankle fracture in the third quarter, Jones scored two TDs in the final period to cap the comeback.

The injury didn't stop Jones, particularly during November. Twice that month, Jones rushed for more than 200 yards in a game.

He had 240 against Iowa State. Then, one week after the top-ranked Cornhuskers had their national championship hopes doused by No. 2 Oklahoma, Jones capped his career with a 248-yard effort at Colorado, giving him 1,232 for the season. Only 1983 Heisman Trophy winner Mike Rozier had a more productive senior year for the Cornhuskers.

While the 200-yard games remain good memories for Jones, the one that sticks out most in his mind is the 1987 battle against Oklahoma.

"That was the peak," he said. "Even though we lost (17-7), it was just a heck of a game."

Jones was selected by the Los Angeles Rams in the sixth round of the 1988 NFL draft. His professional career was marred by an assortment of injuries and led him to Cleveland and Dallas. But he accepted his fate in stride and made enough impressions to stick through the four years required to qualify for a pension.

"I think if you know how to carry yourself and respect people, you don't have many problems," said the deeply religious Jones.

During his one season in Cleveland, Jones started the first four games, mainly because Eric Metcalf held out. The night before the Browns were to play archrival Cincinnati on Monday Night Football, Jones was told by his coach that Metcalf was ready to replace him in the lineup.

"I was happy for Eric," Jones said, "because that game he made a move on about the 10-yard line, faked out about four guys that had dead-aim on him and took it into the end zone."

The next year, "End Zone" wound up in Dallas.

"Little did I know, that's what Michael Irvin called himself," Jones said. "But one day he came over and said, 'While you're here, you can have it.'"

In Nebraska, though, Jones will forever be known as "End Zone."

"Football has always been fun for me," he said. "I remember when I was really young I played one year for the Swaggers, and I broke a lot of records. From that point on, (people) had high aspirations for me. But it was just a game to me and I was just out there having fun."

Jeff Kinney (35) uses a block from Maury Damkroger to score on a 2-yard run with 1:38 left against Oklahoma November 25, 1971. Kinney's TD, one of his four in the game, gave Nebraska a 35-31 victory in the Game of the Century. (Journal Star Library).

JEFF KINNEY/STATS

LETTERED:	1969-71
HEIGHT:	6-2
WEIGHT:	200
HOMETOWN:	MCCOOK, NEBRASKA
HONORS:	1971 ALL-AMERICAN
	1971 ACADEMIC ALL-BIG EIGHT
	1971 ALL-BIG EIGHT
	1971 ACADEMIC ALL-AMERICAN
	NEBRASKA FOOTBALL HALL OF FAME
PRO EXPERIENCE:	KANSAS CITY CHIEFS 1972-75
	BUFFALO BILLS 1976

derek
brow

Running back Derek Bro
was known for his abilit
leap over the line. Here
scores against Kansas St
in NU's 38-31 victory Octo
19, 1981. (Journal Star
Library)

lawrence
phillips

Lawrence Phillips helped
Nebraska run to an NCAA-
bowl record 524 yards
against Florida in the 1996
Fiesta Bowl. Phillips finished
the game, which Nebraska
won 62-24, with 165 yards
and two touchdowns.
(Journal Star Library)

jeff kinney

Jeff Kinney played on two national championship teams at Nebraska in 1970-71.

calvin jones

Freshman Calvin Jones set NU records with 294 yards and six rushing touchdowns in Nebraska's 59-23 victory against Kansas November 9, 1991. (Journal Star Library)

en
lark

Clark is met in mid-air by
klahoma State defender
ng NU's 48-23 win against
Cowboys, October 21, 1989.
Cowboys held Clark to just
ards and two touchdowns
e game. The previous year,
Husker running back
ed for 256 yards against
(Journal Star Library)

mik
rozi

Mike Rozier started
1983 Nebraska team
was considered by n
the best offensive
college history. (Jou
Star Library)

tom
rathman

Tom Rathman came to NU
from Grand Island,
Nebraska, and went on to
fame in the NFL. (Journal
Star Library)

ahman
green

hman set an Orange Bowl
cord with 206 yards
shing against Tennessee in
98. (Journal Star Library)

THE END OF A HUSKER CAREER

By Don Forsythe

November 4, 1971— Jeff Kinney has thoroughly enjoyed his football career at the University of Nebraska . . . but he wouldn't want to start it over again.

"No, I don't think I'd like to start over. I'm happy with the way it has turned out," explains Kinney, who along with 18 other Nebraska seniors, makes his final appearance at Memorial Stadium Saturday.

"Looking back to this summer, I thought 'boy, what a long season it was going to be,'" says Jeff.

"But it's gone by pretty fast. Now I'm thinking what a short career it's been. It all seems like one year bunched together," he says.

As the McCook senior heads down the homestretch, he owns Cornhusker career records for touchdowns scored (29) and passes caught (81). He's rapidly approaching No. 1 status as Nebraska's all-time rushing leader.

"I don't worry about records. But if I would get it, it would be a great honor. Bobby Reynolds and Joe Orduna were great backs," he says of the two ball carriers who still rank ahead of him.

Chance, not choice, dictated Jeff's emergence as a ball carrier. The former high school quarterback was switched to halfback on the Cornhusker freshman team. The presence of Van Brownson and Jerry Tagge made this shift expedient.

Locked in a battle with Larry Frost for the wingback job in his sophomore year, Jeff suddenly became an I-back when injuries felled Orduna and Frank Vactor.

"At that time, I thought I was a better receiver than a runner," admits Jeff, who won't get any arguments. In the offensive scheme that year, the I-back became a wide receiver when the Cornhuskers went into their spread formation. Kinney was a good one, setting a season record with 44 catches.

But he became a better runner each week. "I wasn't a great runner because I couldn't read blocks very well . . . I just had to learn how to run to daylight. The last two or three games I started coming around," says Jeff.

He "arrived" at Oklahoma, carrying 35 times for 127 yards, scoring three touchdowns. It was the same game that the nation's premier I-back, Heisman Trophy winner Steve Owens, had his long string of 100-yard plus games snapped by the Nebraska defense.

"I had incentive to win and play a good game. I had received letters from all the Big Eight schools but Oklahoma in high school. They told Ken Hulstein, who they recruited from McCook, they didn't think I'd make it," relates Jeff.

Kinney has definitely "made it," thanks to patience on the part of backfield coach Mike Corgan and head coach Bob Devaney.

"I fumbled three times against Oklahoma State as a sophomore. They took me out of the game for awhile, but put me back in. That showed me they had confidence in me," says Jeff.

Now he ranks as one of the nation's leading backs. When *Sports Illustrated* spotlighted the nation's top running backs last week, Kinney was ranked among the top 10 seniors. "I was very pleased with the article, but I didn't realize I was that slow," says Jeff, referring to the line "It would be unfair if he had real speed."

"I think I have adequate speed. I think I'm faster now than I've ever been," says Jeff. "I don't run for speed. I run under control to read the blocks so I'm able to move either way.

"Coach Corgan says, 'Read it like you see it' and I can always find a crack or something. I can read the holes at a faster speed because of experience. It's sort of like a judgment call by an official," explains Jeff.

With the options afforded by his offensive line and fullbacks, it's been one good call after another for Jeff.

HUSKERS KNOCK OU, 35-31

By Hal Brown

November 26, 1971— It was billed as the Game of The Decade. It turned out to be the Game of The Century. And Nebraska Coach Bob Devaney called it "the greatest victory of my career."

It was a game in which Nebraska found a way to beat the Oklahoma wishbone-T—outscore it, which the Huskers did Thursday afternoon, driving 74 yards in the closing minutes for a come-from-behind 35-31 victory with the Big Eight, as well as the national championship, riding on every signal barked by quarterback Jerry Tagge during the do-or-die march.

"It's the greatest victory of my career," a happy Devaney told a crowded roomful of writers as he appeared before them, dripping wet from a trip to the showers, courtesy of his jubilant squad.

"The way we did it, coming from behind against a great Oklahoma team, makes me very proud of this team. It will make for a very happy Thanksgiving for everyone back in Nebraska."

But when Oklahoma went ahead 31-28 with only 7:10 left in the game, some of the less-confident Husker backers may have been wondering about the happiness of

this Thanksgiving.

Devaney wasn't among them.

"I figured we could score," Devaney said. "I was worried that we might score too quickly and give them a chance to come back."

The Huskers took 5:32 to march the 74 yards in 12 plays for the winning touchdown and when they turned the ball over to the Sooners on the ensuing kickoff, Oklahoma had 81 yards between it and the Husker end zone and only 1:38 to get there.

The Nebraska Black Shirts, who had yielded 31 points and 467 yards, nearly 300 above their give-up average, weren't about to give up any more.

Oklahoma quarterback Jack Mildren first tried to pass. It went incomplete. He then kept for 5 yards, but on the next play, Husker tackle Larry Jacobson, who only Tuesday had been named the nation's outstanding lineman by the Football Writers Association, got to him before he could get rid of the ball for an 8-yard loss, and the Sooners were faced with a fourth-and-13 from their own 16.

Jacobson and middle guard Rich Glover took care of the final Sooner hope, with Glover batting Mildren's pass attempt down as the

two chased the Sooner quarterback.

That gave the Huskers the ball at the Sooner 16 with 1:10 remaining and, with no desire to "run up the score," ran out the clock to clinch their third straight Big Eight championship and assure themselves of at least the United Press International's national championship with the coaches' panel choosing not to take a post-bowl vote.

Nebraska will have to put its claim to the Associated Press' national title on the line one more time—against Alabama in the Orange Bowl on New Year's night, where the Huskers won their first national crown a year ago with a 17-12 victory over LSU.

Thursday's victory was typical of so many of the Husker victories under Devaney—a come-from-behind one with a length-of-the-field drive as the clock ran down.

Devaney-coached teams have done it at least 10 times in his 10 years at the Husker helm, but never have they done it with so much riding on the do-or-die effort.

Coming from behind was a new thing for this 1971 team. They had not trailed in 10 previous victories this season. But when they did fall behind—and they did twice Thursday before a record Owen Stadium crowd of 63,385— there was no panic, another trademark of Devaney-coached teams.

The winning drive started immediately after Oklahoma had gone ahead 31-28 on a 69-yard drive in 12 plays that ended with Sooner split end Jon Harrison beating All-Big Eight defensive back Bill Kosch for the third time in the game, on a 16-yard pitch from Mildren.

The drive was in trouble when it reached a third-and-8 at the Sooner 46. But Johnny Rodgers made a shoestring catch of a Jerry Tagge pass at the Sooner 35 to keep it alive.

The drive was never in trouble again as Jeff Kinney went for 13 to the 22. Rodgers gained 7 and Kinney added 7 more for a first-and-goal at the 8.

It was Kinney for 2, Kinney for 4 and Kinney for the final 2. And when Kinney trotted off the field with his fourth touchdown of the afternoon, his tear-away jersey was in shreds.

Six Husker backs wore tear-away jerseys for this game for the first time this season.

It took such an exciting finish to top the excitement generated for Nebraska fans by Rodgers early in the game.

When the Nebraska Black Shirts stopped Oklahoma on the Sooners' first possession, one of the few times the Black Shirts did stop the wishbone, and forced a punt from the OU 38, Rodgers fielded it at the Husker 28.

Before he gave up the football, he was in the OU end zone, having jitterbugged down the sideline in full view of the Oklahoma bench and the 72 yards wiped out the Big Eight's season punt return yardage record of 515 yards set by Jack Mitchell of Oklahoma in 1949.

The 72-yard return gave

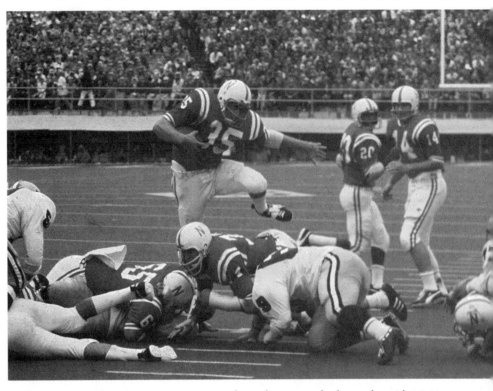

Jeff Kinney ended his career at NU in 1971 as the Huskers' career leading rusher with 2,244 yards, touchdown scorer with 29 TDs and receiver with 81 receptions. (Journal Star Library).

Rodgers 534 for the season, and the Huskers were ahead 7-0 with only 3:32 gone in the game.

The Sooners came right back to march from their own 15 to the Husker 13 before the Black Shirts held and John Carroll kicked a 30-yard field goal with 5:53 left in the first quarter.

Oklahoma was driving again when All-American Greg Pruitt fumbled at the Husker 46 and Jim Anderson scooped it up.

The Huskers used 12 plays to drive the 54 yards to go ahead, 14-3, with 11:06 left in the first half, with Kinney going over from the 1 for his first touchdown.

The only pass completion in the drive was a 12-yarder from Tagge to Rodgers, with the rest coming on the running of Kinney and Tagge.

But that was the end of the Husker offense in the first half, as

the Sooners battled back to take a 17-14 halftime lead.

The Sooners drove 80 yards in 13 plays to close the gap to 14-10 with 5:10 left in the half, Mildren going in from the 2.

Oklahoma later forced a Husker punt with only 1 minute remaining in the first half and turned to the pass to go 78 yards in four plays.

With a first-and-10 at their own 32, Mildren hit Harrison with a 43-yarder as Kosch lost track of the ball while trying to cover the Sooner receiver.

Now with a first-and-10 at the Husker 24 and only five seconds left in the first half, Harrison again beat Kosch, this time in the end zone, and Mildren hit him to put the Huskers behind for the first time this season, 17-14.

And statistically, things looked even worse for the Huskers

as they trotted to the dressing room to talk things over.

Oklahoma enjoyed a 14-5 margin in first downs and a 311-191 edge in total offense.

But the proud Huskers, who were trying to extend their unbeaten string to 30 straight, soon turned the momentum around.

Going primarily to a running game in the second half, they marched 53 yards in six plays the second time they got the ball after the intermission.

Dave Mason gave the Husker offense the ball at the NU 47, recovering a Mildren fumble.

Tagge kept the Huskers on the ground all the way, eating up 32 of the yards by himself on an option play to put the ball at the OU 3.

Kinney bulled his way in for his second touchdown with 8:54 left in the third quarter to give the lead back to the Huskers, 21-17.

The Black Shirts held again and forced a punt that gave the ball back to the offense at its own 39 and NU drove the 61 yards in nine plays, again staying on the ground except for two plays of the nine, a 20-yard and a 10-yard pass from Tagge to Rodgers.

This time Kinney went in from 1 yard out with 3:38 left in the third quarter and the Huskers had what some thought was a safe lead with things going their way at 28-17.

But it didn't last as Oklahoma scored the next two times it got the ball, going 73 yards in seven plays and 69 in 12 to go ahead by 31-28, setting up the do-or-die situation for the Huskers.

THE HUSKERS DID.

Jeff Kinney's 174-yard, four-touchdown performance in the Game of the Century was "the greatest performance by a running back I've ever seen," Coach Bob Devaney said. (Journal Star Library).

GAME OF THE CENTURY WAS PINNACLE OF KINNEY'S CAREER

By John Mabry

Former Nebraska running back Jeff Kinney paused after being asked if the Game of the Century was the game of his life.

"It was obviously an important game," Kinney said, referring to the Huskers' Thanksgiving Day victory over Oklahoma in 1971. "There were so many my senior year."

But the 35-31 win in Norman, Oklahoma, was the one that gave Nebraska an 11-0 record, a Big Eight title and the chance to face Alabama in the Orange Bowl. If the Huskers don't beat the Sooners, they don't end up with their second straight national championship.

Kinney's fourth touchdown of the game, on a 2-yard run, capped a 74-yard drive that put the Huskers ahead for good with 1 minute, 38 seconds left in the game.

Kinney had runs of 17 and 13 yards during the march. He finished the day with 31 carries for a game-high 174 yards.

After the game, Nebraska fullback Maury Damkroger sat with Cornhusker Coach Bob Devaney on the bus ride from the stadium to the airport.

"All he could talk about was Jeff Kinney," Damkroger said. "He said it was the greatest performance by a running back he'd ever seen."

Devaney had little trouble in getting Kinney to come to Lincoln from McCook (Nebraska) High School. There was no doubt in Kinney's mind that he wanted to be a Cornhusker.

He was born November 1, 1949 in Oxford, Nebraska, and it didn't take long for him to discover Nebraska football.

"I would go out hunting and listen to the Huskers' games on the radio," Kinney said. "I couldn't wait for the Sunday paper to read about them."

He became a star in Lincoln a little earlier than expected. Because starting I-back Joe Orduna was injured, Kinney took on much of the running load as a sophomore.

The numbers from Kinney's first game, a 31-21 home loss to No. 5 Southern California, were less than spectacular. He rushed four times for 17 yards and caught two passes for 18.

But he came back strong the following week against Texas A&M. Kinney carried 24 times for 78 yards and a touchdown, and he had 32 yards receiving on three catches.

He followed that with big games against Missouri (154 total yards) and Kansas (174 total yards).

Then came a clunker, but what turned out to be a valuable clunker.

Kinney fumbled three times against Oklahoma State. The Huskers, however, still managed to win the game, 13-3, and Kinney managed to keep the faith of his coaches.

"Coach Devaney expressed a lot of confidence in me," Kinney said. "He hung in there with me."

Devaney knew what he was doing. In the last game of the season, Kinney tore through the Oklahoma defense, a sign of bigger things to come. He rushed for 127 yards and three touchdowns in a 44-14 victory in 1969.

"Jeff did a tremendous job for a sophomore," Devaney said that December. "I believe he is the most impressive and versatile sophomore back we've had at Nebraska."

"Versatile" was the key word. Kinney, who was picked as the top offensive sophomore in the conference, finished the season with 590 yards rushing, 455 yards receiving and 12 touchdowns.

He caught 41 passes in 1969, which through the 1997 season was still the record for an NU running back.

"I was a flanker that they would send out in a spread formation," Kinney said.

Orduna returned in 1970, and that, combined with the emergence of wingback Johnny Rodgers, made it harder for Kinney to get his hands on the football.

His numbers that year were still solid—661 yards rushing and 179 receiving—and he found out how it felt to be on the No. 1 team in the country.

Nebraska won its first national championship with an 11-0-1 season that was capped by a 17-12 victory over LSU in the Orange Bowl. Against the Tigers, Kinney carried 13 times for 33 yards and caught two passes for 27 yards.

After NU was voted No. 1 in the final Associated Press poll, Kinney was asked how he thought the 1971 team would respond to the pressure of being defending national champion.

"Can we handle it?" Kinney said. "We'll find out next year."

The answer came in the form of 12 routs and one game for the ages.

With Kinney, Rodgers and quarterback Jerry Tagge leading the offense, Nebraska marched through the first 10 games of the '71 season with ease, at least until the November 25 visit to Norman.

The Huskers started the season as the No. 2 team in the country and quickly took over the No. 1 spot after whipping Oregon 34-7 in the season opener.

The closest game before the Oklahoma thriller was a 31-7 thrashing of No. 9 Colorado in Lincoln.

While the team was rolling, Kinney was creeping up on the 1,000-yard mark without being overworked.

"A lot of games, I would play one series in the second half," Kinney said.

Then came the No. 1 vs. 2 showdown with the 9-0 Sooners, a classic that went back and forth several times. Nebraska led 14-3, then Oklahoma led 17-14. Nebraska led 28-17, then Oklahoma led 31-28.

"People didn't realize the importance until it was played over and over (in the media)," Kinney said.

Just as Kinney scored over and over against Oklahoma.

Kinney 1 run.
Kinney 3 run.
Kinney 1 run.
Kinney 2 run.

The last touchdown put the Huskers ahead for good in what became known as the Game of the Century.

Damkroger, who got a first-hand look at Kinney's work during the game, said it was an amazing performance.

"That second half," he said, "they just couldn't bring him down."

Kinney recalled the game from the perspective of the opponent.

"What gets overlooked is that OU had a pretty good football team," he said. "It was a bitter loss for them. It was so close."

The Huskers' last two games of the season were not. Nebraska pounded Hawaii 45-3 in the regular-season finale and manhandled No. 2 Alabama 38-6 in the Orange Bowl.

In the victory over the Crimson Tide, Kinney carried 20 times for 99 yards and a touchdown.

He finished the season with 1,037 yards rushing and he finished his career with 2,244 yards rushing, which at the time was the top total in Husker history. He was inducted into the Nebraska Football Hall of Fame in 1981.

Not bad for a back who occasionally was criticized for his lack of speed.

"I felt like I had adequate speed," Kinney said. "I ran a 4.6 in

the 40, which back then wasn't too bad."

Dick Rupert, one of the linemen who helped create running room for Kinney, said Kinney was successful because he knew where to take the ball.

"He had a real knack for letting us block and going in that direction," Rupert said. "We thought if we gave him the ball, we could gain 5 yards.

"I have cleat marks on my back that I can thank Jeff for."

Bob Newton, an All-America tackle in 1971, appreciated the way Kinney appreciated his linemen.

"I remember playing Minnesota my senior year, and Jeff would come back to the huddle and compliment the line for making the holes for him," Newton said. "He knew how to inspire the linemen."

Kinney went on to play four seasons for the Kansas City Chiefs of the NFL. He also spent a year with the Buffalo Bills. Kinney did not have an outstanding pro career, and after being a star in college, he had a difficult time adjusting to the precarious life of a pro athlete.

Kinney later found success in the insurance business and was able to look back at those tough times in the NFL as valuable learning experiences.

"Life's disappointments are God's appointments," Kinney said.

And when he does get down, Kinney always has the memory of a 1971 Thanksgiving Day appointment with the Sooners to pick him up.

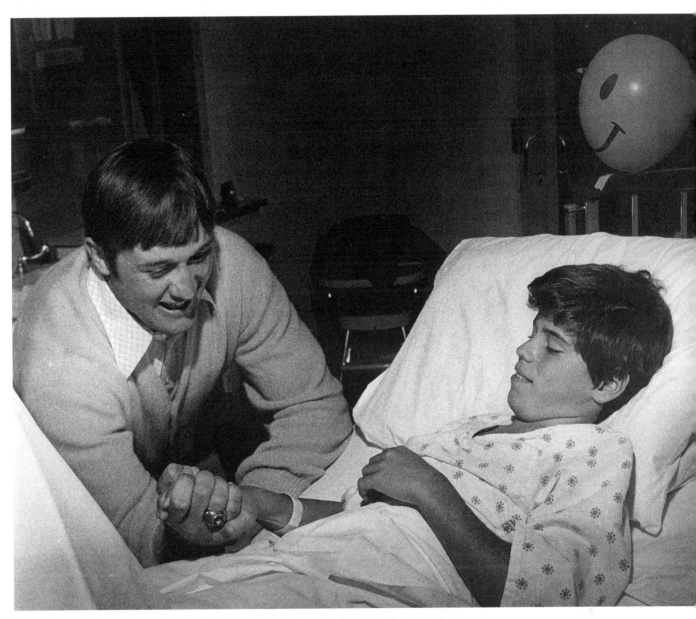

Nebraska I-back Jeff Kinney paid a visit to Bryan Memorial Hospital in September 1971. Among those he visited was 10-year-old Barry Bauer. (Journal Star Library).

PHILLIPS

LAWRENCE

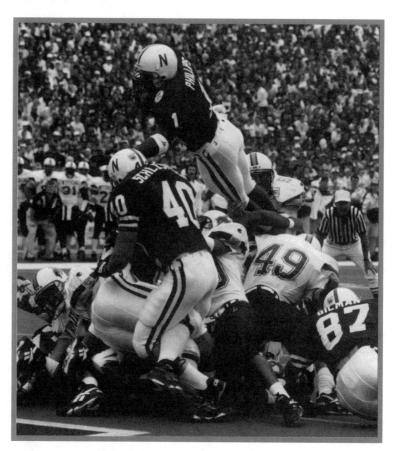

I-back Lawrence Phillips (1) jumps over the top of the pile to score in NU's 42-32 victory against Wyoming on October 1, 1994. (Journal Star Library).

LAWRENCE PHILLIPS/STATS

LETTERED:	1993-95
HEIGHT:	6-0
WEIGHT:	200
HOMETOWN:	WEST COVINA, CALIFORNIA
HONORS:	1994 ALL-BIG EIGHT
PRO	
EXPERIENCE:	ST. LOUIS RAMS 1996
	MIAMI DOLPHINS 1997

FRESHMAN PROVES HE'S NU'S NO. 1

By Mike Babcock

April 24, 1994—Lawrence Phillips was the last player to come to the South Stadium varsity lounge for interviews following the Nebraska football team's annual Spring Game. The freshman I-back showed up, after everyone else had gone, carrying two pens.

His white football pants were marked, generously, with black ink from those pens. He had spent the better part of a half hour immediately following the game signing autographs.

Saturday afternoon at Memorial Stadium, kids, especially, in the crowd of 28,999, were requesting autographs from any muscular young male near the field who looked like a football player. But it's reasonable to assume by the end of the game, they knew who Phillips was, if not by name then by his No. 1 jersey.

Phillips rushed for 156 yards on 16 carries, mostly against the No. 1 defensive unit, to lead the Red team to a 43-19 victory.

Spring game facts, however, aren't particularly significant. The most accurate way to assess Phillips' performance was to listen, carefully, to what Coach Tom Osborne had to say about it.

Osborne was asked if there were questions regarding the I-back position because of Calvin Jones' early departure for the NFL. Although there were those who would have Saturday (some fans can be quick to discard yesterday's stars). Osborne did not respond with: "Calvin who?"

But he was enthusiastic about Phillips, in his typically understated, if not unenthusiastic, way. "I didn't see many questions he (Phillips) can't answer today." Osborne said.

That's about as ecstatic as Osborne gets. A Barry Switzer equivalent, for example, would have been something like: "Wooooeee, that Phillips is incredible. He's another Mike Rozier, only better. He'll win the Heisman Trophy if the voters stay sober."

Phillips has shown the potential to be as good as any I-back NU has had, Osborne said, returning to his more reserved mode. But "he still has to stand the test of time."

Assuming he remains healthy, and doesn't declare for the NFL draft in the immediate future, there is no good reason to think that the 6-foot, 200-pound Phillips won't stand the test of time.

A couple of his runs Saturday were of highlight-film quality. The best, to an untrained eye, was probably a 19-yarder that set up the first touchdown of the second half, when he put a hand down and kept his feet and broke through several frustrated defenders.

Phillips is fast, with good balance. "He's strong," said freshman Mike Minter, NU's No. 1 strong safety.

"It's hard to square up on him. He'll slide off you. You've got to grab him and pull him down. You're not going to put your shoulder into him. The best thing is probably to get an angle on him."

Phillips returned the compliment. Even though the offense seemed to dominate most of the game, "I don't think anybody is going to run through our defense," he said. He, however, did.

It was appropriate that on the day before the NFL draft Phillips would perform as he did. Last year, Derek Brown (who was busy signing autographs on the sideline Saturday) left early for the NFL and Nebraska had Jones. Now, Jones is leaving for the NFL and the Cornhuskers have Phillips, as well as Damon Benning, Clinton Childs and Marvin Sims. Oh yes, and Brian Knuckles, a highly regarded junior college transfer, scheduled to arrive in the fall.

Osborne said the other I-backs shouldn't be ignored, that praise for Phillips shouldn't detract from what they've accomplished this spring. Nebraska appears to be well-stocked at the position.

Few programs, particularly those so dependent on an I-back, could lose a player of Jones' ability and remain optimistic.

"It's too early to compare this guy (Phillips) to Rozier," Osborne said. "He's got to show us some things over a period of time, like hanging in there with the program, doing the right things.

"But he could be pretty good."

Pretty good? Consider the source.

I-BACK RUNNING RUGGED

By Ken Hambleton

September 16, 1994—Lawrence Phillips claims there is one aspect of his football playing he'd like to improve as he prepares to face 13th-ranked UCLA at 2:30 p.m. Saturday in Memorial Stadium.

He explained, "I've gotten better, but I still don't have a big, hard head like Cory Schlesinger." Schlesinger starts at fullback and often leads the way through the defense for Phillips.

"You don't want to give him a 5-yard start before he runs into you. He's tough."

Phillips has shown a certain toughness as well.

Last September, in his first game for Nebraska, the sophomore I-back entered the game in the second quarter and burst into the UCLA defense for 137 yards and a touchdown.

"Last year, in Los Angeles, was special because there were a lot of people in the stands looking for me," said Phillips, a graduate of Baldwin Park High School in suburban Los Angeles. "I was happy because I established that I could play at this level.

"This year, I know I'm starting and I pretty much know what to expect."

He knows to expect a lot of attention from the UCLA defense and the national media.

After Phillips beat Damon Benning and Clinton Childs for the top I-back spot in the spring, he started to get plenty of local attention. Of course, it's only natural for Nebraska's most famous position. Phillips was going to be the next in line after Mike Rozier, Jeff Kinney, Roger Craig, Calvin Jones, Keith Jones, Derek Brown, I.M. Hipp, Doug DuBose, Bobby Reynolds and others who ran to Nebraska glory.

In Phillips' first two games as a starter, he hasn't disappointed anybody and even impressed head coach Tom Osborne.

In the second quarter of the Texas Tech game, Phillips picked up 7 yards behind the blocking of tackle Zach Wiegert, then gained another 13 on his own, breaking three tackles before he was run out-of-bounds.

"That was the most impressive run he's had there," Osborne said. "The last game he showed what he could do. He has the ability to break tackles, show balance and speed and shows potential to rank up with the finer running backs we've had here if he keeps his direction straight on and off the field."

Phillips was named Big Eight Offensive Player of the Week for his 175 yards and two touchdowns against Texas Tech.

"Just about everything is going his way," said Frank Solich, Nebraska running backs coach. "He's able to do things the average back can't do and he's getting better every game."

He is showing signs of maturity on and off the field, according to Solich.

"You go back to last season and you can see by the Orange Bowl, it just started to come together for Lawrence," Solich said. "He's become a big-play producer because of what he did in the spring and fall practices and the work he put in over the summer. He's had three or four big plays already and he's learning how to take advantage of our offensive line, the blocking of the receivers and the other backs as well."

Phillips is also happier to be in Lincoln. He is no longer bothered by the homesickness that made him stay away from practice after last year's Oklahoma game and, by vote of the team seniors, almost kept him from playing in the Orange Bowl.

"I was scared of the cold here," Phillips said. "But it wasn't as bad as I thought it would be. And I've learned to get along and slow down to the life in Lincoln.

"It's a lot more fun to be here. It's more fun to come to practice and I'm just getting the hang of things here."

PHILLIPS SHOWED STAMINA

By Curt McKeever

October 20, 1994—Nebraska sophomore I-back Lawrence Phillips relied on speed and elusiveness to become the second player in school history to reach 1,000 yards rushing in six games.

Saturday at Kansas State, Phillips showed that his package includes much more than exceptional physical talent.

Running against a defense whose main purpose was to stop him because of Nebraska's fragile situation at quarterback, Phillips carried 31 times for 117 yards and one touchdown to rescue the Cornhuskers in their 17-6 victory.

"That, to me, ranks as high as any of the games that he's played this year," said assistant head coach Frank Solich, who has coached NU running backs the last 12 seasons.

Phillips' rushing total was his lowest in a game this season. But to Solich, that number didn't reflect what Phillips helped Nebraska accomplish.

"I think it was pretty evident to the people that are close to the program, to the people at Kansas State, that we were going to be very limited in the number of options that we ran," Solich said. "So you're talking about running a power-type of offense with plays that generally are 4-, 5-, 6-yard gains with two, three people hitting you. It's not a deal where one guy brings you down, so his physical stamina showed.

"The fact that he had patience in the game, a lot of young backs would just get frustrated (with) the 3- and 4-yard gains. Almost every game he's played in he's made the big play, and now the big play wasn't there. A lot of young backs would just get frustrated, and then all of a sudden their game starts to unravel and fall apart. It never happened. He worked hard for every yard that he got, came back to the huddle and took the handoff the next play and just kept doing the same things, play after play. That all adds up."

Kansas State's defense eventually began to crack, and when the Wildcats cheated too much on Phillips, Nebraska caught them with fullback traps, including one that Jeff Makovicka carried 15 yards for a touchdown.

Phillips said Saturday's game reminded him of his senior year at Baldwin Park High School in West Covina, California.

"Our starting quarterback got hurt about the fourth or fifth game, and we brought a sophomore up from the jayvee team, so it turned into a lot of teams focusing on the run and playing run real tough," he said.

So when Kansas State stacked eight players on the line of scrimmage to try to stop him, Phillips was more than happy to hammer away.

"It's a time when you know you're just going to have to pound it out and get whatever you can, and hopefully maybe once or twice you might get a 20-, 25-yarder," he said. "When it's that type of game, you've got to get into a mindset of what's going to happen than when it's another type of game where you've got to be a little more elusive."

Phillips' toughness also showed after he took a blow from a helmet late in the first half that left him wondering whether his left thumb was broken. X-rays taken at a hospital during halftime turned up negative, and despite severe swelling, Phillips returned to action midway through the third quarter and gained 64 of his yards thereafter.

"I think it was one of my most characteristic performances of the year," Phillips said.

That kind of character has put Phillips, currently the third-leading rusher in the country with 1,123 yards for a 160.4-yard average, in the running for the Heisman Trophy.

"Right now, he's probably (a dark horse) because he wasn't well-known," said NU quarterback Tommie Frazier, a Heisman candidate before blood clots ended his season after four games. "But I guarantee you after this year, or maybe later on this year, you will hear a lot of people talking about him for Heisman."

Phillips seems unaffected by his name being mentioned with the Heisman and says his focus is on helping Nebraska, currently ranked second and third in the major polls, win a national championship. The Huskers will attempt to improve to 8-0 when they play at 1 p.m. Saturday at Missouri.

"I guess it's all right to be on the Heisman watch, but I think with the situation we're in we've got to concentrate more on trying to win games," he said.

Phillips credits his high school coach, Tony Zane, for helping him to keep things in perspective.

"He didn't really baby any of the athletes," Phillips said. "Some

schools, they have their athletes and you don't have to do much, and he didn't have that. It didn't matter who you were – you worked and there was no easy way out with him. So I guess he kind of helped me develop that trying not to be the star."

Phillips got an early chance to play last season after Calvin Jones was injured in Nebraska's opener. After gaining 80 yards in his first game, Phillips responded with a 137-yard effort at UCLA.

"He's really showed the whole package from the time he came here," Solich said.

Lawrence Phillips runs for some of his 96 yards in the 1995 Orange Bowl game against Miami of Florida. The Huskers' 24-17 come-from-behind win gave Coach Tom Osborne his first national championship. (Lincoln Journal Star).

PHILLIPS HAD THE WHOLE PACKAGE

By Steve Sipple

Two wood and glass display cases greet visitors of the Hewit Center for Student-Athletes at the University of Nebraska at Lincoln.

One of the displays features Mike Rozier's 1983 Heisman Trophy, an enlarged photograph of Rozier and his red and white jersey with No. 30. Nearby is a display featuring Johnny Rodgers' 1972 Heisman, photo and jersey No. 20.

If not for troubles off the field, Nebraska might well have a third Heisman to display, one with a photograph of Lawrence Phillips and his jersey No. 1.

Former Nebraska head coach Tom Osborne said Phillips "is probably the most-talented running back we have ever had here."

Phillips had the whole package: strength, size, breakaway speed, instincts, attitude, everything. He put it all on display in his final appearance as a Cornhusker—the 1996 Fiesta Bowl in Tempe, Ariz. At times, Florida's defenders looked like junior high players trying to corral him during Nebraska's 62-24 victory.

The 6-foot, 215-pound Phillips carried 25 times for 165 yards and scored three touch-downs, including one on a 42-yard run during which at least five Florida defenders missed opportunities to tackle him.

"He's the best running back in college football, by far," Nebraska defensive lineman Jason Peter said after the Fiesta Bowl win, which gave the Huskers their second straight national championship. "He can run through you, jump over you or go around you. He showed what he can do."

It was vintage Phillips.

Ohio State running back Eddie George captured the Heisman Trophy voting that season. Early in the year, however, Phillips looked as if he would be the runaway winner of college football's most prestigious award.

The native of West Covina, California, devastated defenses in the first two games, rushing for 153 yards on only 12 carries against Oklahoma State before running through and over the Michigan State defense for 206 yards and four touchdowns despite a badly sprained ankle.

"There's no question he was a Heisman Trophy-type running back at that point," said Nebraska head coach Frank Solich, who then served as running backs coach. "He got off to a tremendous start that season.

"I came out of the Michigan State game thinking I had the best running back in the nation—there was no question in my mind. He showed tremendous instincts running inside, great body control, great balance and great acceleration. When he broke free, he never got run down (from behind)."

For Phillips, the future seemed to hold so much promise. Then, one tumultuous incident changed everything. The unstoppable I-back was halted, but not by tacklers. The best way to put it is Lawrence Phillips stopped himself. He was suspended for the next six games for an assault on a girlfriend. The incident, which occurred in the pre-dawn darkness the morning after the Michigan State game, rocked the entire state, creating controversy that dragged on the entire season, and beyond.

Upon returning from his suspension, Phillips was noticeably bigger, and he ran sluggishly. He came off the bench and rushed for 68 yards against Iowa State, 47 against Kansas and 73 against Oklahoma.

"There's no question that he was not in great shape," Solich said at the time. "It took him quite a while to get back in shape."

In pre-Fiesta Bowl workouts, however, Phillips was exceptional. Anybody who witnessed the practices knew he had returned to form and was primed for a big night in Tempe. He was running like the franchise back that he was.

"He was certainly ready to play," Solich recalls. "As I remember Lawrence, he was always a top-effort guy. He always worked hard in practice—he was probably one of the hardest-working guys we ever had."

Phillips' ability and work ethic helped him at Baldwin Park High School, where he rushed for 1,752 yards and 25 touchdowns as a senior. He drew nationwide recruiting attention, turning down Southern Cal, Washington State, Arizona State and Illinois.

"Wherever you go, there are going to be good players," Phillips said. "I knew that. So I wanted to go where they'd win."

Phillips was third on Nebraska's first depth chart in the fall of 1993, but moved up when Calvin Jones was injured against North Texas in the opener. Phillips sat out that game, suspended for fighting with a teammate. The next week, he rushed for 80 yards on 14 carries.

Phillips enjoyed the first 100-yard game of his college career the next week against UCLA in the Rose Bowl. After entering in relief of starter Damon Benning—who fumbled twice—Phillips carried 28 times for 137 yards and a touchdown in a 14-13 win. It was evident Nebraska had a big-time back.

After finishing his freshman year with 508 rushing yards, Phillips enjoyed a huge sophomore season, rushing for 1,722 yards on 286 carries, an average of 6.0 yards per carry. His most-productive day came against Oklahoma State, when he rushed for 221 yards in a 32-3 victory. It was the next two games, however, that showed Phillips has much more than just physical talent.

Against Kansas State, Phillips carried 31 times for 117 yards and one touchdown running against a defense whose main purpose was to stop him. Nebraska had to rely heavily on Phillips because its top two quarterbacks were sidelined, leaving walk-on Matt Turman at the controls.

Nebraska ran few options, choosing instead to hammer away between the tackles and pick up yards in small chunks. Forty of the Huskers' 61 plays went between the tackles. The final: NU 17, KSU 6.

What's more, sometime during the first half, he suffered a blow from a helmet that caused severe swelling in his thumb. The injury continued to bother Phillips in the next game, a 42-7 win at Missouri in which he rushed for 110 yards on 22 carries.

"Lawrence is playing with one arm," Osborne said afterward.

"It's been a challenge, but if that's what it takes, fine," Phillips said. "If I need to run the ball 50 times for us to win, that's OK."

Phillips ended the season with a 19-carry, 96-yard effort in Nebraska's 24-17 victory against Miami in the Orange Bowl, a triumph that gave the Huskers the national crown.

Phillips finished eighth in the Heisman voting and was a consensus second-team All-American. Entering the 1995 season, however, he was the No. 1 preseason Heisman candidate in at least two national publications. Soon, such hopes faded in the early morning hours after his brilliant performance against Michigan State.

Some have said that the assault on his girlfriend would not have received nearly the publicity it did had it not taken place so close to the exoneration of O.J. Simpson. Many Nebraska teammates say the public has never had a chance to see the other side of Phillips—the one who volunteered two years in a row at a shelter for abused women in Lincoln, the one whose impressions of comedian Eddie Murphy could leave friends weak with laughter.

"If Lawrence is a beast, he's like the beast in 'Beauty and the Beast,'" Benning, who was a close friend of Phillips, told the *St. Louis Post-Dispatch*. "What you see on the outside is not really who he is."

Coaches and teammates said Tom Rathman ran more like an I-back than the fullback he was. In 1985, Rathman set a Nebraska record for a fullback with 881 yards rushing. (Journal Star Library).

TOM RATHMAN

TOM RATHMAN/STATS

LETTERED:	1983-85
HEIGHT:	6-1
WEIGHT:	235
HOMETOWN:	GRAND ISLAND, NEBRASKA
HONORS:	NEBRASKA FOOTBALL HALL OF FAME
PRO	
EXPERIENCE:	SAN FRANCISCO 49ERS 1986-93
	LOS ANGELES RAIDERS 1994

FULLBACK RATHMAN RUNS WILD

By Mike Babcock

September 9, 1984—Tom Rathman ran like a bull in a china shop Saturday afternoon.

Wyoming's defense wasn't as fragile as fine china, of course.

Rathman just made it look that way.

The Nebraska fullback carried 13 times for 108 yards and one touchdown in the Cornhuskers' 42-7 victory over Wyoming at Memorial Stadium.

His yardage was the most by a Nebraska fullback since Andra Franklin rushed for 122 yards on 20 carries against Oklahoma in 1980.

"If they want to give it to me, I'll carry it," said Rathman, who made mundane trap plays exciting.

His performance was far from trite.

"I was really surprised at how much I got the football. You don't usually see a fullback here gaining that many yards," Rathman said.

What Cornhusker fullbacks usually do is block for Cornhusker I-backs, a responsibility Rathman didn't shirk on Saturday. "He did a heck of

a job blocking" said I-back Jeff Smith.

"I heard a lot of cracks out there, and a lot of them were Rathman," Nebraska center Mark Traynowicz said. "He'll hit you, and you'll feel it."

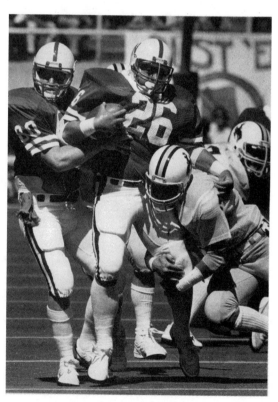

Husker fullback Tom Rathman battles for yardage against Wyoming September 8, 1984. The Grand Island native rushed for 108 yards and one touchdown in NU's 42-7 win. (Journal Star Library).

With Rathman, Traynowicz, and the rest of the offensive line clearing the way, Smith carried 28 times for 170 yards, the second-most productive opening game for a Cornhusker I-back in 22 years. Jarvis Redwine rushed for 179 yards against Utah in 1980.

Much of Smith's yardage came on isolation plays, designed to go inside, with Rathman blocking a linebacker.

"I was killing that linebacker on the 'isos', said Rathman.

Rathman's touchdown, the second of his career, and his first rushing, came on a 16-yard run off-right tackle.

"It was a well-blocked play, and I saw a big hole," he said. "I just had to cut off one block, either by the wingback or the split end. I don't know which.

"I was only concerned about getting in the end zone because I'm so familiar with that feeling."

His other Nebraska touchdown came on a 9-yard pass from Turner Gill in last year's victory over UCLA.

Rathman's previous best rushing total was 48 yards on

Nebraska's Tom Rathman dives head-first into the end zone for a touchdown against Kansas State October 27, 1984. Rathman tied the school record for TDs by a fullback with 12 from 1983-85. (Journal Star Library).

five carries against Oklahoma. His career yardage was 143 on 26 attempts.

Being Mark Schellen's backup, the most Rathman had ever carried in one game was six times.

He ran the ball nine times, for 80 yards, in the first half on Saturday.

Smith's only other 100-yard afternoon came during his sophomore season in 1982, when he rushed for 126 yards on seven carries against New Mexico State. His best a year ago was 99 yards against Miami in the Orange Bowl.

"I knew we were going to run the ball a lot," Smith said. "Our of-

fensive line did a real good job. If it hadn't been for those turnovers in the first half, we would have had an awesome game."

"We were just beating ourselves in the first half," said Rathman, who lost a fumble inside the Wyoming 10-yard line late in the first quarter.

That proved the Cowboy defense was no china shop. "I had both hands on the ball, the way the coaches tell you, but I got hit pretty good," Rathman said.

The 6-1, 235-pound junior from Grand Island ran more like an I-back than a fullback on Saturday. He averaged 8.3 yards per carry,

with five of his carries going for 10 or more yards.

"Rathman's a different breed of fullback. He's got a lot of acceleration," said offensive guard Harry Grimminger, another Grand Island athlete. "Tom can give you that 20- or 30-yard gain."

Rathman is deceptively fast.

The last time he was timed, electronically, in the 40-yard dash, "I only ran :04.88," Rathman said.

"You're a lot faster when guys are chasing you, though," said Nebraska wingback Shane Swanson.

"Definitely," Rathman said.

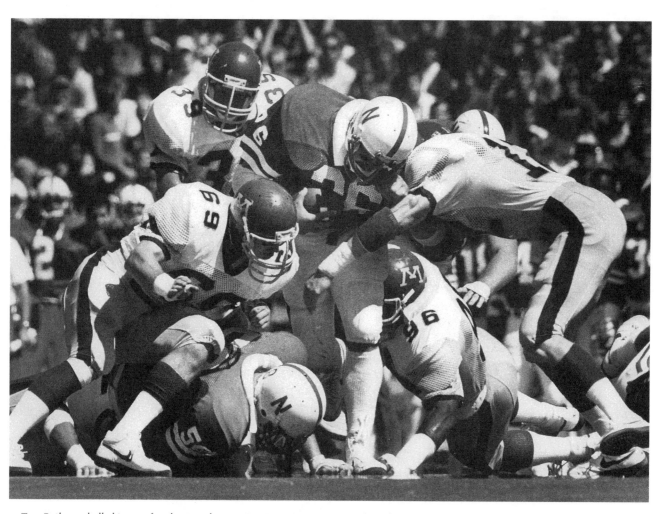

Tom Rathman bulls his way for short yardage against Minnesota in 1984. (Humberto Ramirez/Lincoln Journal Star)

BUFFALOES INCUR WRATH OF RATHMAN

By Virgil Parker

October 27, 1985—About the time they turned the lights on at Memorial Stadium for Saturday's late-starting, nationally televised football game, Nebraska's Tom Rathman turned them off on Colorado.

The fullback from Grand Island broke open a tight defensive struggle late in the third quarter with an 84-yard touchdown run to snap a 7-7 tie. Dale Klein, who kicked seven field goals to beat Missouri last week, then added a 42-yarder to give the Cornhuskers a 17-7 victory.

The win extended Nebraska's dominance over the Buffs, who haven't beaten the Huskers since 1967.

Rathman already had the longest run by a Big Eight Conference player this season after scoring from 60 yards out against Florida State.

"It was a great feeling to go 84 yards," Rathman said. "That's the longest run of my career. I wanted to do something good today because Grand Island was saluting me. And it turned out to be the big play of the game."

Rathman said the key to the play—a 38-trap—is the tight end's block on the linebacker. "He seals off the linebacker and I'm to cut off his block," Rathman explained. "But this time I cut it back early and jumped over a pile of players on the ground. Suddenly, there was nobody there. It was a matter of me trying to outrun the defensive back."

The 6-foot 220-pound Rathman wasn't sure he was going to be able to do that. "I tried to pick up my blockers downfield," he said, "but the defensive back was in front of them. I think he would have caught me if I'd tried to go straight for the end zone. So I made another cut at about the 5 and had enough power to get into the end zone."

Nebraska Coach Tom Osborne noted that 'there are not too many fullbacks with his size—guys who can block like he can—who can also go 84 yards. But Tom is a remarkably good football player and has been playing very well for us."

Tom Rathman is all alone on an 84-yard touchdown run against Colorado on October 26, 1985. (Journal Star Library).

FULLBACK RATHMAN STILL GETTING SWEETER, RUNNING LIKE I-BACK

By Ken Hambleton

November 3, 1985—Nebraska I-back Paul Miles said that fullback Tom Rathman has all the right ingredients to be a member of the club.

"He likes to think he's an I-back and certainly runs like one," Miles said. "But he needs a little more sweetener. He wears the sweetness towels in practice and all, but he's still got some sweetness to go.

"Otherwise, he's a full member of the I-back club," Miles said with a smile.

For the second straight year, Rathman rushed for a pair of touchdowns and picked up the slack when the Husker running game was stymied somewhat by the KSU defense.

A year ago Doug DuBose was held to less than 100 yards, marking the first time in 20 games that no Husker back had gained 100 yards rushing.

The Wildcats geared up for the NU I-backs again, allowing DuBose 82 yards on 18 carries and Miles 83 yards on 11 carries.

"They were sending a defensive back on the I-back every play," Miles said. "They had a pretty good defensive plan and they made us really work and struggle for everything we got."

Quarterback McCathorn Clayton agreed that the K-State defense was geared to take away the option and cover the pitch.

"I had to keep every option and we tried a couple of different things," he said. "The thing that helped break things loose were the plays to the fullback—Rathman."

The only running play that went for more than 4 yards in the first quarter was a trap play by Rathman that was good for 37 yards and the first touchdown of the game.

In the second quarter, Rathman broke a trap play for 11 yards and the only other run longer than 7 yards in the period was a 21-yard touchdown run around left end by Miles that put NU ahead 14-3.

Miles' touchdown run followed a clutch, 22-yard screen pass from Travis Turner to Rathman.

Rathman scored on a 5-yard run on the next drive to give the Huskers a 21-3 lead.

His three runs for 19 yards helped set up Dale Klein's 50-yard field goal in the third quarter.

"We had to go to the fullback plays and they worked," Clayton said. "In the second half, the pitch plays worked."

Husker left guard Brian Blankenship, who suffered from the flu early in the game, said off-guard plays to the fullback worked well.

"They had the outside covered pretty well and we had to get the yards inside," he said. "Rathman is a good runner and he's learned to play right in behind the blocks."

DuBose rushed for 23 yards on a pitch play in the third quarter to set up a 52-yard field goal attempt by Klein that missed.

"They might stop the I-back stuff some, but they couldn't stop both the I-backs and the fullback," Miles said. "It's a one-or-the-other thing, and it's a compliment to Rathman that he's doing the job.

"The line did a great job, but we all had to earn our yards against K-State's effort."

Rathman, who broke away for an 84-yard touchdown to break open the Colorado game a week ago, credited his achievements to his line and confidence in himself.

"I don't think I'm a breakaway threat without the blocking. Nobody can be," Rathman said

"They're making the holes, and because I'm not so worried about hanging onto the ball the way

I was last year, I have more time and more concentration on reading the holes.

"Last year by midseason, I was having troubles with fumbles and holding onto the ball was my primary concern. It still is a concern, but I can run better without the worry about fumbles."

The change is evident, in that the senior from Grand Island has 596 yards this season, only 32 fewer than Miles and 296 fewer than DuBose.

Rathman has six touchdowns this year, the same as DuBose and one more than Miles, and he is just three TDs short of the season scoring record for fullbacks and two short of the career scoring record for fullbacks at Nebraska. He is 121 yards short of the season rushing record for fullbacks.

"I think Coach Osborne has more confidence in me this year because I'm running better and I'm not fumbling," he said in an effort to explain his success. "I had one fumble in the Florida State game, but since then, no problems.

"We have a team goal about leading the stats in turnover ratio and we have an edge of 14 now and that's high nationally," he said.

"The big gains have to happen up front with the blocking. If we take care of the ball and take advantage of what the line gives us, we can get the yards and get the scores.

"The offense is improving. We had a lot of trouble the last two games getting the ball into the end zone when we get in scoring territory," Rathman said. The Huskers had just two touchdowns and eight field goals in 14 drives inside the opponent's 35 in the last two games.

However, Rathman pointed out, "When we don't stop ourselves, we can do a lot."

FORMER HUSKER RATHMAN LOOKS TO PAY BACK PROGRAM

By Ken Hambleton

April 27, 1991—Former Nebraskans Tom and Holly Rathman are going to try to give back something for the benefits they received from the University of Nebraska and the state.

Tom Rathman, who just completed his fifth year with the San Francisco 49ers, said Friday that he and his wife will donate up to $250,000 to the Husker Beef Club in the form of annual $25,000 installments.

"We feel fortunate to be able to come back and have this special day to announce the scholarship to endow a position on the Nebraska football team," Rathman said. "I'm the first, and hopefully there will be others who will want to give back to the program that helped them so much. It would be great to see other former players and others endow the other positions."

Rathman said he got the idea from Southern Cal, which has endowed almost every one of its positions.

"I'll probably be calling some of the other former Cornhuskers to see if they are interested in doing the same thing," he said.

Rathman said he might begin Saturday when he is the main speaker for the annual Husker Beef Club luncheon at 11 a.m. at the Devaney Sports Center. Current pros Dean Steinkuhler of the Houston Oilers and Neil Smith and Marc Munford of the Kansas City Chiefs are among the former Cornhuskers expected at an autograph session (10 a.m.) and luncheon Saturday.

"When Holly and I first got out of college, we did not foresee something like this happening," Rathman said. "But since I've become a 49er and had the opportunity they've given me, I've finally got the chance to give something back to Nebraska."

The money will go to the Nebraska athletic department to use to fund scholarships for fullbacks. The players receiving the scholarships will be chosen by Athletic Director Bob Devaney, head coach Tom Osborne and running backs coach Frank Solich.

"I'd like to see the scholarships go to someone noted for toughness and the ability to block—two things that signify the fullback at Nebraska," Rathman said. "It's not a famous position, known for scoring touchdowns, but noted for the rugged play."

Rathman, who caught five passes in his career at Nebraska, has been one of the leading receivers for the 49ers, who won the Super Bowl in 1989 and 1990 and finished as the NFC runner-up in the 1991 playoffs.

"I'd like to see the fullbacks catch more passes here, too," Rathman said. "I know they still rely on the option, but there are situations where you have to throw the ball."

RATHMAN EPITOME OF HUSKER FULLBACK

By Mark Derowitsch

You won't find Tom Rathman's name listed among the top 10 leading rushers in Nebraska football history. Heck, Rathman didn't even crack the top 25 during his four-year career as a Cornhusker.

Rathman's contributions on the football field can't be measured in yards or feet or inches.

Try hits. As in punishing, long, run-springing blocks.

If Nebraska running backs were measured by those standards, Rathman would likely have been at the top of the list.

Not that Rathman couldn't run. He did gain 1,425 yards, rushed for 100 yards or more in a game four times and scored 12 touchdowns on the ground as a Husker. Following the 1997 season, Rathman stood as the 28th-leading rushing in school history, which isn't bad considering he only touched the ball 220 times from his position at fullback. Mike Rozier, the Huskers' all-time leading rusher, had more than three times the chances that Rathman did.

But when the Huskers needed a first down or a big play, chances were that the I-back would get the ball, running behind the powerful blocks of Rathman, a native of Grand Island.

Former Husker quarterback Steve Taylor, who as a freshman played with Rathman during the 1985 season, wished they had lined up in the same backfield throughout his career.

"He was one of the best blockers I've ever seen," Taylor said. "When I think of Rathman, though, I think of the trap. He was tough to bring down and I don't think I ever saw him tackled for a loss. When he got the ball, you knew he was going to get some tough yards."

Rathman's ability to run with the ball set him apart from the rest of the fullbacks. Among Husker fullbacks, Rathman ranks fifth, but two of the players in front of him also spent time at I-back.

Yes, Rathman could deliver as deadly a blow with the ball in his hands as he could leading the way for an I-back or quarterback. In Rathman's senior season, 1985, the Huskers defeated Colorado 17-7. The turning point came when Rathman scampered 84 yards for a score to snap a 7-7 tie in the third quarter. Rathman finished the game with 115 yards on 11 carries, but it was his long touchdown run that everybody was talking about after the game.

"There are not too many fullbacks with his size—guys who can block like he can—who can also go 84 yards," said Nebraska Coach Tom Osborne. "But Tom is a remarkably good football player."

Rathman finished his senior year with 881 yards—the most ever by a Husker fullback during a single season. He teamed with Doug DuBose to form a backfield that gained more than 2,000 yards combined.

That's what made the Husker backfield so good. Frank Solich, then the Husker running backs coach, said having Rathman lined up behind the quarterback was like having two I-backs in the game at once.

"He is what you look for in a fullback," Solich said. "His size, toughness, and his ability to catch—as he showed with San Francisco—were all perfect for us. Most teams get to have a complete I-back and a complete fullback, but with Rathman we had both. He was as tough to bring down and he was one of those guys who wanted to be a great blocker. He was just about everything as a fullback."

He could also catch the ball, but that wasn't discovered until after he left Nebraska.

Rathman didn't catch a pass as a Husker. But when the San Francisco 49ers picked Rathman in the third round of the NFL draft in 1986, an triple-threat offensive star was born.

He played nine years in the NFL—the first eight with San Francisco and the final season with the Raiders, who were then based in Los Angeles—and caught 320 passes for 2,684 yards. Most of the time, he teamed with Roger Craig—another former Husker standout—to give the 49ers one of the best running back tandems in the league.

When Rathman joined the 49ers, Craig was already an established veteran. But he moved to halfback to make room for Rathman in the starting lineup.

Craig also played a part in bringing Rathman to San Francisco.

"I remember (49ers Coach) Bill Walsh called me into his office and asked about Rathman, 'Do we want this kid?'," Craig said. "I said you've got to get this guy. He's tough, knows how to block and he can run. I can work with him on the catches.

"The next year, when I was the most valuable player, we were in the same backfield. We knew each other really well."

As a 49er, Rathman played on two Super Bowl-winning teams, including the 1989 contest in which San Francisco rallied late in the game to beat Cincinnati 20-16. The next season, the 49ers whipped Denver, 55-10, in the most lopsided Super Bowl victory ever.

"Probably the ultimate was playing against Denver in Super Bowl XXIV," Rathman said. "We were so far ahead, we were celebrating at halftime."

In nine years in the NFL, Rathman rushed for 2,020 yards and scored 34 touchdowns. In 1989, he led all professional running backs with 73 receptions for 616 yards.

Rathman's last year with the Raiders was marked by a neck injury that limited his effectiveness. He carried the ball just 26 times and gained 194 yards. He could have returned for one more season with Los Angeles, but decided to walk away from the game before he was more seriously injured and because he grew tired of working in one city and living in another (San Francisco).

"It was kind of difficult commuting from L.A. to the Bay area where my family was," he said. "And I hurt my neck that year. There were a lot of reasons for retiring, really. I decided it wasn't worth it anymore. Financially, I could've been a lot better off, but I decided money's not everything. Your health is the most important thing."

Retirement didn't mean the end of Rathman's involvement with football. After spending some time as an assistant coach at Serra High School in San Mateo, California, he joined the 49ers' staff as a running backs coach.

He also hasn't forgotten his Nebraska roots. In 1991, Rathman, along with his wife, Holly, gave $250,000 to the Husker Beef Club in the form of annual $25,000 installments. The money goes to Nebraska's athletic department to fund scholarships for fullbacks.

"When Holly and I first got out of college, we did not foresee something like this happening," he said. "But since I've become a 49er and had the opportunity they've given me, I've finally got the chance to give something back to Nebraska."

JARVIS REDWINE

Nebraska's Jarvis Redwine earned All-America honors in 1980 after leading the Big Eight Conference in rushing with a 124.3-yards-per-game average. (Journal Star Library).

JARVIS REDWINE/STATS

LETTERED:	1979-80
HEIGHT:	5-11
WEIGHT:	204
HOMETOWN:	INGLEWOOD, CALIFORNIA
HONORS:	1979 ALL-BIG EIGHT
	1980 ALL-BIG EIGHT
	1980 ALL-AMERICAN
PRO EXPERIENCE:	MINNESOTA VIKINGS 1981-83

REDWINE PROVES WORTH

By Mike Babcock

May 6, 1979—When you're a transfer at Nebraska, you try harder. . . much harder. Ask Jarvis Redwine about that.

Becoming a Cornhusker after beginning your college football career somewhere else takes a lot of perseverance. NU coaches are not easily convinced.

"The No. 1 reason it's so hard proving yourself to the coaches here is that they want to know why you transferred. They wonder if something is wrong with you, and you have to show everybody you're capable," Redwine said after Saturday's annual Red-White Spring Game.

Redwine came to Lincoln from Corvallis, Oregon, home of Oregon State University.

He spent last fall on the Cornhusker scout squad and this spring trying to prove himself to NU Coach Tom Osborne and his staff.

Saturday afternoon, Redwine's proof included 94 yards rushing on 16 carries. Some 20,000 Husker fans—according to Jarvis, a crowd the size of some of those at Oregon State's regular-season home games—left convinced that the speedy I-back from Los Angeles, was indeed a player.

Now Nebraska is "home" for Redwine.

"It was home the minute I decided to pick up roots and leave Oregon. This had to be the place," he said.

Only once did Nebraska fans have cause to disown the 6-foot 195-pounder with :04.4 speed. That came when Redwine fielded the second-half kickoff and his momentum carried him out-of-bounds inside his own 1-yard line.

"I don't know what it is with me," he said with a smile. "I always seem to make a mistake like that.

"I misjudged the wind, which was blowing the ball that way. It was my first time being on the kickoff team, and I felt I could field it," Redwine said.

The situation was quickly salvaged when quarterback Jeff Quinn connected with veteran receiver Tim Smith on a 36-yard pass play that got the Red team out of trouble.

And Redwine redeemed himself time after time with quick bursts through and around the line. His longest effort of the afternoon was a 17-yard sprint up the middle on the day's first scoring drive.

Redwine's emergence during the spring has given Osborne some welcome depth at running back.

Isaiah Hipp, who missed Saturday's game with a broken thumb, and Omaha junior-to-be Craig Johnson join with Redwine to give the Cornhuskers a special kind of triple-threat.

"I feel real good that we have three players at I-back who can run like that," Osborne said. "I don't worry about that situation at all.

"The way football is now, you have to have three guys at that position," he said.

Osborne isn't complaining about his I-back situation for the fall. Barring injury, Hipp should become Nebraska's all-time leading career rusher. He's gained over 1,000 yards in each of his last two seasons after walking on from Chapin, S.C.

"If I had to rank-order them right now, Hipp would be first because he has the experience," Osborne said. "But there's no way to differentiate between Craig or Jarvis as No. 2 and No. 3. . . They're right together."

Jarvis Redwine had proved himself a worthy transfer.

REDWINE COLLECTS T-SHIRT, 100 YARDS

By Mike Babcock

September 30, 1979—Jarvis Redwine tore the clear plastic wrapper off a powder-blue T-shirt that read: "Penn State Nittany Lions."

Nebraska's junior I-back pulled it on as he explained where the T-shirt came from. "An eastern writer called me Wednesday night (for an interview), and I asked him if he would bring me and my wife (Frances) something with 'Penn State' on it," Redwine said.

"He said, 'What if you lose?' I told him he could bring it anyway, but I wouldn't wear it."

Redwine began his collection of opposition T-shirts last week in Iowa City; he couldn't get one from Utah State. Saturday, he picked up No. 2, with his first 100-yard rushing performance as a collegian, and wore it after Nebraska's 42-17 victory over Penn State.

His previous yardage high was a 95-yard (16 carries) effort in one half against Tennessee during his sophomore year at Oregon State. One week after that game, he quit the team.

The swift transfer gained 124 yards in 22 carries against a physical Penn State defense. He ripped through—and around—the Nittany Lions almost as easily as he ripped the wrapper on his new T-shirt . . . or as easily as Lion defenders ripped jerseys off him.

According to the NU equipment room, he lost six tearaway jerseys during the afternoon.

"I just hope this game was telecast on the West Coast," said Redwine, meaning specifically Inglewood, California, his home and Corvallis, Oregon, where he played before transferring to Nebraska.

"I don't mean that to get revenge with anybody. I just want to show that I can run," he said.

Viewers in Oregon may have been surprised with the Redwine they saw tearing up the artificial turf in Memorial Stadium. He didn't head for the sidelines each time Tim Hager handed him the ball.

Saturday, a more physical Redwine dealt out punishment instead of just taking it. "At Oregon State I was getting a lot of hits and it started shaking me up so I began using the sidelines," he said.

Not so against Penn State. Redwine was turning up-field, picking out defenders and making them pay for bringing him down. Like the safety he slammed into at the Nittany Lion 21-yard line following a 19-yard gain in Nebraska's first touchdown drive.

Redwine hit the defender chest high, and knocked him over backwards. "That typified what I've been trying to do; I'm more satisfied with the way I was delivering the blows than anything," he said, recalling the hit.

Nebraska offensive backfield coach Mike Corgan was pleased with Redwine's physical play. "This is a little different kind of football than he's been used to playing," said Corgan.

"The thing is, on the wide stuff, he's been exposing himself to some open shots (from the tacklers). Like a billiard shot in the corner, they've been banging him around.

"But today he ran inside tough, and he read pretty well," Corgan said.

Even Bruce Clark, Penn State's super-strong, All-America defensive tackle, wasn't exempt from Redwine's new-found, "muscle 'em around" attitude.

Their personal battle began when Clark crashed through to throw Redwine for a 4-yard loss one play after his 19-yard burst, only to be called for a facemask penalty, which moved the ball to the Nittany Lion 11-yard line.

"He grabbed it (the mask) and stuck his whole hand in my eye," said Redwine. "I told the official, 'Hey, facemask,' and he said, 'Yeah, I got it.'"

According to Redwine, "Clark said a couple of things" early in the game, and he (Jarvis) responded by sticking his hand in Clark's facemask "one time when he had me down on the ground.

"I remember him saying something like 'Yeah, buddy, yeah,'

and I told him to go someplace. I told him to go to hell, but I didn't mean it that way," said Redwine.

"Coach (Tom) Osborne tells us not to talk, but if they try to intimidate you, I guess sometimes you can't help it. You can't do an excessive amount of talking, but you can tell a guy where to get off," Redwine said.

Redwine had 70 of his rushing yards in the second half and his confidence kept increasing each time he handled the ball. Andra Franklin's 34-yard run late in the

first half was particularly inspirational.

"I had all the confidence in the world after Andra broke that long one," he said.

Even when the Cornhuskers trailed 14-0, 12 minutes into the game, Redwine wasn't worried. His confidence didn't waiver. "All the time we were behind, we knew we could come back," he said. "Those are the national championship teams; they can keep their heads up even when they're playing a good team like Penn State and get behind."

REDWINE SURE INJURY NOT FROM ACCIDENTAL HIT

By Randy York

November 4, 1979—Football is a game requiring the acceptance of injuries, but the shot that put Nebraska's Jarvis Redwine on the sidelines Saturday may be a different story.

Redwine doesn't have all the evidence. But the Huskers' leading rusher who was destined to be on the cover of Sports Illustrated this week is fairly convinced his injury in the game against Missouri was intentional, not accidental.

Redwine suffered a bruise behind his right knee on the extra-point attempt following Nebraska's second touchdown, which gave the Huskers a 14-6 lead with 11:02 remaining in the second quarter.

"After we scored our first touchdown, I heard a couple Mis-

souri players say: 'Let's get him. Let's get him,'" Redwine said.

"I didn't pay much attention, though. Then they started saying the same thing after the second touchdown. I looked around and the next thing I knew, I was on the ground.

"I don't know if it was dirty or not," Redwine said. "All I know is what I heard, what I felt and what my teammates told me. It looked pretty intentional to them."

"I don't think they were going for a blocked kick," Nebraska Coach Tom Osborne said. "If they weren't and they were going for something else, that's not players. That's coaching."

Redwine, who entered the game as the nation's seventh-leading rusher with an average of 127

yards a game, came out of it with only 36 yards on nine carries.

His last attempt was a gain of 6 yards shortly before halftime.

Redwine, thus, may have suffered a Sports Illustrated jinx before a cover shot was even published.

He was scheduled to join other Heisman Trophy candidates from highly ranked teams on this week's cover.

The publicity, however, was the last thing on his mind in Faurot Field.

He was more interested in watching third-team I-back Craig Johnson, one of his favorites, fill in admirably in his absence.

While Redwine watched the last 30 minutes of the game, Johnson took over from I.M. Hipp to carry the load in the second half.

He finished with 98 yards on 17 carries, but was particularly effective on the Huskers' final scoring drive, capped by Dean Sukup's 19-yard field goal with 4:16 remaining.

CORGAN: JARVIS BECOMING 'PRETTY DARN GOOD BACK'

By Mike Babcock

October 28, 1979—You want impressive? Try this.

Jarvis Redwine moved into the 24th position on the all-time career rushing list at Nebraska Saturday afternoon. That's after seven games as a Cornhusker and only 117 carries.

Redwine is moving up on the leaders at the rate of 7.6 yards per run. Against Colorado, in Nebraska's 38-10 romp, he gained 206 yards, averaging 11.5 of them each time he took a handoff or a pitch-out.

Compare that to Southern California's Charles White, who needed 44 carries to gain 198 yards against California. Give the ball to Redwine that many times and he'd probably gain enough yardage to reach Ceresco.

"I've never seen anything like it," one press box observer remarked.

Such a "can you believe that?" attitude surfaced nearly every time Redwine touched the football Saturday.

The Big Eight's leading rusher handled the ball four times in the second half, breaking two runs for touchdowns—he had three for the afternoon—and gaining 73 net yards to push him over 200 in one game for the first time since his senior year at Inglewood (California) High School.

In a game against Serra High, "I think I gained 206 yards," Redwine said.

Actually, he topped 200 yards twice against Colorado. His change-of-direction, 13-yard touchdown run left him with 202.

Then he was stopped for a 4-yard loss by Steve Doolittle on his next carry before ripping through the Buffaloes for 8 yards on his final run of the game to set up Andra Franklin's 2-yard touchdown.

"He's getting to be a pretty darn good back," said NU backfield coach Mike Corgan, emphasizing "darn good."

The praise implicit in such a statement from Corgan is comparable to the gushy ramblings of a Hollywood press agent or the puffery spewed forth in the name of advertising.

Using Corgan's terminology, Billy Sims is a "darn good back." It translates into Heisman Trophy material.

Redwine's 206-yard effort was the best in the Big Eight this season, and it was the fifth best single-game rushing total in Nebraska history. Richard Berns had afternoons of 255 and 211 yards in his career. Isaiah Hipp has had one-game totals of 254 and 207.

Hipp holds the single-season rushing record at 1,353 yards (in 1977). With his 889 yards and four regular-season games and a possible bowl appearance remaining, Redwine is within reach of that.

His five straight 100-yard performances also ties a Hipp record set during the 1977 season.

In a jammed Nebraska dressing room after the game, NU Chancellor Dr. Roy Young stopped at locker No. 12 to shake Redwine's hand.

Most of the media questions dealt with his 13-yard touchdown run, the one on which he started right, reversed his field and pushed guard John Havekost into the final Buffalo defender before diving into a corner of the end zone.

"It's not in the playbook, but it's something you can feel when you're out on the field. I could see it out of the corner of my eye; their whole defense had over-pursued," Redwine said.

"It was a gamble, but when things are going good for the team, you can get away with stuff like that . . . and any time you score it's all right."

Corgan agreed with such an assessment, adding that he was pleased Redwine deviated from the preconceived plan only the one time in Saturday's game.

"Once in a while you can get away with it, but normally that's not real practical," said Corgan. "You can't tell anybody that's the thing to do. Jarvis just did it on sheer speed.

"He's getting a lot more confidence. He feels more like he's the boss now, and that's what he has to do," Corgan said.

Redwine's first touchdown came on a 23-yard-run, with Tim Smith making the final block on CU cornerback Mark Haynes near the goal line. His second covered 56 yards on the second play from scrimmage in the second half; it was his longest run of the season.

Redwine slowly worked through the myriad post-game interviews with which he was confronted and then prepared to play host to Kevin Nelson, brother of Stanford's Darrin Nelson and a prospective Husker recruit visiting Lincoln from Pius X High School in Los Angeles.

Want someone impressive for such an assignment? Try Jarvis. Like some fine red wines, he just gets better with age.

REDWINE HAPPY TO BECOME BIG RED BACK

By Steve Sipple

The phone call excited Gene Huey. He remembered watching Jarvis Redwine at Inglewood High School in Los Angeles. And now, Redwine was calling Huey to say he wanted to transfer from Oregon State to Nebraska.

"I knew the caliber of running back he had been in high school, and more importantly, I knew what kind of person Jarvis was," said Huey, a former Cornhusker assistant coach who is now an aide with the NFL's Indianapolis Colts. "I knew he would give more to the program than he would ever take from it."

Redwine, a 5-foot-11, 205-pounder, provided Nebraska with big-time production during his two seasons as a Cornhusker, 1979 and 1980, despite missing considerable time because of injuries.

A two-time All-Big Eight and consensus All-America selection, Redwine rushed 156 times for 1,119 yards and nine touchdowns as a senior despite playing in only nine games because of a rib injury.

As a junior, Redwine replaced injured I.M. Hipp in the Cornhuskers' fourth game and exploded for five straight 100-yard games, finishing the season with 1,100 yards on 165 carries despite knee and ankle injuries.

Redwine will be remembered as one of Nebraska's most exciting I-backs, what with his graceful style and breakaway speed. Yet one must wonder how much more he could have accomplished without the injuries.

"He wasn't a back who would overpower you," Huey said. "But once he got outside, forget about it, because nobody was going to catch him."

Huey was an assistant at New Mexico when he first made contact with Redwine, who rushed for 1,300 yards as a high school senior and attracted the attention of schools such as UCLA, Notre Dame and Arizona State.

Redwine was also drafted out of high school by the Oakland A's.

Huey failed to lure Redwine to New Mexico, losing out to Oregon State.

"I was looking to play a lot as a freshman," Redwine said.

Redwine saw action in seven varsity games in 1977, gaining 95 yards and scoring a touchdown against Tennessee in the seventh game. He quit the next day.

"I'd had enough," he said. "There was so much pressure on us to win, and it wasn't getting done. You couldn't confide in a coach. There was no togetherness. When I was at Oregon State, I figure I got junior college experience; that's all."

In November 1977, Redwine was watching the Nebraska-Oklahoma game with Oregon State teammates when the cameras zoomed in on Cornhusker Coach Tom Osborne. Huey, then in his first season as an NU assistant, was standing next to Osborne.

"Hey," Redwine said. "That's Coach Huey, the man who tried to recruit me to New Mexico."

Redwine didn't call Nebraska immediately. He worked a construction job that summer in Corvallis, Oregon. But he began to realize how much he missed the game. So he looked up Huey, who had no problem remembering Redwine.

"Jarvis was possibly the neatest, most interesting player I ever recruited," Huey said. "I remember his bedroom was decorated with *Sports Illustrated* covers. It was neat and orderly. It was interesting like a museum of sports memorabilia. And he was a great conversationalist—very mature in his thinking and his actions.

"I still remember him showing up in Lincoln (Nebraska) with

his wife. They had a U-Haul truck and a car in tow."

Redwine spent the 1978 season as a redshirt on the scout squad and earned a reputation as a hard-hitter. He burst into prominence in 1979 with five straight 100-yard games, including 206 in game seven, a 38-10 triumph against Colorado. At that point, he was seventh in the nation in rushing during a particularly strong season for college running backs. The big names included Charles White of Southern Cal (the eventual Heisman Trophy winner), George Rogers of South Carolina (the 1980 Heisman recipient) and Freeman McNeil of UCLA, to name a few.

The next week, however, Redwine's injury problems began. He suffered a knee bruise when Missouri nose guard Norman Goodman dove at his right leg while Redwine was blocking for an extra-point kick. Redwine maintained the hit was intentional. The Huskers' star I-back tried to come back too soon and suffered an ankle injury the following week. He played well below form the rest of the season.

Redwine began his senior season with a flourish, climaxed by a 189-yard effort on national television in Nebraska's 21-7 triumph against Penn State in the third game. He was the talk of the nation after slow starts by quarterbacks Mark Herrmann of Purdue and Art Schlichter of Ohio State, the early favorites for the Heisman Trophy.

Then came the fourth game against Florida State, in which Redwine was carried off the field late in the game with painfully cracked ribs. He had gained 145 yards on 25 carries.

In the blur of the moment, according to the *Chicago Tribune*, Redwine remembers hearing a Florida State defender boast, "I think I got him. I think it was my hit."

Redwine missed the next two weeks before returning for the Colorado game. He was forced to leave early when he suffered a thigh injury.

Next up was Missouri. Like the previous season, tempers flared after the game when Redwine complained of a cheap shot on a play in which he reinjured his ribs when he was tackled out-of-bounds on the final play of the first half. According to the *Lincoln Journal*, Osborne said Missouri's Kevin Potter "put his knee in Jarvis' chest and gave him a good shot. He had to take himself out."

Redwine, an introspective and thoughtful young man, began wondering if there was a way to control football violence and injuries without changing the game. The thought

Jarvis Redwine was a popular figure during the Big Eight Skywriters' visit to NU in 1980. (Journal Star Library).

Jarvis Redwine ran through the Iowa defense for 89 yards in NU's 24-21 win on September 22, 1979. (Journal Star Library).

of players intentionally trying to injure others made him ill.

"It just seems like the more publicity you get, the more it activates things, the more that everybody tries to be after you, to see if you can live up to that publicity," he told the *Chicago Tribune*. "What they try to do is bust you."

Redwine managed a total of 108 yards in the next two games before gaining 152 on 21 carries in the final game of the regular season, a 21-17 loss to Oklahoma in Lincoln. Midway through the first quarter against the Sooners, Redwine broke free and raced 89 yards for a touchdown.

When it became clear none of the Oklahoma defenders would catch him, he turned and pointed

at them, a seemingly harmless expression of exuberance. But it was a breach of decorum that earned him a week's worth of discipline in the form of grass drills.

Redwine was selected to play in both the Hula and Japan Bowl all-star games, yet he didn't start for his own team in the 1980 Sun Bowl against Mississippi State. Osborne said the demotion was the result of a subpar performance against Oklahoma, noting a half-dozen missed assignments. Many, however, believed his benching stemmed from the finger-pointing incident.

Whatever the case, Redwine came off the bench to rush for 42 yards on 13 carries in NU's 31-17 victory. The Huskers managed only

159 yards on the ground after leading the nation during the regular season with a 378.3-yard average.

Redwine—who now lives in Los Angeles and works for Northwest Airlines—said in a 1985 interview that the demotion affected his future as a pro player. The Minnesota Vikings selected him with the 24th pick of the second round, and he played three seasons, mostly as a kick returner.

"A lot of pro scouts were at that (Sun Bowl) game," Redwine told the *Lincoln Journal*. "They might have thought, 'He has an attitude problem.'"

He said he never could shed that reputation.

BOBBY REYNOLDS

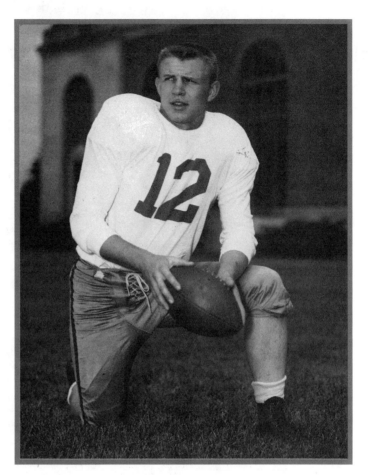

Nebraska's sophomore sensation, Bobby Reynolds, led the nation in rushing, touchdowns and scoring in 1950. The All-America halfback from Grand Island, Nebraska, rushed for 1,342 yards and scored 157 points in NU's nine games in 1950. Injuries hampered Reynolds his junior and senior seasons, but he still finished his career with 2,196 yards. (Journal Star Library).

BOBBY REYNOLDS/STATS

LETTERED:	1950-52
HEIGHT:	5-11
WEIGHT:	175
HOMETOWN:	GRAND ISLAND, NEBRASKA
HONORS:	1950 ALL-BIG SEVEN
	1950 ALL-AMERICAN
	NATIONAL FOOTBALL HALL OF FAME
	NEBRASKA FOOTBALL HALL OF FAME
PRO EXPERIENCE:	LINCOLN CHIEFS (BASEBALL)

REYNOLDS—GREATEST EVER AT NU?

October 23, 1950—On an unseasonably warm September 30 afternoon this fall, a 5-foot, 11-inch, 175-pound sophomore left halfback ripped into the left side of the Indiana line and with two tacklers hanging on to his body plunged into the end zone for his first collegiate touchdown.

Before the day was over, Bobby Reynolds, the most heralded high school football player to come out of Nebraska, had scored twice more—once on a 45-yard gallop—and kicked two extra points as the Cornhuskers tied the Hoosiers, 20-20.

On successive Saturdays, the Grand Island wonder boy accounted for a pair of touchdowns, including one for 67 yards, and extra points in Nebraska's 32-26 conquest of Minnesota, and tallied all the Huskers' points in their 28-19 loss to Colorado and 19-0 win over Penn State.

Nebraska politicians, who are making the pre-election circuit these days, have stuffed their speeches into their hip pocket and are talking about what every Nebraskan wants to hear—Bobby Reynolds and the Cornhusker resurgence.

It didn't take young (19-year-old) Reynolds long to squelch the skeptics who thought he was just a high school flash and couldn't stay with the "big boys".

A game-by-game breakdown of Reynolds' phenomenal running clearly shows why he leads the nation in net yards gained per game rushing.

Through four games, Reynolds has lugged the ball 78 times for 679 net yards and an average 8.7 yards per carry and 169.8 yards per game.

Which is nifty running in anyone's league.

Reynolds' 11 touchdowns and six placements for 72 points put him far ahead of other Big Seven Conference scorers. The Husker speedster has yet to master many of the fine points of running. He combines a keen sense of finding the-line-of-least-resistance and natural speed to shake off would-be tacklers.

His shotgun starts prompted one Nebraska linesman to remark:

"Reynolds is through the line and into the secondary before we can throw the initial block."

One Nebraska sportscaster dubbed Bob as "Mr. Hot Rod" because Reynolds' amazing get-away and sustained gait reminds one of a teenager's souped-up car.

Reynolds is not limited to ball carrying. He has completed one of three passes thrown, caught seven of quarterback Fran Nagle's tosses for 96 yards and two touchdowns, both against Colorado, and averaged 38.8 yards for 23 punts, none of which have been blocked.

For three years Bob quarterbacked the Grand Island High school football and basketball teams. He was also a hurdler on the track team. During his junior and senior years, the Islanders were mythical state football champions and won the basketball title in the state tournament.

Oddly enough, it wasn't the gridiron ivory hunters who camped on Reynolds' front lawn but major league baseball scouts. He played second base for the Grand Island American Legion team and hit over .300 as a shortstop in a Nebraska amateur league last summer.

Since his opening-game scoring spree, Reynolds has been the idol of the fans and the despair of visiting scouts who must report his cavorting to their superiors.

Grade school boys on the sandlots already are imitating the dashing sophomore while opposing coaches are devising new defensive tricks in an effort to slow him down.

Frank Patrick, Penn State's

chief undercover man, who has trailed the Cornhuskers like a gumshoe for three weeks, wasted no words when he summed up Reynolds to the Nittany Lions.

"This Reynolds isn't just another sophomore. He's got class, plenty of it. Sure, he's a runner, a good one, but he's also a good pass receiver and an exceptional punter."

Patrick, who played on those great Sutherland-coached Pittsburgh teams with Nebraska Coach Bill Glassford, likens Reynolds to Marshall Goldberg of Pitt fame—"Just like him," he says, "—only faster."

Sheldon Beise forewarned the Minnesota horde about Reynolds, but the Gopher giants could do little to hobble him.

Nebraskans, who have longed for an individual hero and a winning team for a decade, have taken to Reynolds and this year's team like a budget-conscious housewife to hamburger at 49 cents a pound.

Many Husker followers believe him to be the greatest Nebraska back of all time. Some of the old-timers want to see more.

Whatever the personal opinion, sophomore Bobby Reynolds has shown in four games that he is a real team player and places the reason for his meteoric debut on the "boys up front."

"Give the blockers the credit," he says.

NU's Bobby Reynolds earned All-America honors in football, but also played professional baseball with the Lincoln Chiefs. (Journal Star Library).

COLLIERS VISITS MR. REYNOLDS

By Norris Anderson

September 27, 1951—On the newsstands today is *Colliers* magazine with a 2,000-word feature, replete with pictures, on Nebraska's Bobby Reynolds.

Labeled "Nebraska's Mr. Touchdown," the article by Bill Fay is designed more for good reading than for factual content. It does make good reading.

Bobby said he didn't know where the author got some of the details.

Three excerpts, in particular, mystified the young All-American:

(1) The fact that he came to Nebraska unheralded in football, but as a basketball star.

"Gosh, basketball is not my best sport—I don't think."

(2) That he keeps a Ted Williams bat in his room and handles it as he studies.

"Why, the guys would laugh me out of the fraternity!"

(3) That he turned down a big-league bonus offer with the statement that his grandfather had already left him a lot of money.

"That was really news to me."

Otherwise, the article is well done. It goes a long way towards justifying Colliers' mistake of leaving Reynolds off even its All-Mid-west team picked early in the 1950 season. The same author made the omission.

Some excerpts from the article that should interest you: Averaging 2.4 touchdowns per game for the season, he rolled up 157 points (22 touchdowns and 25 conversions) for the highest total since Jim Leech compiled the all-time high of 210 points (26 touchdowns, 48 conversions and two field goals) for Virginia Military Institute in 1920.

Excluding Leech, only three other college players have ever accumulated more points in one season than Reynolds. Jim Thorpe counted 198 for Carlisle in 1912; Jerry DePrato racked 188 for Michigan State in 1915; and Bill Ingram tallied 162 for Navy in 1917.

Only four of his 22 touchdowns originated from inside the 10-yard line; the other 18 scoring dashes ranged from 11 to 80 yards (average: 28.5).

As an interviewee, Fay says Reynolds definitely does not belong to the shucks-I-was-just-lucky school of bashful athletic heroes. Bobby is articulate and factual; he discusses his touchdown runs objectively, and has no illusions about the difficulties of duplicating or sur-passing his 1950 scoring exploits.

"A touchdown," he remarked, "is a chain of circumstances involving 22 players. Very often, the fellow who carries the ball across the goal line is the least important link in the whole chain."

"Take our Oklahoma game last year," he went on. "Oklahoma was leading us 14-0 when we recovered a fumble. Up to that point, we weren't even in the ball game. So we got our first scoring chance on a break.

"In the huddle our quarterback, Fran Nagle, picked a play on which I was supposed to feint to the right, then cut back through center. But—and here's the important link in the touchdown chain—as we came out of the huddle, Fran noticed that Oklahoma's big eight-man line was bunched in close. So Fran yelled a warning signal—what we call an "automatic"—which completely changed my part in the play. Instead of cutting back through the middle, I went wide outside the right end— and got loose."

"In other words," Bobby concluded, "the difference between my running into a mass of Oklahoma tacklers at center and going for the touchdown around end was Nagle's alertness in detecting a defensive weakness and instantly redirecting our offense to exploit the weakness."

Reynolds recalls that six of his 22 touchdowns were scored on Nagle's "automatics"—plays that were redirected a split second before the center snapped the ball.

About his famous 100-yard run against Missouri: "That actually was a dumb play—I should have passed the ball, instead of fading back at the risk of being tackled for a big loss."

Bobby will continue having fun playing football. If it wasn't fun,

he wouldn't be playing, because he is that rarest of college athletic phenomena—an unsolicited, unproselytized (and virtually unstoppable) halfback.

Other facts by Mr. Fay:

That his, Bobby's father, Gil, was a third-string halfback on the 1923 Cornhusker team. That his mother, the former Blenda Olson, captained Nebraska's senior girls basketball team in 1925, the year she married Gil.

That three of the biggest buildings on the Nebraska campus were built by Charles Olson, his

grandfather. They are the Student Union, Library and Engineering Hall.

That Bobby was born in Omaha in 1930, right next door to Dave Noble, who still ranks as one of the most dangerous running backs in Nebraska history.

That he didn't walk until he was 13 months old, causing his parents to fear he might turn out to be awkward.

That his athletic career started at age 5, when he used to shag flies for his dad.

That his two-year scholastic average in the school of business administration is 79.

Bobby Reynolds was a lifetime Nebraska fan. The Reynolds family, including sons (from left) Rush, Tom and Rick, and wife Sarah, prepares to head to a Husker game. (Harald Dreimanis/Lincoln Journal Star).

MR. TOUCHDOWN'S ANNIVERSARY

By Dave Sittler

October 31, 1975—Seated somewhere in Saturday's sellout crowd of more than 68,000 fans at the Nebraska-Missouri game in Columbia will be a man celebrating a silver anniversary.

Instead of a wedding anniversary, it will be a football celebration.

Nebraska football fans may find it hard to believe, but it was 25 years ago this weekend that a Cornhusker halfback named Bobby Reynolds ran a touchdown against Missouri, making the player and the play legend in Nebraska football.

When football buffs recall past Cornhusker gridiron glories, the conversations usually start with Reynolds' run against the Tigers in Memorial Stadium a quarter-century ago.

"I didn't realize it had been that long ago," Reynolds said Thursday.

For those too young to recall the run, or not fortunate enough to have seen it on film or had it explained by a Big Red fan, read on.

The Cornhuskers had driven to Missouri's 33-yard line when they faced a fourth down-and-short yardage situation with only 6 minutes left in the game.

What happened next? This is the way Bob Broeg, covering the game for the *St. Louis Post-Dispatch*, described it to his readers:

"Reynolds, starting wide on a lateral, was trapped behind the line. When he saw he was about to be tackled, he swung back in the other direction. But again he was trapped, and again he reversed his field, dropping back to his own 40, nearly 30 yards behind the line of scrimmage.

"He hand-faked one guy, swivel-hipped another and set out for the goal line now 60 crow-flight yards away. He picked up three nice blocks, stepped away from another tackler and took advantage of two more blocks. It was an astounding run. The kid stands out like a neon light."

The zig-zag romp, sending the crowd into a frenzy, took so long that many stories have developed through the years.

According to *Omaha World-Herald* writer James Denney, one of his favorite stories concerned Nebraska tackle Charley Toogood.

Toogood, so the story goes, threw a block during the run and then remained lying on his Missouri opponent. The Tiger player said, "Let me up; the play's over."

"Not necessarily," replied Toogood. "He might come back this way again."

Reynolds went on to score 22 points that afternoon as the Cornhuskers outlasted the Tigers in a 40-34 battle. He finished the year with 22 touchdowns and an astounding 157 points scored while rushing for 1,342 yards. He also earned the nickname Mr. Touchdown.

Despite all those impressive figures, when fans talk about Bobby Reynolds, they still speak of his run against Missouri.

"Sure, it still goes through my mind when Nebraska plays Missouri," Reynolds said. "And a lot of people still bring it up."

Reynolds described the run as "one of those freakish plays that just happened to work."

Nebraska, which finished 6-2-1 that season under Bill Glassford, were led by—in addition to Reynolds and Toogood—such players as Don Strasheim, Art Bauer, Dick Regier, Nick Adduci, Bob Mullen and Fran Nagle. And another player named Don Bloom.

Bloom made a run later that season against Kansas State, a run that Reynolds considers better than his own jaunt against Missouri.

"It was a kickoff," Reynolds recalled of the 88-yard run. "He (Bloom) cut from one side of the field to the other. It was a better run."

Maybe it was a better run in your eyes, Mr. Touchdown, but thousands of fans might beg to differ.

Happy 25th anniversary.

REYNOLDS REMEMBERED FOR 'THE RUN'

By Jeff Korbelik

Bobby Reynolds' light never shone more brightly than it did on November 4, 1950.

The teenager from Grand Island ran for 175 yards on 25 carries and scored 22 points on three touchdowns and four extra points in Nebraska's 40-34 homecoming victory over the Missouri Tigers.

But it was Reynolds' fourth-quarter run for one of those touchdowns that captured a nation's imagination and spawned a football hero.

Bobby Reynolds became "Mr. Touchdown."

Leading 33-27 with seven minutes remaining, Nebraska faced fourth-and-1 at the Missouri 33, so, of course, the Cornhuskers went to their bread and butter, their 19-year-old sophomore halfback.

In the eyes of *St. Louis Dispatch* reporter Bob Broeg, the play was far from ordinary.

"Reynolds, starting wide on a lateral, was trapped behind the line," Broeg wrote. "When he saw he was about to be tackled, he swung back in the other direction. But again he was trapped, and again he reversed his field, dropping back to his own 40, nearly 30 yards behind the line of scrimmage."

"He hand-faked one guy, swivel-hipped another and set out for the goal line now 60 crow-flight yards away. He picked up three nice blocks, stepped away from another tackler and took advantage of two more blocks.

"It was an outstanding run. The kid stands out like a neon light."

Asked if he remembered any one play that made Reynolds stand out, former Nebraska quarterback Fran Nagle quickly recounted the run against Missouri.

"The whole thing took about five minutes," Nagle recalled. "That was one for the books. There was never anything like it again. It was 30 yards to the end zone, but Bobby made it a 150-yard run."

Nebraska senior linebacker and co-captain Robert "Moon" Mullen said the run seemed like "300 yards." He had a great view of it from the NU sideline.

"He ran all over the place, but he always knew where he was at on the field," Mullen said. "He would just stop and go. He had a sixth sense."

Great running backs have come and gone from the Nebraska program since. But only 1983 Heisman Trophy winner Mike Rozier may have had a more magical season than Reynolds did in 1950.

Maybe.

"Bobby was part of the new era, in my opinion," Carl Brasee, Reynolds' Nebraska teammate, said. "He was the leader in that era of the new era for Nebraska. Bringing it off its knees. He did it as a sophomore and did it basically in one year."

Had injuries not plagued Reynolds' junior and senior seasons, Nebraska fans often wonder what could have happened? How good could he have been?

Yet, that one season made Reynolds more mystical and all that more legendary.

"Why do we have heroes?" asked Brasee, an NU linebacker and three-year letterman. "You have them because you have personalities and circumstances that develop. The public needed something to grab a hold of."

In post-World War II Nebraska, the masses clung to Reynolds, a 5-foot-11, 175-pound, baby-faced football player.

"He was just a kid that everybody liked," Nagle said. "He really, truly, was an All-America-type of kid. He was always easy to talk to and very modest. He just enjoyed life."

To understand Reynolds' impact, you need only turn to the record book.

In 1950, he scored a then-NCAA record 157 points (22 TDs, 25 PATs) in leading the Bill Glassford-coached Huskers to a 6-2-1 record—the team's first winning season since 1940. His duties weren't limited to the backfield. He also punted and played defense.

Heading into the 1998 college football season, Reynolds' single-season scoring total ranked him fifth all-time among Division I-A players. Rozier was second with 174 points on 29 touchdowns.

During the magical 1950 season, Reynolds scored at least one touchdown in every game, and in three of the Huskers' nine games, he accounted for all his team's points. He finished averaging 17.4 points a game—a record that stood for 38 years until Oklahoma State's Barry Sanders eclipsed it. Sanders, the 1988 Heisman Trophy winner, averaged 21.3 points per game and scored a record 234 points.

Comparisons to Rozier and Sanders stop at statistics. Reynolds never ran over would-be tacklers like Rozier did, and didn't have the blazing, break-away speed of Sanders. He possessed something different.

"He was not a fast runner, but an elusive runner," Mullen said. "Bobby had that sense of knowing where he was on the field at all times. He set up his blockers and he used those blocks."

He had some great names in front of him. The line included Big Seven all-conference picks Charley Toogood at tackle and Don Strasheim at guard. The other linemen were Walt Spellman, Arthur Bauer, Verl Scott and Joe McGill.

"Bob had several things that, you know, made him what he was," said Brasee, who co-captained NU's 1952 team with Reynolds. "He had a tremendous sense of balance and timing. The closest that I've seen anybody here with that balance was Johnny Rodgers (Nebraska's 1972 Heisman Trophy winner) when he used to do those runs leaning over sideways. That was one of the things Bob had. He had a tremendous sense of the game."

Reynolds wound up at Nebraska after a stellar prep career at Grand Island High School. He led the Islanders to undefeated state football championship seasons in 1947 and 1948. He also played on two state championship basketball teams that combined for a 44-1 record and was a standout in baseball and track.

Mullen knew Reynolds was something special before the youngster stepped on the NU campus. He watched Reynolds lead Grand Island to a 25-14 football victory over rival Lincoln High in 1947. The game drew so much interest that it was moved to the Huskers' Memorial Stadium. More than 20,000 fans attended.

So Mullen wasn't surprised when the sensational sophomore nearly led the Huskers to an upset of Bud Wilkinson's unbeaten Oklahoma Sooners in '50. Reynolds scored three touchdowns in the first half to put the Huskers ahead, but the Sooners' depth eventually overwhelmed Nebraska and OU went on to post a 49-35 victory en route to a national championship.

The Huskers, however, had made a statement. The year before,

Oklahoma had whipped Nebraska 48-0 in Lincoln's Memorial Stadium.

"He was as loose as a goose," Mullen said of Reynolds. "I don't think anybody ever had a great shot at him. They never got him flat-footed. I don't think anybody could really nail him to the floor."

Injuries got to him instead. Reynolds was never able to duplicate his spectacular 1950 season. He suffered a shoulder separation in 1951 during preseason drills. When he did come back, an eye injury sidelined him even longer. He scored only two touchdowns as the Huskers ended up 2-8. The next year, he separated the other shoulder. He played in only four games and scored four touchdowns and kicked 13 extra points for a 5-4-1 Husker team.

A broken leg during the 1953 baseball season ended Reynolds' dream of playing either football or baseball professionally. Ironically, he broke it while trying to score, sliding into home. He tried semi-professional baseball, but he never could regain his athletic prowess. The injury even left him with a slight limp.

With his playing days over, Reynolds turned to the private sector, becoming a successful insurance executive in his hometown. He died of a heart attack in 1985 at the age of 54.

The state mourned his passing.

"If I was reincarnated and could come back, I would want to be someone like Bobby Reynolds," Nagle said.

And why not? After all, Reynolds was an All-America boy. He was "Mr. Touchdown."

MIKE ROZIER

Mike Rozier is Nebraska's only Heisman Trophy-winning running back. (Journal Star Library).

MIKE ROZIER/STATS

LETTERED:	1981-83
HEIGHT:	5-11
WEIGHT:	210
HOMETOWN:	CAMDEN, NEW JERSEY
HONORS:	1983 HEISMAN TROPHY
	1982 ALL-AMERICAN
	1983 ALL-AMERICAN
	BIG EIGHT CONFERENCE
	CAREER RUSHING LEADER
	1982 ALL-BIG EIGHT
	1983 ALL-BIG EIGHT
	NEBRASKA FOOTBALL HALL OF FAME
PRO EXPERIENCE:	PITTSBURGH MAULERS (USFL) 1984
	JACKSONVILLE BULLS (USFL) 1985
	HOUSTON OILERS 1985-90
	ATLANTA FALCONS 1990-91

ROZIER MAKES NOT QUITE SO GRAND ENTRANCE

By Chuck Sinclair

August 12, 1981—How do you suppose Mike Rozier, the most celebrated of Nebraska's 1981 football recruits, made his grand entrance into Lincoln for the start of fall workouts?

Rozier, a 5-11, 210-pound sophomore running back out of Camden, New Jersey, via Coffeyville Junior College in Kansas, and recently tabbed by *Playboy* magazine as one of the top newcomers in the nation, didn't fly in Monday in a private Lear Jet.

He didn't fly commercially, either . . . or drive up in a shiny new sports car.

Rozier slapped his money on the counter a couple of days ago and began a 34-hour Greyhound bus trip from Camden that pulled into Lincoln at 2 a.m. Monday to join his brother Guy as one of 110 new faces for Nebraska football fans to familiarize themselves with.

While freshman Guy will join 108 other freshmen for their first organized practices Wednesday, Mike Rozier will continue to work out with the varsity in informal evening get-togethers at Memorial Stadium in preparation for Picture

Day Sunday prior to Monday's opening day of practice.

Had it not been for the elder Rozier catching a cold a week ago, he would have caught a plane to Lincoln with his brother instead of catching a late-arriving bus.

"With that controllers' strike, my mom didn't want me to catch a plane back east," Rozier said, "and I wasn't crazy about it either. I didn't want to risk a crash."

Thirty-four hours later, his thoughts had shifted from getting to Lincoln to trying to live up to his expectations.

"In a way there's been a little pressure put on me," Rozier said. "But I like to play ball. I think I can cope with it. I don't have any confidence problems."

"Back home there are a lot of people looking forward to seeing me play on national television," Rozier added. "I want to prove to them that I can play anywhere. I want to do a good job for myself, and for my family and friends."

Rozier did plenty of proving last year as a freshman at Coffeyville Community College.

The speedster with a :04.45 40-yard dash and a bench press of

340 pounds to his credit rushed for more than 1,100 yards last year despite missing two games with a shoulder injury.

That was out of the wishbone formation. Rozier's coach at Coffeyville, Dick Foster, said he could have gained 2,500 yards out of an I-formation like Nebraska uses.

All the previous publicity, and the additional preseason status accorded him by *Playboy*, isn't causing Rozier to complain, but he's not exactly basking in the limelight.

"It's kind of nice, but I think I would have rather come in on my own without so much publicity," he said. "Then if things went well, it would have been a surprise, not something everyone expected."

Still, Rozier is grateful for the year of adjustment at Coffeyville, where he raised his grade average in order to accept a scholarship at Nebraska that was offered him out of high school.

"I appreciate going to the junior college instead of a university right away," Rozier said. "I learned a lot about college, and more about football. And I know I played more than I could have here as a freshman. I'm just happy to be here now.

"Nebraska is a great football school," Rozier said. "I was told the atmosphere is a lot like professional ball. That's what I was looking for. I didn't want to stay back east. I was used to the city life. I just wanted to go somewhere away from home and play ball."

After arriving in Lincoln, Rozier took up residence with an old friend, sophomore wingback Irving Fryar.

"Irving and I used to play against each other in high school," Rozier said. "He was a defensive back then. Did he hit me? He couldn't catch me. We're real close," he added. "My mom grew up with his parents. We're tight besides on the football field."

There's no question Rozier is looking forward to his future in Lincoln . . . and proving the new man wearing jersey No. 30 can play.

Mike Rozier knew the importance of his offensive line: "I don't care how great a back you are, you have to have those guys doing the job up front." (Journal Star Library).

Mike Rozier finished his three-year career as NU's career leading rusher. His 4,780 yards and 49 touchdowns are easily NU's best. (Journal Star Library).

HE'S ONLY A NUMBER?

By Mike Babcock

April 18, 1982—The way Mike Rozier describes it, he's a little bit like the people in those American Express card television commercials, the ones with the celebrities whose names are more familiar than their faces. When Rozier and Nebraska football teammate Roger Craig "walk into a store, everybody knows Roger, but he has to introduce me," said Rozier.

"Everybody always says, 'So you're that Rozier kid.'

"They know my (jersey) number is 30, and they know my name. But they don't know what I look like," Rozier said.

Because of that, Rozier still considers himself something of an unknown, although he could hardly be termed "low-profile" in this, his first year at Nebraska.

Rozier rushed for 943 yards and scored six touchdowns last fall. He earned first-team all-conference recognition from both AP and UPI and was named the Associated Press "Offensive Newcomer of the Year" in the Big Eight.

Even so, "I haven't established myself yet," he said. "People don't know who I am: they really don't."

Rozier wasn't complaining; he was just stating what he considers to be a fact. "People know Roger (Craig) because he's been around here for three years," Rozier said.

"They don't know me."

The sophomore from Camden, N.J. is still going through his first spring of practice, after transferring from Coffeyville, Kansas, Junior College. He has yet to feel the pressure of public recognition which goes with being a first-team Nebraska I-back. That's fine, he says.

"I'm not that high on 'pub,' anyway."

Rozier was an immediate success as a football player in a career that began at age 8. He was a running back in a league that required players to weigh at least 80 pounds.

"I was really big even then, big-boned and heavy," he said.

"I've always been bigger than everybody else. I was always one of the biggest guys in school. I was kind of the bully, you might say, and everybody was scared of me," said Rozier.

He's always had the strength to run over tacklers and the speed and quickness to run around them. He's much more compact than Craig, his I-back counterpart. Rozier is at least three inches shorter but only about 10 pounds lighter.

Sharing I-back duties is no problem.

At least, "I don't mind it," Rozier said. "Roger and I are pretty close friends. If he wasn't really a top running back, I might be upset (about alternating). I wouldn't show it, of course, but it might bother me.

"But Roger does the job, so what more can you ask?"

Rozier, in fact, casts an early, though unofficial, vote for Craig as next fall's Heisman Trophy award winner. "He's worked hard through high school and here, and it's Roger's last season; I'd like to see him get it," said Rozier.

Rozier is bound to draw Heisman attention, too.

It's nice "people would think that way," he said. "But you've got to have a lot of publicity, and if the right people don't see you play, even that doesn't matter."

For now the only endorsements for which Rozier is looking must come from the NU coaching staff and his Cornhusker teammates. He can remain anonymous in public places, but he doesn't want to be ignored by those who count.

Rozier figured his football playing days would end when he finished high school. "I never thought I'd be in this situation," he said. "Everybody else did, but I thought it would all be over by now."

In the context of an American Express card commercial, he might not be recognized without one now, but before long, he'll be able to leave home without it.

Mike Rozier had one of the best rushing seasons in history in 1983—running for 2,148 yards with an astonishing 7.81 yards-per-carry average. (Journal Star Library).

ROZIER RUNS LONGEST (2) YARD(S)

By Mike Babcock

September 25, 1983—He went this . . . oops, that way.

Scott Raridon, Nebraska's offensive right tackle, pulled and ran to his left, presumably to lead I-back Mike Rozier on a "49-pitch" play.

The Cornhuskers snapped the ball just 2 yards from the UCLA goal line.

After moving a few steps to his left, however, Raridon caught a glimpse of Rozier looping back to the right.

"He (Rozier) should've kept coming my way; I had the end sealed off," wingback Irving Fryar said. "But he turned around and went the other way."

Fryar had lined up wide to the left.

"I went left and cut down both the tackle and the linebacker," said fullback Mark Schellen, who was hard-pressed to explain Rozier's sudden and dramatic change of direction. "There must have been someone (a defender) left."

Rozier didn't see an opening.

"They told me the hole was there, but I didn't see it and I was the one running with the ball," he said.

"That was the longest 2-yard run I've ever seen," said the 280-pound Raridon. "I came off the field, and Coach (Clete) Fischer told me I looked tired. I said I was; I'd just run 60 yards."

Rozier could rest. Raridon couldn't; he had to snap for the extra-point kick.

After a fumbling start, Nebraska's top-ranked football team showed its offensive punch again Saturday afternoon in a 42-10 victory over UCLA.

The Cornhuskers broke long runs and completed long passes, but no play was longer than Rozier's 2-yard touchdown run with 8:16 remaining in the third quarter.

When he finally stepped into the west corner of the south end zone, Rozier had covered approximately 75 to 80 yards and "proved why he should win the Heisman (Trophy)," Schellen said.

"That's the kind of athlete he is."

The play unfolded like this:

Quarterback Turner Gill pitched the ball to Rozier. NU left guard Harry Grimminger blocked UCLA cornerback Ron Pitts at about the 6-yard line.

Rozier, however, appeared to be contained near the east sideline and began running back to his right, eluding Bruin free safety Don Rogers and giving ground as he went, back to the 18.

UCLA tackle Frank Batchkoff had Rozier in his grasp at the 18 but couldn't hold on, and Rogers missed another opportunity to tackle Rozier, who was now angling toward the end zone.

Gill avoided clipping Rogers and blocked inside linebacker Gene Mewborn out of the play.

Raridon shoved outside linebacker Doug West to the ground.

The Bruins' Neal Dellocono, another outside linebacker, had the final shot at tackling Rozier, but by the time Dellocono dived over another Grimminger block, Rozier was in the end zone for his second touchdown of the game.

Rozier ascribed no special significance to the run, which led to a 21-10 NU advantage and brought back memories of Bobby Reynolds' historic run against Missouri in 1950 and a Jarvis Redwine touchdown against Colorado in 1979. "Everybody blocked real well and I scored," Rozier said.

"That wasn't so bad. The

hard ones (yards) are those up the middle."

Rozier's run had little impact on his afternoon's 159-yard rushing total, but it was dramatic enough that CBS television broke into its coverage of the Iowa-Ohio State game to show a video replay.

On such things are Heisman Trophy winners decided, a fact which pleased NU offensive backs coach Frank Solich.

"The coaches upstairs (in the press box) said Mike might have had a little crease. We'll have to look at the films for that," said Solich.

However, crease or no crease, he scored, and that's the bottom line. Solich wasn't complaining and neither was Fryar. "He's 'Michael Heisman,'" Fryar said. "He can do anything he wants."

Most foes had a very tough time bringing down Mike Rozier, who Coach Tom Osborne said was a complete player. "He runs inside with strength, power and balance." (Journal Star Library).

ROZIER MAKING STRIDES

By Randy York

October 30, 1983—Someone has said the only thing standing between Mike Rozier and the Heisman Trophy is the trainer.

After Nebraska's 51-25 victory over Kansas State Saturday, that may not even be true.

Rozier took two more small steps past two more great Big Eight running backs.

And his first 200-yard rushing performance of the season may just be the giant leap he needed to make reservations for the Heisman Trophy banquet in New York on December 8.

"He's the best back I've ever seen. He's better than anybody in the nation," K-State free safety David Ast said after watching Rozier rush for 227 yards and three touchdowns on 23 carries against the Wildcats.

"I can't find nobody, really, to compare him with," KSU defensive end L.E. Madison said of Rozier. "The only backs I know like him are in the pros."

K-State Coach Jim Dickey, who has seen Rozier rush for 584 yards and six touchdowns in three years against his Wildcats, has compared the nation's leading Heisman Trophy candidate with John Riggins and Billy Sims in the past.

Saturday, Dickey saw nothing to change his mind.

"He'd liked to have killed two or three of our defensive backs. He's a great runner," Dickey said.

Rozier, who has averaged more than 11 yards per carry in 53 career carries against the Wildcats, scored all three of his touchdowns in a 127-yard first half.

Even though an unexpectedly dramatic second half helped him add another 100 yards to his total, Rozier wasn't all that excited about his rare route-going performance.

"I'm ready to go the distance any time I have to," he said. "But it was cold, boring and rainy. What can I say? I wanted to come in, get it over with and go home."

Rozier returned to Lincoln Saturday night with 4,076 career rushing yards. In becoming the 16th player in NCAA history to reach that 4,000-yard milestone, he passed two ex-Oklahoma greats on the all-time Big Eight rushing chart.

Joe Washington (3,995) and Steve Owens (3,867) had owned the Nos. 2 and 3 spots on that chart before Rozier posted the fourth 200-yard or better game of his career.

Now, Rozier must average 169 yards in his final three regular-season games against Iowa State, Kansas and Oklahoma to overtake Oklahoma State's Terry Miller, the all-time Big Eight rushing leader with 4,582 yards.

Rozier confided Saturday that he's aware of the record because "somebody pulled out a newspaper clipping at a store and showed it to me. I know about it, but all I can do is go out and keep punching as hard as I can."

Saturday, that was his only goal, especially after fielding the opening kickoff, running out of the end zone, then going back in and downing the ball for an unintentional, and embarrassing, safety.

"I changed my mind," Rozier said. "I wasn't sure about the rule. But I got it straight now. I was upset with myself. That was stupid."

Frank Solich, NU's offensive backfield coach, said "there's no reason for that kid to feel stupid.

"He's been a little banged up and we took him off the kickoff return team. He wanted back on it and wanted to do a good job. He wanted to come out and heard a teammate tell him to stay in, so he put a knee down."

That minor bit of confusion was about the only thing that went wrong for Rozier Saturday.

REYNOLDS: ROZIER AS GOOD, IF NOT BETTER, THAN WALKER

By Randy York

November 7, 1982—Superlatives aren't Bobby Reynolds' style, but the former Nebraska All-American couldn't avoid them Saturday after watching Mike Rozier break his 32-year-old single-season rushing record.

"He's as good as anybody they're touting for Heisman. He runs like Herschel Walker, if not better," Reynolds said of Rozier, who rushed for 251 yards to break Reynolds' record by 37 yards.

The timing could not have been better. Rozier's record came in Nebraska's ninth game, the same number of games Reynolds used to set his record in 1950.

"I've been sitting in the stands, cheering all these years for somebody to break it," Reynolds said. "Thirty-two years is a long time. It's amazing somebody didn't break it before."

Rozier, admitting he thought I.M. Hipp or Jarvis Redwine "probably held the record" until *The Sunday Journal and Star* informed him otherwise earlier in the week, said there won't be another 32-year lapse between records.

"There's always someone better than you," Rozier said. "My

record won't last as long as his record lasted, believe me. There are just too many good running backs around now."

Barring injury, Rozier is likely to set an unbelievable standard for future record-chasers. If he just maintains his 153-yard average for his final three regular-season games against Iowa State, Oklahoma and Hawaii, he will finish the season with 1,838 yards rushing.

That would be the sixth-best single-season effort in NCAA history—behind Southern Cal's Marcus Allen (2,342 in 1981), Pitt's Tony Dorsett (1,948 in '76), Georgia's Walker (1,891 in '81), Cornell's Ed Marinaro (1,881 in '71) and Southern Cal's Ricky Bell (1,875 in '75).

According to Bill Hancock, Big Eight Service Bureau Director who watched Saturday's game from the press box, Rozier will not be penalized in NCAA statistics for playing in the extra game at Hawaii.

If he duplicates his average and continues his assault, Rozier will slip past the single-season bests of such legendary runners as USC's Charles White, South Carolina's George Rogers, Oklahoma's Billy Sims, Texas' Earl

Campbell and USC's O.J. Simpson.

Nebraska fullback Mark Moravec is one who would like to see Rozier generate more national attention. "He reminds me so much of Tony Dorsett," Moravec said Saturday.

"Like Dorsett, he has such great balance and football sense. He knows when to take off, when to cut and when to really level somebody. He might even have more power than Dorsett. I've seen a lot of big guys get ready to tackle him and he just turns right into 'em. He gives them a licking before they can give it to him."

Rozier appreciates all the endorsements, but it's really not his style. He often wears a T-shirt that says: "I'm a good running back, not a great running back."

"I bought it in New Jersey," Rozier explained Saturday as he signed several dollar bills thrown in his face by young autograph-seekers.

"God gave me a gift. I'm just trying to use it to the best of my ability," he said.

While admitting Saturday's record has increased the attention on him, it hasn't changed him.

"I didn't come into this game

thinking about any records," he said. "This wasn't Mike Rozier against Ernest Anderson. The media built that up. I knew the real match up was Nebraska against Oklahoma State.

"The record's nice, but I've been breaking records since I started playing football. The only thing that really matters is that our team came out on top and we're one game closer to getting back to the Orange Bowl."

Rozier, wearing a New York Yankee cap while being interviewed by reporters, said "coming from New Jersey, I'm conscious and proud of the fact that I represent Eastern football talent.

"But more than that, I represent Nebraska," he said. "I'm proud that Nebraska people have faith in me and want me to break records and all. This is my team."

ROZIER 'THROWS IN' TOWEL; THRILLS CARTER LAKE BOY

October 3, 1983 (AP)—Remember the television commercial where Pittsburgh Steeler lineman "Mean" Joe Greene tossed his jersey to a kid who handed him a cola?

A real-life replay took place in Lincoln on Saturday after the University of Nebraska football team, ranked No. 1 in the nation, defeated Syracuse 63-7.

The principals were Cornhusker running back Mike Rozier and 7-year-old Paul Bradbury, of Carter Lake, a second-grade student at nearby Bellevue, Nebraska, Christian Academy, who had just attended his first Nebraska game.

The Huskers were heading toward the locker room after the game, and Bradbury stopped Rozier— something the Orangemen hadn't been able to do on the field.

"I looked up to him—he was real hot and sweaty—and I asked for an autograph," Paul said. "He said, 'Sure,' and dropped his towel" to sign the autograph.

"I picked up his towel to hand it to him, but Mike smiled down at me and said, 'You can have it.'

"It was the biggest surprise of my life," Paul said.

Paul's father, Rick Bradbury, said Paul was totally taken by the towel.

"It's just a plain old white towel, but Paul thinks he's got the Heisman Trophy," Bradbury said. "The towel was sopping wet, but Paul wouldn't put it down. In fact, he fell asleep with it around his neck on the ride home."

"I asked him if he'd give it up for $5, and he said 'No way.'"

Would he give it up for $100. No.

"How about a million dollars, Paul?"

"No."

"He's telling everybody about Mike's gift," Bradbury said of his son. "I'd say what Mike did is going to be on Paul's mind for quite a while."

MATURING ROZIER SEES NEBRASKA IN NEW LIGHT

By Randy York

October 11, 1983—Mike Rozier plopped down in an empty stadium Monday. He was wearing sweat clothes, eating sunflower seeds and in the mood to be a little bit philosophical.

Admittedly burned out on talking football, Rozier wanted to talk about other things.

The thing that seemed to be at the top of his list was a certain gratefulness for Nebraska and what it has done for him rather than the other way around.

"I owe Nebraska more than they owe me," he said. "I've grown up here. I've matured."

Rozier, Nebraska's All-America running back and the nation's leading Heisman Trophy candidate, said it's easy to measure his maturity.

"When I first got here, I had to call home Friday nights before every game, whether it was home or away," Rozier said.

"Last year, I was better. But I was still homesick all the time," Rozier said. "If we played a road game, I'd make sure I called home before we went back to Lincoln."

This year, Rozier still calls Camden, N.J. after every game. But he waits until he gets to Lincoln to do it.

The gradually changing procedure may not seem like much to most people. But it shows Rozier how much he's changed since his celebrated arrival from Coffeyville Junior College in Kansas.

"I look at Lincoln a lot different now," he said. "I don't look at it as country and a bunch of corn anymore. I can see why people like to live here."

If Rozier is handling the Heisman Trophy hype, he said Nebraska has helped him do it.

"I've met a lot of people here and they've given me their own little comments on life," he said. "They've helped me learn there's no easy road. Football is as up and down as life and if you don't look at it that way, you're not going to learn anything."

Rozier has learned to appreciate things he never thought he would.

"Like that fight song," Rozier said, humming the monotonous rhythm of "There Is No Place Like Nebraska."

When he was a sophomore, "I didn't like that song at all," he said. "Last year, I still didn't like it,

but I didn't mind it. This year, it sounds different to me. I wouldn't go home and put it on my stereo. But I kind of like it now. I finally understand why it riles up the fans."

The maturity of Mike Rozier has been a fascinating case study for Frank Solich, the Nebraska assistant who recruited him and now coaches him.

"People don't realize how strong Mike's family ties are in Camden," Solich said. "It was not natural for him to take to Lincoln."

Solich knows NU fans appreciate Rozier's style off the field as much as they appreciate his style on it.

"When you take into consideration all the publicity he's gotten, he's fairly remarkable," Solich said. "He's not out just to meet his personal goals. He's still very team-oriented. He rises to the occasion whenever the team needs him most."

Never was that more evident than last year's Missouri game, when Rozier came off the bench from a painful hip-pointer and rushed for 139 yards on 17 carries in a 23-19 win.

"Those 139 yards were like 339 yards," Oklahoma State Coach

Mike Rozier flew over and through opposing defenses. (Journal Star Library).

Jimmy Johnson said of Rozier's performance in the Missouri game. "They meant more because his team had to have 'em when he was hurt."

Rozier remembers the situation. "Anybody who's had a hip-pointer knows what kind of pain you go through," he said. "But we'd already lost one game to Penn State and I didn't want to lose another one to Missouri.

"Coach Osborne always says one back can motivate the whole offensive line," Rozier said. "That's all I wanted to do—motivate the rest of the team. That's why I wanted to play so bad. I wanted to win."

To Rozier, winning is all that matters.

"When time ticked down in the Oklahoma State game, I was just as happy as ever," he said. "A four-point win means just as much as a blowout. It wouldn't have mattered to me if we'd won by one point." NU won 14-10.

Rozier's 146 rushing yards were about twice as much as he thought he'd generated. "I thought I had about 76," he said. "I didn't have any long runs. I guess I had to earn my yards in that game."

He expects Missouri to be no different.

"Oklahoma is THE game around here. But Missouri's right behind Oklahoma," Rozier said. "It's important, but we can't make it more important than any other game."

That approach has shaped Rozier's competitive edge. It has reinforced something he has always known—that football is a team game, not an individual spectacle.

"The biggest reason I came here was the tradition of Nebraska's offensive line," he said. "I don't care how great a back you are, you have to have those guys doing the job up front."

This year, when Nebraska seeks to recruit another great running back, Mike Rozier said he will be more than willing to help.

"Wherever the guy's from, I'll tell him straight out that this is a great program and a great place to live," Rozier said. "Two years ago, I couldn't have said that because I didn't know any better."

ROZIER'S RECORD PERFORMANCES DEFY FOOTBALL AXIOM

By James M. Vanvalkenberg
NCAA Director of Statistics

December 11, 1983—It has been an axiom in football statistics that big-yardage season records and per-play season records cannot be accomplished by the same player. In other words, the more times you carry, the harder it becomes to maintain a record average.

Mike Rozier defied that axiom this season with 2,148 yards rushing—second-highest in history—and a record 7.81 yards per rush. The Heisman Trophy winner from Nebraska had truly one of the most remarkable seasons ever in college football.

Consider this: The college game's only previous 2,000-yard rusher, Marcus Allen of Southern California (2,342 in 1981—his Heisman season), averaged 5.81 yards per carry—exactly two yards less than Rozier. The only other runner close to 2,000 yards was

Pittsburgh's Tony Dorsett (1,948 in 11 games—one game less than Rozier in 1976, Dorsett's Heisman season), and Dorsett averaged 5.76.

And the previous record holder in yards per rush at 7.63—Billy Sims of Oklahoma (in 1978—his Heisman season)—gained 1,762 yards or 386 less than Rozier.

If that is not enough, remember that Rozier scored 29 touchdowns and 174 points, both figures equaling the all-time Division I-A records set by Penn State's Lydell Mitchell in 1971. Rozier, the fast and tough 212-pounder from Camden, N.J., ended the season with 480 rushing yards and 54 points more than any other I-A player. But there was plenty of talent on hand—23 rushers gained at least 1,000 yards vs. 18 a year ago.

Rozier's teammate, Irving Fryar, averaged 15.3 yards per play

in all-purpose running, highest by far among those with at least 100 yards rushing. He averaged a remarkable 13.8 yards per rush in gaining 318 yards, and 19.5 per reception, and scored 10 touchdowns on just 83 plays for the season.

On the career chart, Rozier's 4,780 yards ranks sixth. But among three-year players (he played a year in junior college at Coffeyville, Kansas), he is second only to Herschel Walker's 5,259 at Georgia (1980-82).

And Rozier's 7.16 yards per rush broke the career record of 7.09 by Sims.

In career scoring, Rozier's 318 points are tied for sixth; but among three-year players, he is second to Oklahoma's Steve Owens (1967-69), with 336.

VP BUSH PRESENT AS NU'S ROZIER RECEIVES HEISMAN

By Virgil Parker

December 9, 1983—At ceremonies highlighted by the appearance of Vice President George Bush, Nebraska's Mike Rozier officially received his Heisman Trophy Thursday night.

The black tie banquet drew a crowd of 1,700 in the Grand Ballroom of the New York Hilton Hotel.

The audience responded with a standing ovation for Rozier when, immediately following the presentation of the trophy, he turned college football's most coveted award over to his mother, Beatrice Rozier.

"I always said I'd give this to my mom if I won it," Rozier said. "On behalf of the Downtown Athletic Club (sponsors of the Heisman since its inception in 1935) and me, Mom, this trophy is for you."

Mike had his brother Guy, also a member of the Nebraska football team, come to the podium to take the trophy to his mother. Then he admonished her, "Don't drop it, Mom, it was hard to get."

"He's my Heisman Trophy even if he never got the trophy," said Mrs. Rozier. "I appreciate the fact that he hung in there and persevered so far from home."

"It's a great honor to be named the best player in the country," Mike Rozier said. "I'd like to thank my teammates, and especially the offensive line. If it weren't for them, I wouldn't be standing here tonight. I'll try to keep up the good name of the Heisman by doing the best I can when I go out into the world.

"Whatever I do, I do my best and work hard at it," said Rozier. "Jesus Christ gave me the gift of being able to go out and run around: I give back to Him doing the best I can."

Eighteen former Heisman Trophy winners shared the dais with Rozier, Vice President Bush and members of the Heisman Trophy committee.

Bush, the captain of a Yale baseball team in the late 1940s which played for the College World Series championship, took a strong stand on the need for an NCAA championship playoff in football.

First he praised the play of Rozier and the No. 1-rated Cornhuskers. "This is not only a great night for a gifted athlete, but for all football fans," the Vice President said. "It was a joy to meet Mike

and especially his family. I have been impressed with Mike's dedication, hard work and God-given ability.

"I have been particularly impressed with what he said—that as much as an individual honor means to him, the team goals are more important. That unselfishness is a credit to Mike, his family and his coach.

"But, as a politician, I know when to shut up," Bush added, "because I am going home to Texas for the holidays. Undefeated Nebraska has a great team, but undefeated Texas also has a great team. Both will be playing great teams in the bowl games. But it sure would serve a lot of fans if the Cornhuskers and the Longhorns were going to play each other.

"I wish the powers that be would figure out a plan to decide a national champion where it should be decided—on the field of play. It's time for the NCAA to devise a plan to decide the football championship in the same way they do for all the other sports."

Cornhusker head coach Tom Osborne opened his remarks by asking the Vice President "to convey my best wishes to (Texas Coach) Fred Akers. He sounds like a good friend of yours."

Osborne praised Rozier for his "completeness" as a player. "He does so many things so well. He runs inside with strength, power and balance. He reads his blocks well, and runs with speed to the outside. He's a good receiver and a great blocker.

"Mike is a tremendous 'effort' player with a great attitude," Osborne said. "He has broken most of the school and Big Eight Conference records and many NCAA records. The record I appreciate the most is his yards per attempt. He gained 7.8 yards per rush this season and nearly 7.2 for his entire career.

"For a coach, that's very comforting," said Osborne.

Mike Rozier scored on many long runs, including this 46-yarder in 1983. (Journal Star Library).

SIMPLY THE BEST

By Ken Hambleton

He is the standard by which all other Nebraska running backs are measured.

Tom Osborne claimed that Mike Rozier was the best running back he ever coached.

"The games he played while hurt and yet still produced on the field like he did convinced me," Osborne said.

Enough said.

Rozier tore through the Nebraska and Big Eight record books the same way he ripped through dozens of defenses in his three years as a Cornhusker. He won the Heisman Trophy in 1983, carried the Huskers to the national championship game and notched a permanent place in Nebraska football history.

He was impossible to tackle while playing for the Rosedale Vikings, harder to bring down in high school, more elusive in college and made an impact in a pro career shortened because of injuries.

"We all played together for the Rosedale Vikings in Midget League," said longtime friend Kenny Pratt. "We never knew Mike would win the Heisman. But nobody could

stop him, nobody. He was always two steps ahead of us and three steps ahead of everyone else. In junior high, people wouldn't even kick to him. In high school, he made runs that belong on highlight films. People didn't tackle him. They pushed him out-of-bounds.

"When you think about it, he was destined to win the Heisman. Everybody always talked about stopping Mike Rozier but nobody ever did."

Rozier's 7.81-yards-per-carry average on the 2,148 yards and 29 touchdowns he gained in 1983 was considered one of the most remarkable efforts in college history. His 4,780 yards and 49 career touchdowns are far ahead of Nebraska's long list of great running backs.

"He could make you miss with a minimum of movement," Osborne said. "The ability to make you miss him with a little step, a shoulder shake and he would be gone.

"He was also one of the toughest players I've ever seen. He played a game against Missouri (1982) with a hip-pointer. He could barely move before the game. But he had a great game. He usually did."

Rozier said the Missouri game in 1982 was his most memorable. He had only 17 carries, but he gained 139 yards and led Nebraska to a 23-19 victory. "Nobody expected me to play but I wasn't going to sit on the bench," he said. "I really couldn't go to the bathroom because of the pain. But I wanted to play, so I did."

Rozier had plenty of great runs and great days for Nebraska.

He had a 93-yard kickoff return for a touchdown against Oklahoma State in 1981. He had a 93-yard touchdown run against Kansas State that same season.

His famous 2-yard run for a touchdown against UCLA in 1983 was one of the most remarkable runs in Nebraska history. Osborne said it was one of the top runs he ever saw.

Rozier took the 49-pitch to the left and was following offensive tackle Scott Raridon. Rozier looped back to his right, then back to his left at the 18-yard line, then back to the right and finally finished his 75-to-80-yard run by scampering into the end zone.

"He's Michael Heisman," teammate Irving Fryar said. "He can do anything he wants."

Rozier did just about anything he wanted.

Sharing time with Roger Craig, he rushed for 943 and 1,689 yards his first two years at Nebraska after transfering from Coffeyville (Kan.) Junior College. As a senior, he gained 227, 212, 285 and 205 yards, respectively, in his final four regular-season games. Despite a knee injury, he rushed for 147 yards in NU's 31-30 loss to Miami in the 1984 Orange Bowl.

By the time he finished his college career, Rozier had rushed for the second-most yards in NCAA history, the best yards-per-rush average and rushed for more than 100 yards in his last 12 games.

Still, personal records were not a priority.

"When you take into consideration all the publicity he got, he was fairly remarkable," said Frank Solich, his running back coach at the time and now Nebraska head coach. "He wasn't out just to meet his personal goals. He was very team-oriented. He was an adequate blocker and ran out the fakes well."

Rozier proved the point when he had a great scrimmage just before the 1984 Orange Bowl. "It was just a piddly scrimmage, but he ran like it was the national championship," said Nebraska teammate Mark Traynowicz. "I wonder how many other Heisman Trophy winners would have been out there, running like that." Another teammate, Harry Grimminger, added, "He was leaving cleat marks on people's backs."

It was all part of the fun of running the football.

"I had the best time of my life in college football," Rozier said. "It wasn't a business, it was just fun. I would have played without fans in the stands. I would have played for a bad offense. As it was, I played

on a great offense with great guys Turner Gill, Irving Fryar, Roger Craig and a great line.

"Our receivers blocked downfield better than anybody else. They still do. Our offensive line is always the best around."

Rozier made the most of every advantage he had, except two.

"The weight room was not my favorite place," he said. "And school, I just was never motivated for classes. I wasn't good at school and I didn't put in the time I should. But I got by.

"I was gifted by the Lord. I could run. I gave 100 percent every time I ran, from when I was a little kid to when I played junior college at Coffeyville, at Nebraska and in pro football."

Rozier's efforts in high school were noticed.

Solich was recruiting a tight end in New Jersey when, while watching film of the recruit, he spotted Rozier on the opposing team. He quickly contacted officials at Woodrow Wilson High School (where the field is now named for Rozier) and started to recruit the running back.

Rozier visited Arizona and Pittsburgh. He chose Nebraska because he wanted a pipeline to the pros and he appreciated the academic programs in Lincoln.

"I fell in love with Lincoln," Rozier said. "The people there are almost as close as my buddies back here in Camden (N.J.). The coaches, the players and the fans at Nebraska make that a very special place. I still think of Coach Osborne as a very special person in my life."

Rozier ran for fun and to save face with his friends back home.

"I knew if I made a mistake, and we were on TV, I'd hear about it from my New Jersey friends. They didn't care about the four-touch-

down days, just the times I fumbled, missed a block or goofed up. And they let me know about it."

Of course, the goofs were few and far between.

Rozier was good enough to force Nebraska to shift Craig to fullback. He was on a team that included backs Jeff Smith and Doug DuBose. He followed in the footsteps of I.M. Hipp and Jarvis Redwine.

"Running backs at Nebraska, it just goes together," Rozier said. "Back then, when I came to Nebraska, it was the style of running you learned from Mike Corgan. He wanted us to run tough, shearing off the blocks and hitting guys hard before they hit you.

"When Coach Solich took over as running backs coach, we did pretty much the same thing. You have to play tough to play at Nebraska. It became a thing of violence on the field, but it was the only way to go, if you wanted to succeed."

These days, Rozier relaxes with friends and family in Camden.

He signed a $4 million contract with the Pittsburgh Maulers of the USFL in 1984. He played for Jacksonville in the same league the next year. Eventually, he signed a four-year contract with the Houston Oilers in the NFL. After two years with Atlanta, he retired. Rozier finished his pro career with 4,462 yards and 30 touchdowns and caught 90 passes for 715 more yards.

"My knees and my interest in football were done," he said.

"Pro football is not fun. I made enough to live on. I was able to buy the house we all grew up in. I was able to get my mother a house near here. I just retired from almost everything and now I spend my time going to charity events and speaking at local high schools."

Former Husker Heisman Trophy winner Johnny Rodgers tried to talk Rozier into finishing his degree at Nebraska. "Maybe when I settle down, get married, have a family, I'll do that.

"You know, people around there would want to talk a lot of football, too. I'm just not that interested in football any more. I don't watch it. I stay away from football. It's changed a lot and it's all about money, too."

Two years ago, Rozier was injured when a Camden man shot him and a friend. Two bullets went through Rozier's chest and one through his hand. He is completely recovered and, a year after the shooting, an arrest was made.

Because he has a daughter and a son, both 7, in Texas, Rozier said the shooting changed his emphasis on life and deepened his religious beliefs.

"A lot of people don't understand about life," he said. "You better get a grip on it, take advantage while you can. Things you put off today, you better do today. I realize I could be gone, just like that. In a split second, I could have been a dead man."

Instead, he's living life to its fullest.

"To be honest, I never wanted to play football. I just wasn't big enough for basketball. I tried boxing and that was too hard. I was good at football and it gave me a chance to do a lot of things in my life.

"I took advantage of those things and now it's time to move on."

Mike Rozier

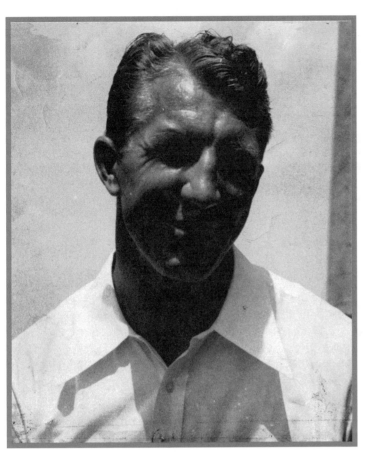

George Sauer earned letters in basketball, baseball, track and football at Nebraska in the 1930s. He received All-America honors as a fullback in 1933. (Journal Star Library).

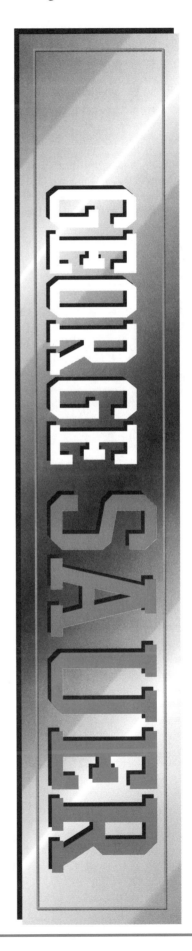

GEORGE SAUER/STATS

LETTERED:	1931-33
HEIGHT:	6-2
WEIGHT:	200
HONORS:	1931 ALL-BIG SIX
	1932 ALL-BIG SIX
	1933 ALL-BIG SIX
	1933 ALL-AMERICAN
	NATIONAL FOOTBALL HALL OF FAME
	NEBRASKA FOOTBALL HALL OF FAME
PRO EXPERIENCE:	GREEN BAY PACKERS 1935-37

SAUER ... SUCCESS ... FOOTBALL ... SYNONYMOUS

By Curt Mosher

There are some who say that George Sauer was the best all-around fullback ever to play in the Big Eight.

His record doesn't do anything to dispute it.

There are some, particularly those around Kansas, who will tell you he was one of the finest college coaches in his time.

His record doesn't hurt him there, either.

Regardless of where he ranks in either category, Sauer's reputation has soared to great heights both in Nebraska, where he was born and where he played, and across the nation.

This reputation has earned him a berth in *The Lincoln Journal* Nebraska Sports Hall of Fame.

A native of Stratton, Sauer moved to Lincoln when he was about 5 years old. He gained his first taste of football glory at Lincoln High, and, except for a stint in the Navy and a brief fling at selling insurance, he has been involved in the football business ever since.

He is as intensely involved as ever in his current capacity of Director of Player Personnel for the New York Jets of the American Football League.

In this role he renewed his ties with Nebraska this past winter when he signed Nebraska fullback Rudy Johnson off last year's Orange Bowl champions.

Perhaps it is unfair to moderns to use the all-around term so much since the modern fullback generally isn't called upon to function as they did in leather helmet days.

But that's just what Sauer was. George recalls the time at Oklahoma when the Cornhuskers held a 13-7 lead over the Sooners late in the ball game.

NU drove deep into Soonerland to about the 15, where the march faltered and fourth down was facing the Cornhuskers. Quarterback Bernie Masterson, the regular field goal kicker, was injured and substitute quarterback Jerry LaNoue was a little uncertain about what move to make.

"We're going to kick a field goal," Sauer said. "Who's going to kick it?" LaNoue wanted to know.

"I am," George replied, and he did. The kick iced the game and NU won, 16-7. He had never kicked one before in competition.

"I don't think Coach (Dana) Bible thought much of that deal until it went through the uprights," Sauer said the other day.

Bible probably thought a lot about a lot of things that year, however, as the Sauer-led Cornhuskers lost only to Pittsburgh that year, 6-0, and Sauer made All-America.

He had been all-conference the two previous years as Nebraska racked up 8-2 and 7-1-1 seasons under the famed coach, who is also a member of the Hall of Fame.

Following his great career at NU, Sauer played three years of professional football with Green Bay and he did the punting.

Sauer cut his professional career short because he wanted to try coaching, but he almost blew his first job because he thought someone was pulling a practical joke on him.

"There was always a lot of kidding around on the club, and one day I got a letter from New Hampshire. It was signed by the college president and asked me if I were interested in the head coaching job.

"The signature was small and looked like a woman's. I went to the library and looked up in the New Hampshire college president's name and the catalog was a year old and the name was different.

"About 10 days later a telegram came from the same name, asking why I hadn't answered the letter. He said he would be in Chicago and if I wanted the interview to be there."

Sauer did go for the interview. He took the job and stayed there four seasons before going into the service. He served in combat on the aircraft carrier Enterprise and was discharged a lieutenant commander.

He landed the Kansas job and shared the title both seasons there—1946 and '47, taking the club to the Orange Bowl that year.

It was at Kansas where he coached Ray Evans, recently voted into the National Hall of Fame.

Sauer regards Evans and Baylor quarterback Larry Isbell as the two finest players he ever coached.

Sauer then moved on to Navy, where he became the first civilian to coach there in over a decade. He didn't have too good a record there, but he showed what kind of stuff he was made of when he resigned after the academy treated two of his assistants unfairly.

From there he went to Baylor, coaching six seasons before stepping aside to devote full time to his athletic directorship.

Sauer still makes his home in Waco. He has two children, and his son, George Jr., will be a junior on the University of Texas football team this fall. He lettered as a sophomore last year.

A flanker back, George Jr. plays at 6-2 and 205, slightly bigger than his father was at Nebraska.

George misses coaching (he only gets to do some in the preseason drills), but he likes his current job real well.

He travels the nation looking for footballers and he often makes a trip back to Lincoln. Huskerland is one of his favorite stops and it should be, for it was the springboard for one of football's great personalities.

SAUER LEGACY REAL, BUT NOT ON VIDEOTAPE

By Mike Babcock

March 29, 1994—Johnny Rodgers. Mike Rozier. Dave Rimington. You can pop a tape in the VCR and see for yourself what made them special.

To know the greatness of athletes who competed in another era, however, requires the eyewitness accounts of those who remain. With the passing of time, such accounts can be lost forever.

"We're getting fewer and farther between," Bill Pfeiff said.

Plus, he added with a laugh, "we're all liars, anyway."

Pfeiff is about as close as we can get to a videotape of George Sauer, who died recently at the age of 83 in Waco, Texas.

Pfeiff was there to watch when Sauer was establishing himself among the greats in Nebraska football history.

Sauer was a multi-sport athlete at Nebraska, earning letters in basketball, baseball and track and field in the early 1930s. But it was as a football player that he excelled, earning All-America recognition from Grantland Rice as a Cornhusker senior in 1933. Sauer played for Coach D.X. Bible, on teams that had a combined record of 23-4-1. In three seasons, they never lost a Big Six Conference game.

Such evidence of Sauer's greatness is readily available in any record book or history. But it lacks the immediacy of a videotape.

Pfeiff watched Sauer compete, first when he, Pfeiff, was a junior high student in Lincoln and Sauer was playing football for Lincoln High School and Coach W.H. Browne, and later at Nebraska.

"I remember going down to the (Lincoln High) 'Oval,'" Pfeiff said. "They were good ballplayers. There was some highly successful football played here in the 1920s and 1930s."

Sauer was a junior in 1928, in a backfield that included Bernie Masterson, Lyle Weyand and Joe Luchinsger. Sauer might have been a senior, but Browne suggested he take an extra semester to graduate, giving him another season of football eligibility.

Browne suggested the same thing to Weyand, who decided not to. "I wanted to get on with my life and go to college," said Weyand, who accepted an athletic scholarship from Cotner College.

In 1930, Browne was hired as an assistant coach at Nebraska by Bible. Sauer, Masterson, Henry Bauer, Bruce Kilbourne and Clair Bishop were among the Lincoln High players who went with him.

"Several Lincoln boys started on those teams," Lee Penney said in a telephone interview from his home in Superior.

Penney, who hitch-hiked to Nebraska from Tabor, Iowa, also played for Bible's Cornhuskers from 1931 to 1933. Like Pfeiff and Weyand, he can provide some insight into Sauer's character. "Everybody liked George," Penney said. "He was a real fine fella."

Apparently, that characterized him as much as his well-documented ability as a single-wing fullback. Red Smith, the New York City sports writer, once described him as "a thoroughly decent guy."

"He was very friendly, with a lot of humor," said Weyand.

"He was a quiet, dedicated guy," said Pfeiff, who last talked with Sauer 10 years ago, at a Lincoln High alumni function. Soon after, Sauer began to show symptoms of Alzheimer's disease. He spent the final years of his life at a Veterans Administration hospital.

Sauer played professional football, coached at the major college level and was athletic director at Baylor before he retired.

SAUER NEVER FORGOT HIS ROOTS

By Steve Hill

George Sauer's life had all the makings of a hometown-boy-makes-good Hollywood script.

A three-year letterman at fullback for Nebraska, Sauer grew up in an immigrant neighborhood in Lincoln, starred at Lincoln High School and earned consensus All-America honors for Dana X. Bible's 8-1 Husker team in 1933.

His contributions on the field were matched by the important role he played in a community battling the tough economic times of the 1930s.

Sauer was someone for the people of Nebraska—specifically his fellow Germans from Russia in Lincoln—to point to with pride.

"It was a time in the depths of the Depression, when you grabbed hold of anything that could lift your spirits just to help you get up and face the world," said Don Bryant, the longtime sports information director at Nebraska and a friend of the late Sauer. "In retrospect, George contributed to Cornhusker football, but also to the spirits of the Nebraska people who were battling drought and depression."

Bill Pfeiff, a 1937 Husker letterman, was one of those who admired Sauer and dreamed of someday following in the Hall of Famer's footsteps.

After watching Sauer, a three-time all-state selection, star at Lincoln High, Pfeiff followed Sauer's career as it blossomed at NU. It was from Memorial Stadium's knothole section that Pfeiff saw Sauer develop into one of the best running backs of his era.

"He could do it all," Pfeiff said.

Indeed, newspaper accounts from the time described Sauer as a "triple threater extraordinary." In other words, he could do more than run the ball from his fullback position. Sauer was a proficient passer and kicker, as well.

In the last game of his collegiate career, for example, Sauer booted a 77-yard punt against Oregon State as the Huskers were struggling to hold onto a 6-0 second-half lead. After the punt, the momentum switched and NU went on to win easily, 22-0.

But running the ball with power, grit and determination was Sauer's trademark. He led the '33 Huskers in scoring, tallying six touchdowns, a field goal and a point-after conversion.

"They talk about (NU senior Joel) Makovicka being one of the great Nebraska fullbacks," said Sauer family friend Ed Schwarztkopf. "He is great, but he's not the greatest fullback we've ever had."

Schwarztkopf, who earned three letters at NU, called Sauer's versatility his greatest asset.

"George did it all. He ran the ball, threw the ball, kicked PATs and field goals. He had everything you needed to go to war on the field.

"He would bust through the line with power and find the holes and then he would transform from a fullback to a halfback."

Nebraska won three conference titles (1931-33) during Sauer's career and he earned All-Big Six honors in each of those seasons. NU didn't lose a league game during that three-year span.

National power Pittsburgh handed the Sauer-led Huskers their only loss in 1933, a 6-0 defeat at Pittsburgh. But Sauer's gridiron greatness was evident even in that game.

"Without Sauer, we would probably have beaten Nebraska by two or three more touchdowns," one Pitt coach told reporters.

In addition to his physical prowess, Sauer was the Huskers' emotional and intellectual leader.

"George gave it 150 percent all the time," Schwartzkopf said. "He was a bright guy—very perceptive. He passed, he kicked. He was a great all-around player."

But perhaps his crowning achievement came following the 1933 season, when Sauer was named the outstanding player of the 1934 East-West Shrine game. In the 12-0 West win, Sauer accounted for both touchdowns.

"He was one of the greats," Pfeiff said. "And he was just as fine a person as he was a ballplayer."

After his performance in the all-star game, Sauer's status in Lincoln grew from star to legend.

"We all had heroes and he was one of mine," Pfeiff said.

Pfeiff was not alone.

According to Schwartzkopf, the entire town and especially the Germans-from-Russia community, idolized Sauer.

"All the kids in the neighborhood would have their mothers sew a 25 (Sauer's jersey number) on their old sweaters and shirts. And it's no coincidence that Herm Rohrig wanted 25 when he came to the University. Alex Fink wore No. 25, too. They all wanted to be like George."

A newspaper photograph from the time shows Sauer addressing a large group of Lincoln schoolchildren shortly after he was named All-American. According to the cutline, the photo is a "familiar scene on the streets of Lincoln."

Another story raves "There is none of the blase acceptance of wide acclaim; not the slightest display of egotism, nor any of the corresponding symptoms of 'swell-headedness' about this truly great gridder. George Sauer not only is an All-America fullback, but an All-America off the football field as well."

Pfeiff agrees.

"George was one of those kind of guys who would make you think you were important," he said.

"I've come up with this definition of a classy person. A classy person is a person you can look up to, but they don't look down at you. That describes George perfectly. He was as humble as could be.

"He was one of the finest role models a kid could have had."

Sauer went on to play three seasons for the Green Bay Packers, helping them win the championship in 1936.

A professional career and a stellar college coaching career helped Sauer rise from his modest beginnings in Lincoln's Russian Bottoms neighborhood, but according to friends, he never forgot those roots.

"He had a good background from the old neighborhood," Pfeiff said. "And, of course, he remained terrifically loyal to his family and the neighborhood."

Schwartzkopf recalled Sauer returning from a season with the Packers and helping his dad at work—a garbage-hauling business. Not long after, according to Schwartzkopf, Sauer took his dad to a local auto dealership and bought him a new car.

"He never forgot where he came from," Schwartzkopf said.

As a coach, Sauer led the Kansas Jayhawks to consecutive conference co-titles in 1947 and 1948, including a berth in the Orange Bowl. He also coached at the University of New Hampshire, Navy and Baylor, where he led teams to the Orange Bowl and Gator Bowl.

Sauer, who died in February 1994 after a 10-year bout with Alzheimer's disease, is a member of the Nebraska Football Hall of Fame and the National Football Foundation Hall of Fame.

Nebraska I-back Jeff Smith rushed for 1,992 yards in his four-year career at NU and was thrown for just 22 yards in losses in 315 carries. (Journal Star Library).

JEFF SMITH/STATS

LETTERED:	1980, 1982-84
HEIGHT:	5-9
WEIGHT:	195
HOMETOWN:	WICHITA, KANSAS
HONORS:	1984 ALL-BIG EIGHT
PRO EXPERIENCE:	KANSAS CITY CHIEFS 1985-86
	TAMPA BAY BUCCANEERS 1987-88

SMITH CAN'T TAKE EASY ROAD WITH HIGH-POWERED NU

By Mike Babcock

October 21, 1982— Jeff Smith and his position coach Mike Corgan got on the elevator together in South Memorial Stadium.

"What weight you at?" Corgan asked.

Smith, who thought the question referred to how much he weighed, replied: "Still 194 pounds."

"No, how much are you lifting now?" said Corgan, who coaches the offensive backs on Nebraska's football team.

Smith, the Cornhuskers' third-string I-back, said the most he's lifting is 225 pounds. Usually, however, he lifts 195 pounds on the weight room circuit, just to maintain his strength.

That's standard in-season procedure for the NU running backs.

When Smith came to Nebraska after earning prep All-America recognition at Southeast High School in Wichita, Kansas, he weighed 170 pounds and could bench press a maximum of "like 210 or 215."

That has increased to 335 pounds.

"The summer before I came here, I felt I was real weak," said Smith. "You could say I've improved a lot."

Smith has improved his strength and gotten bigger as much out of necessity as dedication. When healthy, he's never missed a workout in the weight room, and he's made up every day he's missed because of illness or injury.

Early in his freshman year on the Cornhusker junior varsity, Smith "was hurting after about every practice because I couldn't take the shots," he said.

"I was getting knocked around."

The defenders were bigger, stronger and faster than those with whom Smith had to contend in high school.

High school tacklers rarely got good shots at him. When they did, Smith bounced right back up, even though "a couple of times on blitzes, a lineman missed his block, and the guy (defender) was right there in my face."

Now, despite his added size and strength, he wonders what would happen if a Cornhusker lineman missed a block on an isolation play.

According to Smith, it's a moot point at Nebraska, mere speculation, because "the blocking is so awesome. If you can read blocks here, it's easy."

A look at Smith's rushing statistics this season provides dramatic evidence of that. Smith has played sparingly, behind Mike Rozier and Roger Craig, but he's gained 330 yards and scored four touchdowns, averaging 12.7 yards each time he's been handed the ball.

In 26 carries, he's yet to be thrown for a loss. Six of those carries have resulted in gains of 14 yards or more, including touchdown runs of 19, 68 and 80 yards.

Smith's main asset is his ability "to read quickly. I'm more of a finesse-type runner," he said. "I'm prepared to run in traffic, but my goal is to find daylight.

"I don't look for anybody to run over."

Depending on the health of Rozier and Craig, Smith could play a significant role in this Saturday's Missouri game, against a Tiger defense "that's not going to give you much daylight. You've got to run in a lot of traffic."

"I've been thinking about that lately. It would be a challenge, but I think I could handle it," Smith said of the possibility of his seeing more action.

"I'll be ready."

Drawing recognition as one of the most talented third-string I-backs in college football is small consolation for Smith, who could start at many schools. "It doesn't help," said Smith. "One of my main ambitions is to start."

That's why he's been so diligent in the weight room at Nebraska.

When he played high school football, talent was enough. Smith didn't spend much time after practice trying to become a better player back then because "it always came easy for me.

"After the coach blew the whistle, everybody ran to the weight room for 10 minutes, showered, and ran home."

It hasn't been easy since he became a Cornhusker. The physical demands have been magnified by the emotional burden of having to wait his turn. But "I've been able to handle things," Smith said.

"I know Mike and Roger will play a lot. I just hope they (the coaches) can throw me in there once in awhile."

Jeff Smith used his blockers well during his NU career: "The blocking is so awesome. If you can read blocks here, it's easy." (Journal Star Library).

HUSKER BACK SMITH 'CLEANS UP' IN WEIGHT ROOM

By Mike Babcock

April 4, 1984—The last three football players finished lifting weights at 5:50 p.m. Tuesday afternoon, just 10 minutes before the doors to Nebraska's strength complex were to be locked for the day.

Jeff Smith was one of the three, just as he is almost every afternoon.

"I think Jeff works for a janitorial service and cleans up in there," teammate Paul Miles said with a smile as he left the varsity locker room at the south end of Memorial Stadium and headed for the training table.

Miles was in no hurry; he had plenty of time to get to the table, which stops serving at 6:30 p.m. Smith would have to hustle to make it, but he didn't mind.

No one forces Smith to lift after the daily strength and conditioning exercises required of everyone on the Cornhusker football team. Many players move quickly through the post-practice, weight-lifting routine and are satisfied.

Some, however, are not. "I do a lot of heavy lifting afterward to help my endurance on the field," said Smith, the logical successor to

Heisman Trophy winner Mike Rozier as Nebraska's No. 1 I-back.

Even though he's proved himself a worthy replacement for Rozier heading into his senior season next fall, Smith hasn't become complacent. "I need to build more strength," he said.

Nebraska's strength and conditioning program "is going to help me get stronger and faster," said Smith. "So I believe in it."

Smith has believed in the value of strength training since he arrived at Nebraska nearly four years ago. As a 175-pound freshman, he could bench press 210 pounds. Tuesday, the first day of spring practice, Smith weighed 195 pounds. His personal best bench press is now 345 pounds.

According to NU strength Coach Boyd Epley, Smith has never missed a workout since he became a Cornhusker.

With Rozier gone, Smith moves into the spotlight reserved for those who carry the football in Nebraska's run-oriented offense. The former *Parade Magazine* high school All-American is prepared to meet that challenge.

In three seasons, including four varsity carries as a freshman,

Smith has rushed for 1,057 yards and scored 12 touchdowns. Last fall, he also ranked fourth in the nation in punt returns, averaging 13.9 yards per return.

As a result, Smith can't step in for Rozier unnoticed, particularly after his performance in the Cornhuskers' Orange Bowl loss to Miami. With Rozier sidelined by an ankle injury, he scored two touchdowns in the game's final seven minutes, responding time and again in critical situations.

The two-point conversion pass that could have won the game was intended for Smith. Despite the disappointment, the Orange Bowl experience "helped my confidence," Smith said. "I was pretty involved in that game. It was a big boost to me."

Since that game, Smith has been eager for the start of this, his final spring practice. Rozier's parting advice to him, following the Orange Bowl, was: "It's your turn now. Have a good time."

That's what Smith is doing. Despite the physical toll exacted by a day's workout, he continues his extra lifting, preparing himself for next fall.

Some athletes over-train, said Mike Arthur, an Epley assistant. "But Jeff's been around here for four years. I think he's smart enough to know when it's time to stop."

That's usually about the time the weight room closes.

In addition to running the ball, Jeff Smith was a threat as a punt returner. He was fourth in the nation in 1983 with an average of 13.9 yards per return. (Journal Star Library).

TO MOST FANS, ONE PLAY DEFINES SMITH'S CAREER

By Todd Henrichs

Jeff Smith went about his work for five years at Nebraska. He put on nearly 30 pounds to win the team's lifter of the year honor, was voted favorite Husker by supermarket customers, even made the fabled cover of *Sports Illustrated*.

But after leaving Nebraska in 1985 as the school's 10th-leading all-time rusher, Smith seemingly is remembered for one game. In reality, one play.

Only the fingertips of Miami defender Ken Calhoun prevented Smith from catching a last-minute two-point conversion pass attempt from quarterback Turner Gill in the 1984 Orange Bowl. The Hurricanes' 31-30 victory kept Nebraska from winning the national title, a feat instead claimed by a Miami team ranked as low as No. 5 entering the game.

"Once we didn't execute, the first thing that came to my mind was there goes the national championship," Smith said. "That was the only thing that could go through your mind."

To this day, Smith says, people in his hometown of Wichita, Kansas, still ask him about the play. It's remembered nationally as the climax to one of the most exciting bowl games ever staged.

In fact, Tom Osborne's decision to go for two ranks as perhaps the defining moment in the retired NU coach's 25-year career. Had Nebraska successfully kicked the point-after, the Huskers would likely have stayed No. 1 as the only unbeaten team in college football that season.

Lost somewhere in the memory bank, however, is Smith's role in allowing the Huskers even a chance to tie or win in the final minute. Miami, after surrendering a 17-0 lead, forged back in front 31-17 late in the third quarter. Four plays after Miami's last score, NU's Heisman Trophy winner Mike Rozier left the game with a badly bruised ankle.

In just 18 minutes, Smith—an understudy to Rozier at I-back throughout his junior season—nearly saved Nebraska's perfect season.

"When I got on the field, I was really pumped up and emotional," Smith said. "I was really upset that the offense wasn't doing what we were planning to do. It was a challenge. I just tried to take over the game."

Smith rushed for 99 yards on nine carries and his 1-yard TD run pulled Nebraska within seven midway through the fourth quarter. With time ticking away, one last-gasp success—Smith's 24-yard scoring scamper on fourth-and-8—set the stage for another last gasp for Nebraska. This time, with only 48 seconds to play, the Huskers and Smith came up empty when the batted ball deflected off his shoulder pads.

Years later, Smith supervises 130 offenders in his position at a state probation office, speaks to youth groups, coaches youth teams and helps direct a football camp named for NFL great Barry Sanders, another Wichita native.

Looking back, Smith says his Nebraska career—filled with as many jaw-dropping ups as head-shaking downs—mirrored that Orange Bowl. Through it all, his teammates and coaches say, Smith never backed down.

"He really defined a team player," said Gill, who roomed with Smith for a semester during their second year together in Lincoln. "I guess he was kind of the happy-go-lucky guy on our football team, but he was the hardest worker. The coaches mentioned he needed to get a little bit heavier and stronger and he took that to heart."

A highly recruited star on Wichita Southeast teams that went 32-2 in his high school career, Smith arrived at Nebraska in 1980 measuring but 5-foot-9 and 175 pounds.

Although he saw varsity time as a true freshman—more of a rarity in those days—Smith knew he would have to hit the weights the first time he took a hit in a scrimmage.

"He worked his way onto the team and onto the field," said Frank Solich, then an assistant to Osborne. "He did so much in the off-season that he became strong enough and big enough to play a lot."

Smith, however, had to wait his turn. After a redshirt year in 1981, Smith managed 569 yards on 56 carries as a sophomore in the same backfield with Rozier and future NFL star Roger Craig. Rozier became the Big Eight's all-time leading rusher in 1983, when Smith rushed 78 times for 439 yards.

"I think everybody wants to be the No. 1 star on the team," Smith said. "I had a lot of respect for Mike Rozier, but playing in (his) shadow wasn't as difficult as you think. It made me work hard, and in the long run, it helped him. I pushed him to become a great back."

Many expected Smith to follow in Rozier's footsteps in 1984. Smith was on pace early, leading the nation in rushing after three weeks before disaster struck. Smith

severely sprained an ankle against UCLA. Before the injury, Smith rushed for 473 yards in $2^{1}/_{2}$ games. Yielding time to Doug DuBose the rest of the season, Smith carried for just 462 more yards. He finished just eight shy of 2,000 yards in his career.

"The senior year, to me, was devastating," Smith said. "I started out the first three games thinking I would have a 2,000-yard season. That was my goal.

"Then I got hurt in the third game, and after that I ended up playing at 60 to 70 percent. I just couldn't cut. I didn't have any power behind my legs."

Despite leading the conference in all-purpose yards and earning All-Big Eight honors, Smith said for the first time ever, he just wanted the season to end. He wasn't the same player who twice in his career ran back punts for touchdowns against Kansas, the school Smith once accused of committing recruiting violations.

The ankle injury shattered everything, at least until a phone call on NFL draft day offered Smith a second chance.

A 10th-round pick of the Kansas City Chiefs, Smith regained his stride. He rushed for 118 yards and added 157 yards receiving in addition to his duties returning kickoffs and punts. Not even another ankle injury—suffered the day of his first NFL start—kept Smith from being named the Chiefs' top rookie.

"I knew I had a great year with Kansas City," Smith said. "We would get beat on Sunday, but personally, I always felt like I did the

best job I could. Then to see the team select me as rookie of the year. It was a surprise, of course, but it was a big honor."

Smith was eventually traded to Tampa Bay for an eighth-round draft pick before the 1987 season. As a free agent in 1989, Smith signed with Green Bay but was waived before the team's opening game.

Leaving the Buccaneers may have been a mistake, Smith says now, but not one he looks back on with regret.

"The professional game is all about business," Smith said. "I received my college degree, so I always knew I could walk away from the game. I was just happy I wasn't one of those players that set out to play football the rest of my life."

Instead, Smith is happy back in Wichita where his mother, Juanita, and grandmother still live. Smith is single, allowing him to spend time helping to inspire the city's youth. He started coaching a third-grade football team in 1994 and is working with the same players four years later.

What does he tell wide-eyed pupils who ask about his playing days at Nebraska?

"You reminisce about the relationship with the coaches and the players and also the rapport of how wonderful the fans were and how supportive they were to Nebraska football players," said Smith, whose teams at Nebraska went 34-4 over his final three seasons.

"I had never been around so many people that are so much involved. That sticks with you."

Coach Tom Osborne calls for quiet so that Jeff Smith can speak after being named the team's lifter of the year in 1984. (Journal Star Library).

Frank Solich was not your typical fullback. The native of Cleveland was just 5 feet, 8 inches tall and weighed 135 pounds coming out of high school, but earned All-Big Eight honors in 1965. His 204 yards against Air Force in 1965 stood as NU's single-game rushing record for 10 years. He still holds the Orange Bowl record for return yards with 166, set in 1966. (Journal Star Library).

FRANK SOLICH/STATS

LETTERED: 1963-65
HEIGHT: 5-8
WEIGHT: 158
HOMETOWN: CLEVELAND
HONORS: 1965 ALL-BIG EIGHT
NEBRASKA FOOTBALL HALL OF FAME

PERSISTENT SOLICH FINDS HIDDEN JEWELS FOR NU

By Virgil Parker

August 28, 1983—From the moment Frank Solich joined Coach Tom Osborne's Nebraska football coaching staff, he has been one of the Cornhuskers' best recruiters.

During his first season on the road, Solich recruited both I-back Mike Rozier and wingback Irving Fryar, two of the key cogs in Nebraska's explosive offensive machine this fall.

The big question is: Would Solich recruit Solich?

As a senior in high school, Frank Solich was all-everything in the talent-laden state of Ohio. He led Holy Name High School to the city championship of Cleveland.

But Solich also had to stretch to reach 5-feet-8. And he weighed 135 pounds soaking wet.

"I wouldn't have weighed that much except our high school had a very advanced weight-lifting program," Solich recalls. "I worked hard on the weights, and at trying to gain. Otherwise, I would have been the original 99-pound weakling."

He's glad Nebraska's recruiters didn't bypass him because of lack of size. So were the Husker fans. Solich became a three-year letterman, earning first team All-Big Eight honors in 1965 as a fullback.

He was co-captain of the Huskers his senior season. And Nebraska went undefeated during the regular campaign that year before dropping an Orange Bowl decision to Alabama.

In a 27-17 victory over the Air Force in the second game of the season, Solich set an all-time single-game school rushing record, gaining 204 yards. The mark stood for a decade.

"People all remember that game," Frank says, "but there were other games, in which I gained a lot less yards, where I was more proud of my performance. Against Air Force, I managed to go 80 yards on the very first play for a touchdown. And I had some other long gainers. (His two other touchdowns came on runs of 21 and 41 yards.)

"But I'll never forget the Iowa State game my junior year. (Quarterback Fred) Duda broke his leg and Coach Devaney put in Bob Churchich. It was the first time Churchich had been in a game. He wasn't to try anything fancy. Just stick to the basics. I was the leading rusher with 78 yards. But they were tough, inside yards.

"And the Missouri games back then were hard-nosed, just like those we have with them today,"

Solich added. "My senior year we trailed Missouri, 14-0, at the end of the first quarter. Yet we came back to beat them, 15-14. I didn't gain anywhere near 100 yards that day. But I really knew I'd been in a ball game when it was over."

None of those games were the most memorable to Solich during his collegiate career, however. "The second game of my sophomore season we played Minnesota up there," he recalled. "When I was a little kid, Minnesota was a real national power. They'd had coaches like Bernie Bierman. And famous players of the past like Bronko Nagurski and Leo Nomelini. Yet we beat Minnesota that day, 14-7. It was a magical feeling. When I got to the dressing room I was almost overcome with emotion. I didn't feel like yelling and screaming to celebrate the victory. I just sat in silence and almost cried."

The next year, the Minnesota game was also played in Minneapolis. It was also a lot more fun, Solich remembers. "That was the game where we trailed, 21-12, halfway through the fourth quarter. I got open to catch a 45-yard touchdown pass, but we still were behind, 21-19."

Nebraska got the ball one last

time. A key 14-yard pass to end Freeman White on fourth down got the Huskers out of one jam. Then Duda hit Bob Hohn with a 15-yarder to the Minnesota 18. On the next play, Duda passed again.

"A Minnesota guy was right there. It was a sure interception," Solich recalls. "But the ball went through his hands, hit him on the helmet and bounced up in the air. Kent McCloughan lunged for the deflected ball, caught it, struggled into the end zone from about the 1 and we won the game, 26-21."

By that time, Solich had worked himself all the way up to a 155-pounder. But he was still the lightest guy on the team. He tried to take care of that matter during the weigh-ins prior to his junior year.

"Actually, it was trainer Paul Schneider's idea," Solich says. "He suggested I tape some lead weights around my waist. We were allowed to wear a pair of those grey gym shorts and a tee shirt when we weighed in. I didn't tuck the shirt in. Figured that would hide the weights okay."

Solich says that in addition to shaking the "smallest guy on the squad" image, he also wanted to improve his program weight so people wouldn't laugh about Nebraska having such a small fullback. "I accomplished that," Solich says. "I was listed in the program my junior year at 162 pounds (but back down to 158 as a senior). But I was still the lightest guy on the team. Larry Wachholtz, the defensive back I thought I could pass, still beat me by a pound at 163. If I'd been smart, I'd have hidden 10 pounds of weights in my shorts instead of five."

Knowing what he was able to accomplish at the big-time college football level, Solich says he never

Frank Solich played with an aggressiveness that belied his size. (Journal Star Library).

rules out a prospect on the basis of size—or lack of it—alone.

"I certainly wouldn't scratch him off my list until I had at least seen some film on him," Solich says. "Take Irving Fryar, for instance. He wasn't very highly recruited out of high school because he played tight end his senior year. Although he's certainly a lot bigger than I was in high school, he wasn't big enough to be impressive as a tight end. He was just in the wrong position. We projected him as a wingback from the very beginning. And look what's happened. You can't say enough good things about the way he has played."

Solich says persistence is the key to success in recruiting. "Just as I wouldn't write off a kid because of his size, neither would I give up on someone for any other reason. Mike Rozier didn't spend much time on the books when he was in high school. As a result, he didn't have a

C average and thus didn't qualify for a scholarship.

"A lot of recruiters gave up on Mike right then," Solich recalls. "But I got to know him. I knew he had the ability to do college level work. He just hadn't applied himself."

As a result, Rozier enrolled at Coffeyville (Kansas) Junior College for one year. "After he brought up his grades he transferred to Nebraska," Solich said. "We might never have gotten him if some of the schools which were high on his list hadn't given up on him right away just because he didn't have a C average."

Solich says he was far from a "super student" when in college, "but I dedicated myself to my school work and graduated in four years."

He was immediately hired as the coach at Omaha Holy Name—ironically, a school bearing the same name as the one he had played for as a prepster.

"I was lucky," Solich admits. "It was unusual then—and it would be unheard of now—for a guy to come right out of college and become the head coach of a Class B school." In two years, he turned a 1-9 loser into an 8-2 winner. That led to an offer to be the head coach at Class A Lincoln Southeast. "I had become very attached to the people at Holy Name and wasn't sure I should leave them after such a short stay," Solich says. "But my wife pointed out—correctly—that it would be silly not to make the move to Class A when the opportunity came."

Eleven years of success at Southeast eventually led to a call from Osborne to join the Nebraska staff as the coach of the freshman team. Solich compiled a 19-1 overall record. His last three teams (1980-82) were all 5-0.

LITTLE FRANK BIG EIGHT'S STAR BACK

Nebraska's 158-pound Frank Solich, fullback and offensive captain of a team loaded with brawny giants, squirted through and around Air Force defenders for 204 yards rushing Saturday and was named Big Eight Conference back of the week.

"It certainly was one of the finest running performances I've seen," said Bob Devaney, Nebraska coach. "Frank is a tremendous competitor despite his size."

Solich had touchdown runs of 80, 21, and 41 yards in Nebraska's 27-17 victory. His total of 204 is 10th highest rushing figure in conference history and a Nebraska school record. He carried 17 times.

Mike Corgan, Nebraska backfield coach: "When Solich is at fullback and required to block, we don't call any different plays. We use him as a receiver, ball carrier, faker and blocker. He is very well coordinated in all phases of football."

Now Osborne has tabbed Solich again—this time to be the running back coach for the varsity. As a result, Solich will coach his first recruit, Rozier, in his final game.

But you don't have to look into a crystal ball to know that this isn't the last season Rozier and Solich will be heard from. Rozier's talents are sure to carry him to an outstanding career as a pro. And Solich will continue to recruit and coach other outstanding Husker backs in the years to come.

Frank Solich, who played fullback for Bob Devaney at Nebraska in the mid-1960s, became NU's running backs coach in 1979. Among the many standouts he coached were Jeff Smith (left) and 1983 Heisman Trophy winner Mike Rozier. (Journal Star Library).

FRANK SOLICH: NEBRASKA'S LITTLE BIG MAN

By Ken Hambleton

There are still calls from folks in Cleveland about how good a running back Frank Solich was at Holy Name High School.

"He was a great athlete," Frank Solich Sr. said. "I think it's because he's serious and he knows what hard work means. He always worked hard. He was like that growing up. He's still like that.

"He didn't care that he was compared to his peers and yet he was usually smaller. He didn't think he was small, so he played just like the big kids."

At 5-foot-8 and 160 pounds, Frank Solich Jr. was one of the smallest fullbacks in Nebraska's and the country's modern football history.

He rushed his way for 1,054 yards on 196 carries. His average of 5.15 yards per carry is 34th all-time and his total yards are 42nd all-time on NU rushing charts. He's ninth among Nebraska fullbacks.

Recruited out of Cleveland by Bob Devaney, Solich quickly made an impression on the Lincoln campus. He played for the Husker freshman team, and as a sophomore, made the varsity and immediately had an impact.

"We recruited Frank, who had an offer from Cincinnati, with the idea of using him on kick returns," Devaney said in 1987. "We were running a lot of spread-formation stuff at the time, when we used him at what would have been the fullback slot because of his quickness."

Solich averaged 26.1 yards per kickoff return in 1963, but his season was cut short because of a broken ankle. As a junior in 1964, he led the team with 444 yards and a 5.1 yards-per-carry average but finished the season with a shoulder injury.

As a senior, Solich rushed for a school single-game-record 204 yards against Air Force, scoring on an 80-yard run on the first play of the game. He finished the season with 580 yards for the Huskers' 10-0 Big Eight championship team and earned All-Big Eight honors. Despite suffering a knee injury in NU's second-to-last regular-season game, Solich played against Oklahoma and in NU's loss to Alabama in the Orange Bowl.

Alabama Coach Bear Bryant was so impressed with Solich that, after the game, he crossed the field to shake the Nebraska senior's hand.

"I thought I was tough and had good acceleration and was a pretty good blocker," said Solich. "My size, although I didn't see it as a problem, was probably one of the reasons I finished every season with a pretty serious injury."

But he was still effective, playing alongside quarterback Fred Duda and halfback Harry Wilson. "I was in there because we had to get a lot of our yards up the middle. When we came from behind to beat Missouri, Oklahoma State and Oklahoma that year (1965), a good part of it was our strength up the middle and our ability to hold onto the ball."

While most fans remember the Air Force game in 1965 as Solich's best, he said the 1964 game against Iowa State was one of his favorites. Duda broke his leg during the game and Bob Churchich took over. "Coach Devaney put in Churchich and wasn't going to do anything fancy, just run up the middle. I got 78 of the toughest yards I ever had that day."

Always a running back as a youngster in Smokeless, Pennsylvania, and later in kids' leagues in Cleveland, Solich was a star at Holy Name High School. Playing running back on offense and safety on defense, he helped Holy Name to its first and last city championship. He was named all-area and all-state and was recruited by Notre Dame, as well as Nebraska and other schools.

"I had that tough-minded, bull-headed style that made me a pretty good back in high school and college," he said. "My size was a detriment in a lot of ways, most importantly in getting injuries.

"But I enjoyed football. Every play? No. But overall, football and running the football was a lot of fun," he said.

Solich was a pioneer in having football players lift weights. He helped establish the weight room in high school and was a driving force behind the early days of lifting at Nebraska.

"I had to be as strong as I could be to survive," he said. "It did improve my speed and helped me get a lot of tough yards. That way you never had to think of yourself of going uphill and you just paid attention to being the best athlete you could be.

"I always thought I could make it in a big college and Nebraska gave me the chance. "

Although he hates to discuss the issue, Solich even used weights to weigh in at Nebraska. Word around campus was that Solich was the smallest player on the team. He knew that Larry Wachholz was also small, so Solich taped two weights to his legs during weigh-ins. He still was lighter than Wachholz.

"Oh, no. I'm not going to talk about that ever again," Solich said.

Because his knee injury as a senior was so severe, Solich turned down a chance to try out for the pros. That led to a decision to coach high school football at Omaha Holy Name. Two years later, he was named head coach at Lincoln Southeast and 11 years later was named to Tom Osborne's staff at Nebraska.

"I learned my running style from a lot of people, including Mike Corgan," Solich said of the former Husker running backs coach. "I think I pretty much taught the same way. You run tough and you run hard. He taught that you don't run away from a hit but deliver the hit. He never wanted to see anybody run out-of-bounds.

"I always thought the running back had to be aggressive. It seems to work for us. It worked for me."

As running backs coach at Nebraska from 1983 to 1998, when he was named head coach, Solich maintained that coaching style.

It would be hard to argue the success of some of his backs, including Heisman Trophy winner Mike Rozier, All-American Jarvis Redwine and all-conference backs Ahman Green, Doug DuBose, Tom Rathman, Keith Jones, Ken Clark, Calvin Jones, Lawrence Phillips and Derek Brown.

NEBRASKA INDIVIDUAL RECORDS

(All records since 1946 and exclude bowl games unless noted)

RUSHING

Game

Attempts: 36; Rick Berns, vs. Missouri, Nov. 18, 1978 (255 yards); Lawrence Phillips, at Iowa State, Nov. 12, 1994 (183 yards)

Yards, Quarter: 135, Mike Rozier, vs. Kansas, Nov. 12, 1983 (1st, 14 att.)

Yards, Half: 230, Mike Rozier, vs. Kansas, Nov. 12, 1983 (1st, 26 att.)

Yards: 294; Calvin Jones, at Kansas, Nov. 9, 1991 (27 att.)

Yards Per Attempt: (min. 10 att.)—19.20; Craig Johnson, at Kansas, Nov. 4, 1978 (192 yards, 10 att.); (min. 20 att.)—11.70; Roger Craig, vs. Florida State, Sept. 19, 1981 (234 yards, 20 att.); (min. 30 att.)—9.19; Mike Rozier, vs. Kansas, Nov. 12, 1983 (285 yards, 31 att.)

Touchdowns: 6; Calvin Jones, at Kansas, Nov. 9, 1991

Most Players Gaining 100 Yards: 3; vs. Arizona State, Sept. 24, 1988 (Ken Clark, 122; Steve Taylor, 116; Terry Rodgers, 113)

Most Yards Gained by Two Players: 396; Ken Clark (256) and Steve Taylor (140), vs. Oklahoma State, Oct. 15, 1988

Longest Nebraska Run: 94 (TD); Craig Johnson, vs. Kansas, Oct. 13, 1979; Roger Craig, vs. Florida State, Sept. 19, 1981

Longest Nebraska Run, No TD: 73; I.M. Hipp, vs. Indiana, Oct. 1, 1977

Longest Opponent Run: 99 (TD); Gale Sayers, Kansas, Nov. 9, 1963

200-YARD RUSHING PERFORMANCES (28*):
(INCLUDES BOWL GAMES)

294 Calvin Jones, at Kansas, Nov. 9, 1991 (27 att., 6 TD)

285 Mike Rozier, vs. Kansas, Nov. 12, 1983 (31 att., 4 TD)

256 Ken Clark, vs. Oklahoma St., Oct. 15, 1988 (27 att., 3 TD)

255 Rick Berns, vs. Missouri, Nov. 18, 1978 (36 att., 2 TD)

254 I. M. Hipp, vs. Indiana, Oct. 1, 1977 (28 att., 0 TD)

251 Mike Rozier, vs. Oklahoma St., Nov. 6, 1982 (33 att., 4 TD)

248 Keith Jones, at Colorado, Nov. 28, 1987 (26 att., 2 TD)

240 Keith Jones, vs. Iowa State, Nov. 7, 1987 (15 att., 2 TD)

234 Roger Craig, vs. Florida State, Sept. 19, 1981 (20 att., 1 TD)

227 Mike Rozier, at Kansas State, Oct. 29, 1983 (23 att., 3 TD)

225 Ken Clark, at Kansas State, Oct. 22, 1988 (20 att., 1 TD)

221 Lawrence Phillips, vs. Okla. State, Oct. 8, 1994 (33 att., 3 TD)

214 Ahman Green, at Iowa State, Nov. 16, 1996 (29 att., 1 TD)

212 Mike Rozier, at Colorado, Oct. 9, 1982 (32 att., 1 TD)

212 Mike Rozier, vs. Iowa State, Nov. 5, 1983 (26 att., 4 TD)

211 Rick Berns, at Hawaii, Dec. 4, 1976 (25 att., 4 TD)

209 Ahman Green, vs. Iowa State, Nov. 15, 1997 (15 att., 3 TD)

208 Calvin Jones, vs. Iowa State, Nov. 13 1993 (26 att., 1 TD)

208 Leodis Flowers, at Iowa State, Oct. 27, 1990 (25 att., 3 TD)

207 I. M. Hipp, at Kansas State, Oct. 8, 1977 (23 att., 2 TD)

206 Ahman Green, vs. Tennessee, Jan. 2, 1998 (OB) (29 att., 2 TD)*

206 Lawrence Phillips, at Michigan State, Sept. 9, 1995 (22 att., 4 TD)

206 Jarvis Redwine, vs. Colorado, Oct. 27, 1979 (18 att., 3 TD)

205 Mike Rozier, at Oklahoma, Nov. 26, 1983 (32 att., 1 TD)

204 Frank Solich, at Air Force, Sept. 25, 1965 (17 att., 3 TD)

204 Mike Rozier, vs. Kansas State, Oct. 16, 1982 (21 att., 2 TD)

FRANK SOLICH

202 Ahman Green, at Colorado, Nov. 28, 1997 (29 att., 2 TD)

200 I. M. Hipp, vs. Kansas, Nov. 12, 1977 (23 att., 0 TD)

Note: Since 1946, Nebraska has had 304, 100-yard rushing games by 70 different Husker performers

BEST SINGLE-GAME RUSHING PERFORMANCE BY CLASS

Freshman: 294; Calvin Jones, at Kansas, Nov. 9, 1991 (27 att.)

Sophomore: 254; I. M. Hipp, vs. Indiana, Oct. 1, 1977 (28 att.)

Junior: 256; Ken Clark, vs. Oklahoma State, Oct. 15, 1988 (27 att.)

Senior: 285; Mike Rozier, vs. Kansas, Nov. 12, 1983 (31 att.)

Season

Attempts: 286; Lawrence Phillips, 1994 (1,722 yards)

Yards: 2,148; Mike Rozier, 1983 (275 att.)

Yards Per Attempt:

(Min. 100 att.)—8.33; Calvin Jones, 1991 (900 yards, 108 att.)

(Min. 200 att.)—7.81; Mike Rozier, 1983 (2,148 yards, 275 att.)

Yards Per Game: 179.0, Mike Rozier, 1983 (2,148 yards, 12 games)

Touchdowns: 29; Mike Rozier, 1983

Games Rushing for 100 Yards: 11; Mike Rozier, 1983; Lawrence Phillips, 1994; Ahman Green, 1997 (ties NCAA record)

Games Rushing for 200 Yards: 4; Mike Rozier, 1983

Consecutive 100 Yard Games: 11; Mike Rozier, 1983 (games 2-12); Lawrence Phillips, 1994 (games 1-11); Ahman Green, 1997 (games 2-12)

Consecutive 200 Yard Games: 4; Mike Rozier, 1983 (games 9-12)

1,000 YARD RUSHING SEASONS (22):

2,148 Mike Rozier, IB,1983 (275 att., 29 TD)
1,877 Ahman Green, IB,1997 (278 att., 22 TD)
1,722 Lawrence Phillips, IB, 1994 (286 att., 16 TD)
1,689 Mike Rozier, IB, 1982 (242 att., 15 TD)
1,497 Ken Clark, IB, 1988 (232 att., 12 TD)
1,342 Bobby Reynolds, HB, 1950 (193 att., 19 TD)
1,313 Derek Brown, IB, 1991 (230 att., 14 TD)
1,301 I. M. Hipp, IB, 1977 (197 att., 10 TD)

1,232 Keith Jones, IB, 1987 (170 att., 13 TD)
1,210 Calvin Jones, IB, 1992 (168 att., 14 TD)
1,196 Ken Clark, IB, 1989 (198 att., 12 TD)
1,161 Doug DuBose, IB, 1985 (203 att., 8 TD)
1,119 Jarvis Redwine, IB, 1980 (156 att., 9 TD)
1,095 Scott Frost, QB, 1997 (176 att., 10 TD)
1,086 Ahman Green, IB, 1995 (141 att., 13 TD)
1,060 Roger Craig, IB, 1981 (173 att., 6 TD)
1,043 Calvin Jones, IB, 1993 (185 att., 12 TD)
1,042 Jarvis Redwine, IB, 1979 (148 att., 8 TD)
1,040 Doug DuBose, IB, 1984 (156 att., 8 TD)
1,037 Jeff Kinney, HB, 1971 (222 att., 16 TD)
1,011 Derek Brown, IB, 1992 (169 att., 4 TD)
1,008 Tony Davis, IB, 1973 (254 att., 12 TD)

Career

Attempts: 668, Mike Rozier, 1982-82-83 (4,780 yards)

Yards: 4,780; Mike Rozier, 1981-82-83 (668 att.)

Yards Per Attempt (min. 200 att.): 7.16; Mike Rozier, 1981-82-83 (NCAA record, 4,780 yards, 668 att.)

Yards Per Game: 136.6; Mike Rozier, 1981-82-83 (35 games)

Touchdowns: 49; Mike Rozier, 1981-82-83

Games Rushing for 100 Yards: 26; Mike Rozier, 1981-82-83

Games Rushing for 200 Yards: 7; Mike Rozier, 1981-82-83

Yards Gained Against One Opponent: 599; Ahman Green vs. Iowa State, 1995-96-97 (three games, 176 in 1995; 214 in 1996; 209 in 1997)

2,000-YARD CAREER RUSHERS:

Achieved 2,000 in:

Player (years)	Att.	Net	#Gms.	#Att.
1. Mike Rozier, IB (81-82-83)	668	4780	19	307
2. Ahman Green, IB (1995-96)	574	3880	21	295
3. Calvin Jones, IB (91-92-93)	461	3153	21	262
4. Ken Clark, IB (87-88-89)	494	3037	22	309
5. I.M. Hipp, IB (77-78-79)	495	2814	18	322
6. Lawrence Phillips, IB (93-94-95)	449	2777	21	322
7. Derek Brown, IB (90-91-92)	458	2699	22	326
8. Keith Jones, IB (84-85-86-87)	398	2488	34	347
9. Rick Berns, IB/FB (76-77-78)	440	2449	33	362
10. Roger Craig, IB (79-80-81-82)	407	2446	29	317
11. Jeff Kinney, HB (69-70-71)	545	2244	31	95
12. Doug DuBose, IB (82-84-85)	362	2205	20	320
13. Bobby Reynolds, HB (50-51-52)	378	2196	22*	326
14. Jarvis Redwine, IB (79-80)	304	2161	19	280
15. Tony Davis, FB (73-74-75)	501	2153	31	469
16. Steve Taylor, QB (85-86-87-88)	431	2125	35	398

17. Monte Anthony, IB (74-75-76-77)   463 2077 35 446

* Because of incomplete statistics, the exact carry on which Reynolds hit 2,000 cannot be determined, therefore, the number listed is his total number of carries at the end of the game in which he achieved the 2,000 yards.

POSITION RUSHING RECORDS

Quarterbacks

Attempts, Game: 25; John Bordogna, vs. Kansas St., 1952 (143 yards)

Attempts, Season: 176; Scott Frost, 1997 (1,095 yards)

Attempts, Career: 431; Steve Taylor, 1985-86-87-88 (2,125 yards)

Net Yards, Game: 199; Tommie Frazier vs. Florida, 1995 (16 att.)

Net Yards, Season: 1,095; Scott Frost, 1997 (176 att.)

Net Yards, Career: 2,125; Steve Taylor, 1985-86-87-88 (431 att.)

Touchdowns, Game: 4; Gerry Gdowski, vs. Iowa State, 1989; Mickey Joseph, vs. Missouri, 1990; Scott Frost vs. Missouri, 1997

Touchdowns, Season: 19; Scott Frost, 1997

Touchdowns, Career: 36; Tommie Frazier, 1992-93-94-95

Fullbacks

Attempts, Game: 25; Jerry Brown, vs. Baylor, 1956 (100 yards); Ken Kaelin, at Iowa State, 1986 (126 yards)

Attempts, Season: 162; Dick Davis, 1967 (717 yards)

Attempts, Career: 348; Dick Davis, 1966-67-68 (1,477 yards)

Net Yards, Game: 204; Frank Solich, at Air Force, 1965 (17 att.)

Net Yards, Season: 881; Tom Ruthman, 1985 (118 att.)

Net Yards, Career: 1,738; Andra Franklin, 1977-78-79-80 (324 att.)

Note: Tony Davis gained 2,125 in 1973-74-75 on 501 att., but only 1,117 yards were while playing fullback

Touchdowns, Game: 3; Joel Makovicka vs. Oklahoma, Nov. 1, 1997

Touchdowns, Season: 9; Mark Schellen, 1983; Joel Makovicka, 1997

Touchdowns, Career: 12; Mark Schellen, 1982-83; Tom Rathman, 1983-84-85

I-backs/Halfbacks

Attempts, Game: 36; Rick Berns, vs. Missouri, 1978 (255 yards); Lawrence Phillips, at Iowa State (183 yards)

Attempts, Season: 286; Lawrence Phillips, 1994 (1,722 yards)

Attempts, Career: 668; Mike Rozier, 1981-82-83 (4,780 yards)

Net Yards, Game: 294; Calvin Jones, at Kansas, 1991 (27 att.)

Net Yards, Season: 2,148; Mike Rozier, 1983 (275 att.)

Net Yards, Career: 4,780; Mike Rozier, 1981-82-83 (668 att.)

Touchdowns, Game: 6; Calvin Jones, at Kansas, 1991

Touchdowns, Season: 29; Mike Rozier, 1983

Touchdowns, Career: 49; Mike Rozier, 1981-82-83

NU's Top Freshman Rushing Seasons:

Player (year)	Att.	Yards	Avg.	TD
1. Ahman Green, IB (1995)*	141	1086	7.70	13
2. Calvin Jones, IB (1991)	108	900	8.33	14
3. DeAngelo Evans, IB (1996)*	148	776	5.24	14
4. Monte Anthony, IB (1974)*	109	587	5.39	7
5. Lawrence Phillips, IB (1993)*	92	508	5.52	5
6. Tommie Frazier, QB (1992)*	86	399	4.64	7
7. Derek Brown, IB (1990)	59	375	6.36	5
8. Damon Benning, IB (1997)	55	323	5.90	4
9. Correll Buckhalter, IB (1997)	54	311	5.76	6
10. Mickey Joseph, QB (1988)	24	215	8.96	3

NU's Top 10 Sophomore Rushing Seasons:

Player (year)	Att.	Yards	Avg.	TD
1. Lawrence Phillips, IB (1994)	286	#1,772	6.00	16
2. Bobby Reynolds, HB (1950)	193	1,342	6.95	19
3. Derek Brown, IB (1993)	230	1,313	5.71	14
4. I.M. Hipp, IB (1977)	197	1,301	6.60	10
5. Calvin Jones, IB (1992)	168	1,210	7.20	14
6. Doug DuBose, IB (1984)	156	1,040	6.67	8
7. Tony Davis, FB (1973)	254	1,008	3.94	13
8. Rick Berns, IB (1981)	182	972	5.34	11
9. Mike Rozier, IB (1981)	151	943	6.25	5
10. Ahman Green, IB (1996)	155	917	5.92	7

NU's Top Junior Rushing Seasons:

Player (year)	Att.	Yards	Avg.	TD
1. Ahman Green, IB (1997)	278	1,877	6.75	22
2. Mike Rozier, IB (1982)	242	1,689	6.98	15
3. Ken Clark, IB (1988)	232	1,497	6.45	12
4. Doug DuBose, IB (1985)	203	1,161	5.72	8
5. Roger Craig, IB (1981)	173	1,060	6.13	6
6. Calvin Jones, IB (1993)	185	1,043	5.64	12
7. Jarvis Redwine, IB (1979)	148	1,042	7.04	9
8. Derek Brown, IB (1992)	169	1,011	6.00	4
9. Leodis Flowers, IB (1990)	149	940	6.31	9
10. I.M. Hipp, IB (1978)	173	936	5.41	7

NU's Top Senior Rushing Seasons:

Player (year)	Att.	Yards	Avg.	TD
1. Mike Rozier, IB (1983)	275	#2,148	7.81	29
2. Keith Jones, IB (1987)	170	1,232	7.25	13
3. Ken Clark, IB (1989)	198	1,196	6.04	12
4. Jarvis Redwine, IB (1980)	156	1,119	7.17	9
5. Scott Frost, QB (1997)	176	1,095	6.22	19
6. Jeff Kinney, HB (1971)	222	1,037	4.67	16
7. Jeff Smith, IB (1984)	177	935	5.28	7
8. Rick Berns, IB/FB (1978)	164	933	5.69	11
9. Gerry Gdowski, QB (1989)	117	925	7.91	13
10. Tom Rathman, FB (1985)	118	881	7.47	8

NEBRASKA'S TOP 50 CAREER RUSHERS

(All Positions—Excluding Bowl Games; 100G indicates career 100-yard rushing performances)

Player, Position, Years	Att.	Gain	Loss	Net	Avg.	TD	100G
1. Mike Rozier, IB, 1981-82-83	668	4,837	57	4,780	7.16	49	26
2. Ahman Green, IB, 1995-96-97	574	3,989	109	3,880	6.76	42	19
3. Calvin Jones, IB, 1991-92-93	461	3,215	62	3,153	6.84	40	16
4. Ken Clark, IB, 1987-88-89	494	3,112	75	3,037	6.15	29	12
5. I.M. Hipp, IB, 1977-78-79	495	2,913	99	2,814	5.68	21	10
6. Lawrence Phillips, IB, 1993-94-95	449	2,886	109	2,777	6.18	30	14
7. Derek Brown, IB, 1990-91-92	458	2,784	85	2,699	5.89	23	13
8. Keith Jones, IB, 1984-85-86-87	398	2,577	89	2,488	6.25	32	10
9. Rick Berns, IB, 1976-77-78	440	2,478	29	2,449	5.57	28	9
10. Roger Craig, IB, 1979-80-81-82	407	2,493	47	2,446	6.01	26	7
11. Jeff Kinney, HB, 1969-70-71	545	2,295	51	2,244	4.12	29	6
12. Doug DuBose, IB, 1982-84-85	362	2,250	45	2,205	6.09	16	14
13. Bobby Reynolds, HB, 1950-51-52	378	2,386	190	2,196	5.81	24	9
14. Jarvis Redwine, IB, 1979-80	304	2,213	52	2,161	7.11	17	10
15. Tony Davis, FB/IB, 1973-74-75	501	2,195	42	2,153	4.30	17	7
16. Steve Taylor, QB, 1985-86-87-88	431	2,560	435	2,125	4.93	32	6
17. Monte Anthony, IB, 1974-75-76-77	463	2,126	49	2,077	4.49	18	5
18. Jeff Smith, IB, 1980-82-83-84	315	2,014	22	1,992	6.32	19	5
19. Joe Orduna, HB, 1967-68-70	489	2,070	102	1,968	4.02	26	4
20. Tommie Frazier, QB, 1992-93-94-95	367	2,231	276	1,955	5.33	36	3
21. Andra Franklin, FB, 1977-78-79-80	324	1,753	15	1,738	5.36	10	3
22. Leodis Flowers, IB, 1988-89-90	247	1,668	33	1,635	6.62	18	7
23. Harry Wilson, HB, 1964-65-66	318	1,683	73	1,610	5.06	10	3
24. Damon Benning, IB, 1993-94-95-96	270	1,623	61	1,562	5.79	20	3
25. Scott Frost, QB, 1996-97	302	1,778	245	1,533	5.08	28	3
26. Bob Smith, HB, 1952-53-54	316	1,595	70	1,525	4.83	9	4
27. Dick Davis, FB, 1966-67-68	349	1,564	87	1,477	4.23	4	3
28. Tom Rathman, FB, 1981-83-84-85	220	1,429	4	1,425	6.48	12	4
29. John O'Leary, IB, 1973-74-75	293	1,461	37	1,424	4.86	14	2
30. Tyreese Knox, IB, 1985-86-87-88	209	1,391	33	1,358	6.50	12	6
31. Bill Thornton, FB, 1960-61-62	295	1,388	60	1,328	4.50	12	3
32. Turner Gill, QB, 1980-81-82-83	290	1,593	276	1,317	4.54	18	1
33. Craig Johnson, IB, 1978-79-80	203	1,293	20	1,273	6.27	18	6
34. Bill Mueller, HB, 1947-48-49-50	321	1,406	190	1,216	3.79	5	2
35. Gerry Gdowski, QB, 1987-88-89	152	1,281	70	1,211	7.97	17	3
36. Willie Greenlaw, HB, 1954-55-56	212	1,251	89	1,162	5.48	10	2
37. Willie Ross, HB, 1961-62-63	226	1,188	63	1,125	4.98	8	2
38. Mickey Joseph, QB, 1988-89-90-91	180	1,198	107	1,091	6.06	16	1
39. Jerry Brown, FB, 1955-56-57	226	1,094	6	1,088	4.81	6	2
40. Paul Miles, IB, 1983-84-85	156	1,097	23	1,074	6.88	9	2
41. Bryan Carpenter, FB, 1987-88-89	170	1,069	5	1,064	6.26	7	1
42. Ben Gregory, HB, 1965-66-67	260	1,069	45	1,024	3.94	9	2
43. Frank Solich, FB, 1963-64-65	196	1,054	44	1,010	5.15	6	1
44. Lance Lewis, FB, 1988-90-91-92	163	1,012	4	1,008	6.18	6	0
45. Gary Dixon, HB, 1971-72	269	1,042	35	1,007	3.74	14	1
46. Joel Makovicka, FB, 1995-96-97	150	995	6	989	6.59	11	2
47. Rudy Johnson, HB, 1961-62-63	168	956	26	930	5.54	9	2
48. Clinton Childs, IB, 1993-94-95	135	942	20	922	6.83	9	1
49. Bill Olds, FB, 1970-71-72	148	955	34	921	6.22	2	1
50. Nick Adduci, FB, 1949-50-53	174	930	17	913	5.25	6	2

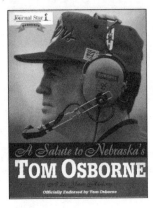
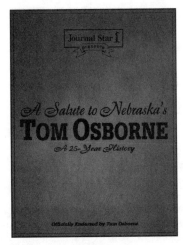